Stir Up Magical Memories With Unforgettable Fare

HOLIDAYS are special times to gather with family, catch up with dear friends and appreciate the blessings in our lives. An attractive spread of home-cooked foods helps make the occasion more joyful and the memories more vivid.

With that in mind, we created *Taste of Home's Holiday & Celebrations Cookbook 2001*. This colorful, photo-filled treasury features 276 mouth-watering recipes to make your Christmas, Thanksgiving, Easter and other celebrations throughout the year easy and enjoyable. We've done the planning, offered menu options and provided timetables to minimize last-minute fuss.

'Tis the Season. From formal sit-down dinners and casual suppers to after-sledding snack parties and dessert buffets, Christmastime is bustling with activities. Take the worry out of what to make for every holiday happening with a merry array of 147 delightful dishes, including Swiss 'n' Bacon Pizza, Poppy Seed Cranberry Bread, Roast Duck with Orange Glaze, Dilled Duchess Potatoes, Caramel Cashew Cheesecake and Chocolate Mousse Torte. Plus, two complete meals (featuring Roasted Beef Tenderloin and meaty Christmas Night Lasagna) make menu-planning a breeze.

Giving Thanks. Do you think your family will resist a twist to the traditional Thanksgiving menu? We guarantee they'll fall for Turkey with Apple Stuffing, Winter Squash Souffle, Sausage Potato Dressing, Refreshing Orange Ice, Pumpkin-Pecan Cake Roll and many more of this chapter's 30 seasonal selections.

Easter Gatherings. Choose from 25 irresistible brunch options, including Crab-Spinach Egg Casserole, French Toast Strata, Asparagus Hollandaise Puff, Fruit Salad with Poppy Seed Dressing and Date Crumb Cake. Our flavorful formal dinner featuring Italian Leg of Lamb will earn compliments for the cook.

Special Celebrations. We offer 74 family-favorite recipes for a host of other gatherings throughout the year. Score a touchdown with a Super Bowl pizza party, shower a bride-to-be with a luscious luncheon or thrill little ghosts and goblins with a Halloween bash. You'll also find a New Year's Eve buffet, a Fourth of July picnic, a selection of sweet brownies and a traditional Hanukkah meal.

Can-Do Decorating Ideas. There are dozens of ideas for creating simple centerpieces (see the beautiful tulip arrangement on page 175), great-looking garnishes (Chocolate Almond Pinecones on page 95 are a dazzling dessert topper) and easy, impressive napkin folds (turn to page 211 for pretty Napkin Roses).

With a splendid assortment of appetizers, side dishes, entrees, desserts, party menus, decorating ideas and more, *Taste of Home's Holiday & Celebrations Cookbook 2001* will make entertaining more fun for you…and unforgettable for your family!

WOULD YOU like to see one of your family-favorite recipes featured in a future edition of this timeless treasury? See page 256 for details!

HOLIDAY & Celebrations COOKBOOK 2001

Editor: Julie Schnittka
Art Director: Linda Dzik
Food Editor: Janaan Cunningham
Craft Editor: Jane Craig
Associate Editors: Kristine Krueger, Heidi Reuter Lloyd
Associate Food Editor: Coleen Martin
Senior Recipe Editor: Sue A. Jurack
Recipe Editor: Janet Briggs
Test Kitchen Director: Karen Johnson
Test Kitchen Home Economists: Sue Draheim,
Peggy Fleming, Julie Herzfeldt, Joylyn Jans, Kristin
Koepnick, Pat Schmeling, Wendy Stenman, Karen Wright
Test Kitchen Assistants: Rita Krajcir, Megan Taylor
Art Associate: Maribeth Greinke
Food Photography: Rob Hagen, Dan Roberts
Food Photography Artists: Stephanie Marchese,
Vicky Marie Moseley
Photo Studio Manager: Anne Schimmel
Production: Ellen Lloyd, Catherine Fletcher
Publisher: Roy Reiman

Taste of Home Books
©2001 Reiman Publications, LLC
5400 S. 60th St., Greendale WI 53129
International Standard Book Number: 0-89821-313-4
International Standard Serial Number: 1535-2781
All rights reserved.
Printed in U.S.A.

For additional copies of this book, write *Taste of Home* Books,
P.O. Box 908, Greendale WI 53129. Or to order by credit card,
call toll-free 1-800/344-2560 or visit our Web site at
www.reimanpub.com.

PICTURED ON THE COVER: Roasted Beef Tenderloin
(p. 8), Special Twice-Baked Potatoes (p. 8), Broccoli Tomato
Cups (p. 12) and Apricot Swan Cream Puffs (p. 10).

'TIS THE *Season*

GIVING *Thanks*

EASTER *Gatherings*

SPECIAL *Celebrations*

'TIS THE Season

From formal meals, casual dinners and sledding parties to planning dessert buffets, baking breads and making cookies and candies, the Christmas season is bustling with activities. You can take the worry out of what to make for every holiday happening by turning to this chapter's appealing assortment of appetizers, side dishes, breads, entrees and desserts. Plus, there are two complete menus and simple decorating ideas for easy entertaining.

'Tis the Season

Holiday Fare

Hints of Home

AT Canton, Ohio's House of Loreto nursing home, Sister Judith LaBrozzi and her food staff delight in providing residents with home-cooked meals throughout the year.

"Just like you and me, the residents here enjoy from-scratch food—not institutional fare—served at an attractive table," says Sister Judith.

So it's no wonder the mouthwatering feast presented at noon on Christmas Day is a favorite.

After starting with Appetizer Stuffed Mushrooms, residents dine on Roasted Beef Tenderloin, Special Twice-Baked Potatoes, Broccoli Tomato Cups and Lime-Pear Gelatin Bells. Saving room for Apricot Swan Cream Puffs and Ice Cream Snowballs is never a problem.

Laughs Sister Judith, "Many folks won't go out with their own families until *after* this dinner with their family at the home!"

Festive Feast

Roasted Beef Tenderloin (p. 8)

Special Twice-Baked Potatoes (p. 8)

Broccoli Tomato Cups (p. 12)

Apricot Swan Cream Puffs (p. 10)

Roasted Beef Tenderloin

(Pictured on page 6 and on cover)

*Beef tenderloin is a simple way to dress up a holiday dinner.
This impressive entree is actually easy to make because it bakes in
the oven unattended, allowing you to prepare other parts of the meal.*

 2 tablespoons Dijon mustard
 1 garlic clove, minced
 3/4 teaspoon coarsely ground pepper
 1/2 teaspoon garlic salt
 1/2 teaspoon onion salt
 1 whole beef tenderloin (about 3-1/2 pounds), trimmed
 1 cup beef broth

In a small bowl, combine the mustard, garlic, pepper, garlic salt and onion salt; brush over tenderloin. Place in a shallow roasting pan. Bake, uncovered, at 425° for 45 minutes or until meat reaches desired doneness (for rare, a meat thermometer should read 140°; medium, 160°; well-done, 170°).

Remove tenderloin from pan; let stand for 10-15 minutes before slicing. Meanwhile, add broth to pan drippings, stirring to loosen browned bits; heat through. Serve with sliced beef. **Yield:** 12 servings.

Special Twice-Baked Potatoes

(Pictured on page 6 and on cover)

*Twice-baked potatoes may take some time to prepare, but we know the
residents really appreciate our efforts. This side dish pairs well with a
variety of meaty entrees and is always a welcome sight on the holiday table.*

 12 large baking potatoes
  1 cup butter *or* margarine, melted, *divided*
  1 to 1-1/4 cups milk, warmed
  8 bacon strips, cooked and crumbled
  1 cup (4 ounces) shredded cheddar cheese
 1/4 cup grated Parmesan cheese
  2 tablespoons minced fresh parsley
  1 teaspoon seasoned salt

Bake potatoes at 375° for 1 hour or until tender. Cool. Cut a thin slice off the top of each potato and discard; scoop out pulp, leaving a thin shell.

In a bowl, mash the pulp with 3/4 cup butter. Stir in milk, bacon, cheeses, parsley and seasoned salt. Spoon or pipe into potato shells. Place on a baking sheet. Drizzle with remaining butter. Bake at 425° for 25 minutes or until heated through. **Yield:** 12 servings.

Ice Cream Snowballs

(Pictured at right)

The House of Loreto residents agree there's no better way to enjoy this festive ice cream dessert than in the warm atmosphere of dinner with friends and family. For extra fun, we sometimes top each snowball with a lit red candle.

1/2 gallon vanilla ice cream
1 package (10 ounces) flaked
   coconut
Fresh mint, optional

Scoop ice cream into 12 balls. Place on a baking sheet and freeze until solid. Roll in coconut. Garnish with mint if desired. **Yield:** 12 servings.

Lime-Pear Gelatin Bells

For festive flair, I use bell-shaped molds for this gelatin salad, but use whatever molds you have on hand. It's such a refreshing way to ring in the holiday season.

1 package (6 ounces) lime
   gelatin
2 cups boiling water
2 cans (15-1/4 ounces *each*)
   sliced *or* halved pears,
   drained
12 ounces whipped cream cheese
1 cup whipping cream, whipped
Leaf lettuce
6 maraschino cherries, halved

In a bowl, dissolve gelatin in boiling water. Place pears in a blender or food processor; cover and process until smooth. Add cream cheese; process until smooth. Add to gelatin and stir well. Refrigerate until cool, about 15 minutes.

Fold in whipped cream. Pour into 12 individual bell-shaped molds or other molds coated with nonstick cooking spray. Refrigerate until firm. Unmold onto lettuce–lined plates. Place a piece of cherry at the end of each bell for clapper. **Yield:** 12 servings.

Apricot Swan Cream Puffs

(Pictured at right, on page 6 and on cover)

Creating unusual desserts is a specialty of our food staff. We serve these pretty cream puffs many times through the year for special occasions or just simply to brighten someone's day.

  1 cup water
1/2 cup butter (no substitutes)
1/4 teaspoon salt
  1 cup all-purpose flour
  4 eggs
FILLING:
1/3 cup sugar
  2 tablespoons cornstarch
1/8 teaspoon salt
  2 cups milk
  2 egg yolks, beaten
  2 tablespoons butter *or* margarine
1-1/2 teaspoons vanilla extract
1/4 teaspoon almond extract
About 3/4 cup chocolate syrup
  2/3 cup apricot preserves
Confectioners' sugar

In a heavy saucepan over medium heat, bring water, butter and salt to a boil. Add flour all at once; stir until a smooth ball forms. Remove from the heat; let stand for 5 minutes. Add eggs, one at a time, beating well after each addition. Beat until smooth and shiny.

Cut a hole in the corner of a pastry or plastic bag; insert a #10 pastry tip. On a greased baking sheet, pipe twelve 3-in.-long S shapes for the swan necks, making a small dollop at the end for head. Bake at 400° for 8-10 minutes or until golden brown. Remove to wire racks to cool.

For each swan body, drop remaining batter by heaping teaspoonfuls 2 in. apart onto greased baking sheets. With a small icing knife or spatula, shape batter into 2-1/2-in. x 2-in. teardrops. Bake at 400° for 30-35 minutes or until golden brown. Cool on wire racks.

For filling, combine sugar, cornstarch and salt in a saucepan; gradually stir in milk until smooth. Bring to a boil over medium heat; cook and stir for 1-2 minutes or until thickened. Remove from the heat. Gradually stir a small amount of hot filling into egg yolks; return all to the pan, stirring constantly. Bring to a gentle boil; cook and stir for 2 minutes. Remove from the heat; stir in butter and extracts. Refrigerate until cool.

Just before serving, spoon about 1 tablespoon chocolate syrup onto serving plates. Cut off top third of swan bodies; set tops aside. Remove any soft dough inside. Spoon 1 tablespoon apricot preserves into bottoms of puffs; add filling. Set necks in filling. Cut reserved tops in half lengthwise to form wings; set wings in filling. Place swans on prepared plates. Dust with confectioners' sugar. **Yield:** 12 servings.

MAKING SWAN CREAM PUFFS

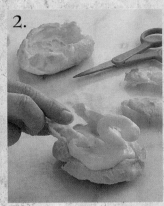

1. To make swan necks, pipe dough into twelve 3-inch-long S shapes onto a greased baking sheet, making a small dollop at the end of each for the head. Bake as directed.

2. To assemble cream puffs, cut off the top third of swan bodies; cut tops in half lengthwise to form wings. Fill bottom of puffs with apricot preserves and filling. Place necks and wings in filling. Place swans on plates topped with chocolate sauce. Dust with confectioners' sugar.

COUNTDOWN TO CHRISTMAS DAY DINNER

A Few Weeks Before:

- Order a 3-1/2-pound whole beef tenderloin from your butcher.
- Make Tea Light Candle Centerpiece (see page 13).
- Assemble and freeze the Ice Cream Snowballs.
- Prepare two grocery lists—one for nonperishable items that can be purchased now and one for perishable items that need to be purchased a few days before Christmas.

Two Days Before:

- Buy remaining grocery items, including the beef tenderloin.
- Bake pastry for the Apricot Swan Cream Puffs and store in an airtight container at room temperature

Christmas Eve:

- Prepare Lime-Pear Gelatin Bells and Special Twice-Baked Potatoes and store in the refrigerator.
- Make the filling for the Apricot Swan Cream Puffs and refrigerate.
- Set the table.

Christmas Day:

- In the morning, assemble Appetizer Stuffed Mushrooms and Broccoli Tomato Cups. Cover (put a damp paper towel over the mushrooms) and refrigerate until baking time.
- Bake the Appetizer Stuffed Mushrooms as guests arrive.
- Prepare and bake the Roasted Beef Tenderloin. Bake the Broccoli Tomato Cups and Special Twice-Baked Potatoes as directed.
- Set out the Lime-Pear Gelatin Bells.
- For dessert, assemble the Apricot Swan Cream Puffs and serve with the Ice Cream Snowballs.

Broccoli Tomato Cups

(Pictured on page 6 and on cover)

Red tomatoes stuffed with a green broccoli mixture make
a colorful addition to the Christmas Day menu.

12 medium tomatoes
 4 cups broccoli florets
 4 tablespoons butter *or*
   margarine, melted, *divided*
1/4 cup seasoned bread crumbs

Cut a thin slice off the top of each tomato. Scoop out pulp, leaving a 1/2-in. shell (discard pulp or save for another use). Invert tomatoes onto paper towels to drain.

In a saucepan, place broccoli in a steamer basket over 1 in. of boiling water. Cover and steam for 5 minutes or until crisp-tender; set aside.

Brush inside of tomatoes with 2 tablespoons butter. Stuff broccoli into tomatoes. Toss bread crumbs and remaining butter; sprinkle over tops. Place in an ungreased baking dish. Bake, uncovered, at 425° for 15 minutes or until heated through. **Yield:** 12 servings.

Appetizer Stuffed Mushrooms

Heat-and-serve convenience foods are forbidden in the House of Loreto kitchen,
and residents appreciate the "real" food we serve.
Everyone reaches for seconds of these tasty morsels.

12 large fresh mushrooms
 2 tablespoons finely chopped
   green onion
 2 tablespoons finely chopped
   green pepper
 1 tablespoon butter *or*
   margarine
 1 slice bread, toasted and
   cut into small cubes
1/4 teaspoon onion salt
1/4 teaspoon garlic salt
1/8 teaspoon pepper
1/8 teaspoon dried thyme
Dash paprika
Grated Parmesan cheese

Remove stems from mushrooms; set caps aside. Finely chop stems; measure 1/2 cup (discard any remaining stems or save for another use). In a skillet, saute chopped mushrooms, onion and green pepper in butter until vegetables are tender and mushroom liquid has evaporated.

Add toast cubes, onion salt, garlic salt, pepper, thyme and paprika; mix well. Stuff into mushroom caps. Place on a greased baking sheet. Bake, uncovered, at 425° for 10 minutes or until heated through. Sprinkle with Parmesan cheese. **Yield:** 1 dozen.

Tea Light Candle Centerpiece

(Pictured at right)

IF HOLIDAY shopping has put your savings account in the red, take comfort in the fact that you don't have to spend a lot of "green" to present guests with a pretty dinner table!

For this eye-catching centerpiece, we simply wrapped pretty ribbon around inexpensive tea light candles (see instructions below) and set them on a tray along with red pillar candles and fresh cranberries.

Affordable tea light candles are easy to find in craft, department, discount and even grocery stores, especially around the holidays. Besides those with traditional metal bases, you may come across colored metal and clear or colored plastic bases. We chose white tea light candles for our centerpiece, but feel free to use whatever color you prefer.

Measure the height of the base of your tea light candles (5/8 inch is fairly standard) so you purchase the cor-
rect width of ribbon, then be creative! We used a solid green ribbon, but you can use a lace braid, plush velvet ribbon, beaded braid, sequin trim or any other decorative ribbon.

You can also mix and match ribbon colors by wrapping half the candles with patterned ribbon and the other half in a coordinating solid color. Make sure the color or colors work with your dishes and table linens.

In addition to making a centerpiece, scatter individual ribbon-wrapped tea lights on the dinner table or group them on smaller trays on other tables or the fireplace mantel.

(These decorated bases can be used even after the candles have burned away. Just remove candles from plain tea light bases and place them in the decorated bases.)

This candle centerpiece can be made weeks in advance. Before your guests arrive, add fresh cranberries and light the candles for a creative table topper.

IT'S A WRAP WITH RIBBON!

WRAP a piece of double-stick tape around the entire metal band on the outside of the tea light. (If you're using a lacy ribbon, be sure the tape is transparent.) Press one end of ribbon (we used 5/8-inch ribbon) onto the tape and wrap it around the tea light until it abuts the starting point. Trim excess ribbon.

A Casual Christmas Dinner

CHRISTMAS NIGHT dinner is informal but special at Nancy Jo Leffler's home, where every room has its own decorated tree.

"December seems so hectic," says the DePauw, Indiana cook, "so Christmas evening is relaxed. Everyone is content to lean back, slip off their shoes and take a deep breath, like, 'Whew, we made it through another year.'"

Nancy's menu sticks to tried-and-true favorites: her signature Christmas Night Lasagna with crunchy Bacon-Cauliflower Tossed Salad, warm Freckled Butterhorn Rolls and dreamy Coconut Cream Pie.

"I like fast-and-easy recipes, but I still want good old-fashioned flavor," says Nancy. "I make everything ahead and then put it in the fridge for a day or so."

A delicious dinner shared with loved ones is the Christmas gift the Leffler family cherishes most.

PLEASING
PASTA PARTY

Christmas Night Lasagna (p. 16)

**Bacon-Cauliflower
Tossed Salad** (p. 16)

Freckled Butterhorn Rolls (p. 18)

Christmas Night Lasagna

(Pictured on page 14)

I tinkered with this recipe four or five times before I got it down to what it is now. It's easy—all you do is mess up two pots—but it tastes as good as the lasagnas that are a big production.

3 pounds ground beef
1 pound bulk pork sausage
1 medium onion, chopped
1 medium green pepper, chopped
2 jars (28 ounces *each*) meatless spaghetti sauce
1 can (10-3/4 ounces) condensed tomato soup, undiluted
1 can (4 ounces) mushroom stems and pieces, undrained
2 teaspoons Worcestershire sauce
1-1/2 teaspoons Italian seasoning
1-1/2 teaspoons salt, *divided*
1-1/2 teaspoons pepper, *divided*
1 teaspoon garlic powder
2 eggs, beaten
2-1/2 cups small-curd cottage cheese

1 carton (15 ounces) ricotta cheese
2 cups (8 ounces) shredded Parmesan cheese
24 lasagna noodles, cooked and drained
12 slices mozzarella cheese

In a large skillet or Dutch oven, cook beef, sausage, onion and green pepper over medium heat until meat is no longer pink; drain. Add the spaghetti sauce, soup, mushrooms, Worcestershire sauce, Italian seasoning, 1 teaspoon salt, 1 teaspoon pepper and garlic powder. Bring to a boil. Reduce heat; simmer, uncovered, for 30 minutes, stirring occasionally.

In a bowl, combine the eggs, cottage cheese, ricotta and remaining salt and pepper. Spread 2 cups meat sauce each into two greased 13-in. x 9-in. x 2-in. baking dishes. Layer each with 1/3 cup Parmesan cheese, four noodles, 1-1/4 cups cottage cheese mixture and three slices of mozzarella cheese. Repeat layers. Top with the remaining noodles, meat sauce and Parmesan.

Bake, uncovered, at 350° for 45 minutes or until bubbly. Let stand for 15 minutes before cutting. **Yield:** 2 casseroles (12 servings each).

Bacon-Cauliflower Tossed Salad

(Pictured on page 14)

I tweaked this tasty recipe from my sister-in-law by using Co-Jack cheese instead of Parmesan.

2 heads iceberg lettuce, coarsely shredded
1 head cauliflower, coarsely chopped
1 pound sliced bacon, cooked and crumbled
1-1/2 cups (6 ounces) shredded Colby-Monterey Jack cheese
6 to 8 green onions, sliced

DRESSING:
1 cup mayonnaise
1/3 cup sugar
1 tablespoon milk
1/2 teaspoon salt
1/8 teaspoon pepper

In a large salad bowl, toss the lettuce, cauliflower, bacon, cheese and green onions. In a small bowl, whisk together the dressing ingredients. Serve with salad. **Yield:** 24 servings.

Coconut Cream Pie

(Pictured at right)

The filling is my mother-in-law's and the crust is mine. My husband and son say they like it better than any other pie I've ever made.

2-1/2 cups all-purpose flour
2 teaspoons sugar
1/4 teaspoon salt
1/4 teaspoon baking powder
3/4 cup shortening
1 egg, *separated*
1/2 cup plus 1 tablespoon cold water, *divided*

FILLING:
2 cups sugar
2/3 cup all-purpose flour
Pinch salt
8 egg yolks
6 cups milk, *divided*
2 cups flaked coconut
2 teaspoons vanilla extract
1 teaspoon coconut extract

MERINGUE:
6 tablespoons sugar
3 tablespoons cornstarch
1-1/2 cups water
8 egg whites
Additional flaked coconut

In a bowl, combine the flour, sugar, salt and baking powder. Cut in shortening until mixture resembles coarse crumbs. Combine egg yolk and 1/2 cup cold water; gradually add to crumb mixture, tossing with a fork until a ball forms. Cover and refrigerate for 1 hour.

Divide dough in half. Roll out each portion to fit a 9-in. pie plate. Place in

plates; trim pastry even with edge. With a small round fluted cutter, cut small circles out of dough scraps. Beat egg white with remaining water; brush over edges of pastry. Arrange dough cutouts around edge.

Line unpricked pastry shells with a double thickness of heavy-duty foil. Bake at 400° for 12-15 minutes or until lightly browned. Cool on wire racks.

For filling, combine the sugar, flour and salt in a large saucepan. Stir in egg yolks and 1 cup milk until smooth; mix well. Gradually whisk in remaining milk. Bring to a boil over medium heat, stirring constantly. Cook and stir over medium heat until thickened, about 3 minutes. Remove from the heat. Stir in coconut and extracts; keep warm.

For meringue, combine sugar, cornstarch and water in a saucepan until smooth. Bring to a boil over medium heat, stirring constantly. Cook and stir for 2 minutes or until clear. In a mixing bowl, beat egg whites until soft peaks form. Pour hot sugar mixture in a small stream into egg whites, beating constantly until stiff peaks form.

Pour warm filling into pastry shells; immediately spread with meringue, sealing edges to crusts. Sprinkle with additional coconut. Bake at 350° for 12-15 minutes or until meringue is golden. Cool on wire racks. Store in the refrigerator. **Yield:** 2 pies (6-8 servings each).

Freckled Butterhorn Rolls

(Pictured on page 15)

From the time they were old enough to talk, my two kids told me these rolls looked like they had freckles. The name stuck.

2 packages (1/4 ounce *each*)
   active dry yeast
2 cups warm milk
   (110° to 115°)
1 cup butter *or* margarine,
   softened
1 cup sugar
4 eggs
2 teaspoons salt
7 to 8 cups bread flour
1/2 cup wheat germ

In a mixing bowl, dissolve yeast in milk. Add butter, sugar, eggs, salt and 4 cups flour; beat until smooth. Stir in wheat germ and enough remaining flour to form a soft dough. Turn onto a floured surface; knead until smooth and elastic, 6-8 minutes. Place in a greased bowl; turn once to grease top. Cover and let rise in a warm place until doubled, about 1 hour.

Punch dough down. Turn onto a lightly floured surface; divide into four portions. Roll each into a 12-in. circle; cut each circle into 12 wedges. Roll up wedges from the wide end and place pointed end down 2 in. apart on greased baking sheets. Curve ends to form a crescent shape.

Cover and let rise in a warm place until doubled, about 45 minutes. Bake at 375° for 12 minutes or until light golden brown. Remove from pans to wire racks. **Yield:** 4 dozen.

CALENDAR FOR CASUAL CHRISTMAS DINNER

A Few Weeks Before:
- Prepare two grocery lists—one for nonperishable items that can be purchased now and one for perishable items that need to be purchased a few days before Christmas.

Two Days Before:
- Make and refrigerate the meat sauce for the Christmas Night Lasagna.

Christmas Eve:
- Assemble the Christmas Night Lasagna; cover and refrigerate.
- Make dressing for Bacon-Cauliflower Tossed Salad; cover and chill.
- Bake crusts for the Coconut Cream Pie; store at room temperature.
- Create the Cutlery Napkin Bundles (see page 19) and set the table.

Christmas Day:
- Prepare Coconut Cream Pie; chill.
- Bake the Freckled Butterhorn Rolls. Cool and store in an airtight container at room temperature.
- Remove the lasagna from the refrigerator 30 minutes before baking.
- Make Bacon-Cauliflower Tossed Salad. Stir dressing; pour over salad or serve alongside. Set out lasagna and rolls.
- Serve Coconut Cream Pie for dessert.

Table Settings for A Crowd

PREPARING CASUAL, make-ahead foods for a holiday buffet certainly makes entertaining easier on the cook. But serving a large group can pose another problem when you realize you don't have enough matching tableware!

Don't panic. You can create a wonderfully festive look by blending the colors and styles of dinner plates, silverware and napkins you do have.

• Present your festive holiday pattern with some solid-colored dishes (as shown above right). Or dust off your formal china and use it alongside your everyday dishes. Give guests the impression that you planned this eclectic look and alternate the patterns when stacking the plates on the buffet table.

• Tie the look together with coordinating colored cloth napkins. By making Cutlery Napkin Bundles (at right), you can also disguise mismatched silverware. For a more finished look, consider arranging the cutlery napkin bundles in a pretty basket or box (see above right) instead of just laying them out on the table.

• If you do a lot of group entertaining, you may want to pick up extra plates, silverware and napkins throughout the year. You can find some real bargains at end-of-season sales and on the clearance tables. Play it safe and select items within the same color schemes. That way, you can mix and match things in a variety of ways.

Be creative and don't worry if the tableware doesn't match exactly!

CUTLERY NAPKIN BUNDLES

THESE easy-to-hold bundles are great for buffets. Start with a cloth napkin folded into a square.

1. Place a set of cutlery diagonally on the napkin, leaving about a third of the napkin showing at the bottom. Fold the bottom corner over the cutlery.

2. Fold the left side of the napkin over the cutlery.

3. Fold right side of napkin over cutlery; tuck under.

4. Securely tie the bundle about halfway down with foil garland, raffia or ribbon.

After-Sledding Snacks

WHEN THE winter blues settle in, it's easy to lift spirits with the promise of food and fun!

Start by inviting family and friends to meet at your favorite toboggan hill for an afternoon of splendid sledding.

When everyone's had their share of spills and thrills, head back home for a savory spread of hot and cold appetizers and thirst-quenching beverages.

Rich and hearty Savory Appetizer Cheesecake, Chicken Ham Pinwheels and Bacon Water Chestnut Wraps will squelch hunger in a hurry. With their fresh flavor, Fruit 'n' Cheese Kabobs and Vegetable Wreath with Dip make appealing accompaniments. (All shown at right.)

But don't limit your buffet to the recipes mentioned above. You'll find a host of innovative appetizers and beverages on the following pages.

WINTER WARM-UPS
(Clockwise from top left)

Savory Appetizer Cheesecake (p. 22)

Chicken Ham Pinwheels (p. 26)

Bacon Water Chestnut Wraps (p. 24)

Fruit 'n' Cheese Kabobs (p. 27)

Vegetable Wreath with Dip (p. 29)

APPETIZER AND BEVERAGE BASICS

AN APPETIZER and beverage buffet is a fun twist on entertaining and lends itself to a less formal atmosphere than a traditional sit-down dinner. But don't be intimidated by such an undertaking...these helpful hints make it a snap!

- For an appetizer buffet that serves as the meal, offer five or six different appetizers (including some substantial selections) and plan on eight to nine pieces per guest. If you'll also be serving a meal, two to three pieces per person is sufficient.
- In order to appeal to everyone's tastes and diets, have a balance of hearty and low-calorie appetizers as well as hot and cold choices.
- So that you can spend more time with guests, look for appetizers that can be made ahead and require little last-minute fuss.
- Chill all punch ingredients before mixing so that you don't have to dilute the punch with ice to get it cold. Or consider garnishing a cold punch with an ice ring (which lasts longer than ice cubes) made from punch ingredients instead of water.
- For hot beverages, avoid shattering the serving bowl by making sure the bowl is heat-resistant and by warming the bowl with warm water before adding the hot punch. If you don't have a heat-resistant bowl, serve the punch in a chafing dish, fondue pot, slow cooker or in an attractive pan on the stovetop.

Savory Appetizer Cheesecake

(Pictured on page 20)

I love to experiment with new recipes, and my family is always willing to taste-test. This warm bacon cheesecake is welcome at family get-togethers.
—Joy Burke, Punxsutawney, Pennsylvania

6 bacon strips, diced
1 large onion, chopped
1 garlic clove, minced
1 carton (15 ounces) ricotta cheese
1/2 cup half-and-half cream
2 tablespoons all-purpose flour
1/2 teaspoon salt
1/8 to 1/4 teaspoon cayenne pepper
2 eggs
1/2 cup sliced green onions
Assorted crackers and fresh fruit

In a skillet over medium heat, cook bacon until crisp. Remove with a slotted spoon to paper towels. In the drippings, saute onion and garlic until tender; remove with a slotted spoon.

In a mixing bowl, combine the ricotta, cream, flour, salt and cayenne; beat until smooth. Beat in eggs. Set aside 3 tablespoons bacon for garnish. Stir green onions, sauteed onion and remaining bacon into egg mixture. Pour into a greased 8-in. springform pan.

Bake at 350° for 40 minutes or until center is set. Cool slightly on a wire rack. Sprinkle with reserved bacon. Serve warm with crackers and fruit. **Yield:** 16-20 servings.

Eggnog Punch

(Pictured at right)

Lemon-lime soda gives this rich beverage a delicate flavor. Even people who don't care for eggnog won't be able to resist a creamy glassful. It's a hit at our Christmas parties.
—Lorrie Sexauer, DeSoto, Texas

4 cups half-and-half cream, *divided*
6 eggs, lightly beaten
1/2 cup sugar
3 teaspoons vanilla extract
1/2 teaspoon ground nutmeg, optional
4 cups whipping cream
6 to 8 cups lemon-lime soda, chilled
1 quart vanilla ice cream
1/2 cup chopped maraschino cherries

In a saucepan, combine 2 cups half-and-half cream, eggs and sugar. Cook and stir over medium heat until mixture reaches 160° or is thick enough to coat a metal spoon, about 9 minutes. Remove from the heat; stir in vanilla, nutmeg if desired and remaining half-and-half. Cover and refrigerate for at least 3 hours.

Pour into a punch bowl. Stir in whipping cream and soda. Top with scoops of ice cream and sprinkle with cherries. Serve immediately. **Yield:** about 4 quarts.

Creamy Chipped Beef Fondue

My mother often served fondue on Christmas Eve and I've since followed in that tradition. It's nice to offer a hearty appetizer that requires very little work.
—Beth Fox, Lawrence, Kansas

1-1/3 to 1-1/2 cups milk
2 packages (8 ounces *each*) cream cheese, cubed
1 package (2-1/2 ounces) thinly sliced dried beef, chopped
1/4 cup chopped green onions
2 teaspoons ground mustard
1 loaf (1 pound) French bread, cubed

In a saucepan, heat milk and cream cheese over medium heat; stir until smooth. Stir in beef, onions and mustard; heat through. Transfer to a fondue pot or slow cooker; keep warm. Serve with bread cubes. **Yield:** about 4 cups.

Bacon Water Chestnut Wraps

(Pictured on page 21)

The holidays around our house just wouldn't be the same without these classic wraps.
Through the years, Christmas Eve guests have proven it's impossible to eat just one.
—Laura Mahaffey, Annapolis, Maryland

1 pound sliced bacon
2 cans (8 ounces *each*) whole
  water chestnuts, drained
1/2 cup packed brown sugar
1/2 cup mayonnaise *or* salad
  dressing
1/4 cup chili sauce

Cut bacon strips in half. In a skillet over medium heat, cook bacon until almost crisp; drain. Wrap each bacon piece around a water chestnut and secure with a toothpick. Place in an ungreased 13-in. x 9-in. x 2-in. baking dish.

Combine the brown sugar, mayonnaise and chili sauce; pour over water chestnuts. Bake, uncovered, at 350° for 30 minutes or until hot and bubbly. **Yield:** about 2-1/2 dozen.

Mandarin Chicken Bites

Instead of a big Christmas meal, our family enjoys nibbling on an all-day appetizer buffet.
Each year we present tempting new dishes alongside our favorites.
This is one of those tried-and-true dishes that's a "must".
—Susannah Yinger, Canal Winchester, Ohio

1 cup all-purpose flour
1/2 teaspoon salt
1/4 teaspoon pepper
1 pound boneless skinless
  chicken breasts, cut into
  2-inch cubes
2 tablespoons butter *or*
  margarine
1 can (11 ounces) mandarin
  oranges, drained
2/3 cup orange marmalade
1/2 teaspoon dried tarragon

In a large resealable plastic bag, combine the flour, salt and pepper. Add chicken, a few pieces at a time, and shake to coat. In a skillet, brown chicken in butter until juices run clear. In a saucepan, combine the oranges, marmalade and tarragon; bring to a boil. Pour over chicken; stir gently to coat. Serve warm with toothpicks. **Yield:** 12-15 servings.

Chili Cheese Snacks

(Pictured at right)

I've been collecting appetizer recipes for more than 20 years and have a host of tasty treats. These handheld morsels are perfect for parties because they allow folks to walk around and mingle.
—Carol Nelson, Cool, California

2 packages (3 ounces *each*)
   cream cheese, softened
1 cup (4 ounces) shredded
   cheddar cheese
1/4 cup chopped green chilies
1/4 cup chopped ripe olives,
   drained
2 teaspoons dried minced onion
1/4 teaspoon hot pepper sauce
2 tubes (8 ounces *each*)
   refrigerated crescent rolls

In a small mixing bowl, beat cream cheese. Add the cheddar cheese, chilies, olives, onion and hot pepper sauce. Separate each tube of crescent dough into four rectangles; press perforations to seal.

Spread cheese mixture over dough. Roll up jelly-roll style, starting with a long side. Cut each roll into 10 slices; place on greased baking sheets. Bake at 400° for 8-10 minutes or until golden brown. **Yield:** 80 appetizers.

Swiss 'n' Bacon Pizza

My family enjoys this pizza so much, I usually make it as a main course. But when we're invited to various gatherings, I like to serve it as an appetizer.
—Vicki Robers, Stratford, Wisconsin

2 tubes (12 ounces *each*)
   refrigerated buttermilk
   biscuits
1 pound sliced bacon, cooked
   and crumbled
1 medium tomato, chopped
1 medium onion, chopped
1 cup (4 ounces) shredded
   Swiss cheese
1/2 cup mayonnaise*
1 teaspoon dried basil

Split each biscuit into two halves. Press onto a greased 14-in. pizza pan, sealing seams. In a bowl, combine the remaining ingredients; spread over crust. Bake at 350° for 20-23 minutes or until golden brown. Cut into thin wedges. **Yield:** 8-12 servings.

*Editors Note: Reduced-fat or fat-free mayonnaise may not be substituted for regular mayonnaise.

Chicken Ham Pinwheels

(Pictured on page 21)

*These pretty pinwheels have been a part of our annual Christmas Eve appetizer buffet
for many years. I love them because they can be made a day in advance
and taste great alone or served with crackers.*
—*Laura Mahaffey, Annapolis, Maryland*

4 boneless skinless chicken
  breast halves
1/8 teaspoon plus 1/2 teaspoon
  dried basil, *divided*
1/8 teaspoon salt
1/8 teaspoon garlic salt
1/8 teaspoon pepper
4 thin slices deli ham
2 teaspoons lemon juice
Paprika
1/2 cup mayonnaise
1 teaspoon grated orange peel
1 teaspoon orange juice

Flatten chicken to 1/4-in. thickness. Combine 1/8 teaspoon basil, salt, garlic salt and pepper; sprinkle over chicken. Top each with a ham slice. Roll up jelly-roll style; place seam side down in a greased 11-in. x 7-in. x 2-in. baking dish. Drizzle with lemon juice and sprinkle with paprika. Bake, uncovered, at 350° for 30 minutes or until chicken juices run clear. Cover and refrigerate.

Meanwhile, in a bowl, combine the mayonnaise, orange peel, orange juice and remaining basil. Cover and refrigerate until serving. Cut chicken rolls into 1/2-in. slices. Serve with orange spread. **Yield:** 24 servings.

Hot Crab Dip

*I like to keep these ingredients on hand as a last-minute snack for unexpected company.
Sometimes I double the horseradish for a little extra kick.*
—*Mary Williams, Lancaster, California*

1 package (8 ounces) cream
  cheese, softened
1/4 cup shredded Monterey Jack
  cheese
2 tablespoons milk
1/2 teaspoon prepared
  horseradish
1/4 teaspoon salt
1/4 teaspoon dill weed
Dash pepper
1 can (6 ounces) crabmeat,
  drained, flaked and cartilage
  removed

1/4 cup sliced green onions
Additional dill weed *or* snipped fresh dill, optional
Assorted crackers *or* sliced French bread

In a mixing bowl, combine cream cheese, Monterey Jack cheese, milk, horseradish, salt, dill and pepper. Stir in crab and onions. Spread evenly into an ungreased 9-in. pie plate. If desired, sprinkle with additional dill in the shape of a Christmas tree. Bake, uncovered, at 375° for 15 minutes. Serve with crackers or bread. **Yield:** 12 servings.

Fruit 'n' Cheese Kabobs

(Pictured at right and on page 20)

The home economists in our test kitchen came up with this colorful combination. It's a simple, nutritious snack that's a snap to put together, much to the delight of busy holiday cooks!

1 block (1 pound) Colby-Monterey Jack cheese
1 block (1 pound) cheddar cheese
1 block (1 pound) baby Swiss cheese
1 fresh pineapple, peeled, cored and cut into 2-inch chunks

1 to 2 pounds seedless green *or* red grapes
3 pints strawberries

Cut cheese into chunks or slices. If desired, cut into shapes with small cutters. Alternately thread cheese and fruit onto wooden skewers. Serve immediately. **Yield:** about 3 dozen.

PREPARING A CHEESE PLATTER

FOR A SIMPLE addition to an appetizer buffet, consider offering a simple cheese platter. Whether served by itself or alongside fruits, vegetables, crackers or bread, cheese appeals to people of all ages. Best of all, it requires little effort on your part. Here are a few suggestions to help you prepare a pleasing platter:

- Plan on about 2 ounces of cheese per person and use four or five varieties.
- Include an assortment of colors, textures and tastes. Some mild cheeses are baby Swiss, Colby, Colby-Jack, Havarti, mild cheddar and Monterey Jack. For a mellow flavor, turn to brick, Brie, Camembert, Edam, Gouda, medium cheddar and Swiss. Be sure to also include some robust varieties like Asiago, blue, Gorgonzola, Gruyere, Parmesan, provolone and sharp cheddar.
- Add eye appeal by cutting cheeses into different shapes, such as rectangles, squares, triangles, cubes and sticks. (For the holidays, use small festive cutters.)
- For best results, use a sharp clean knife and cut cheese while it's cold. Cutting can be done early in the day. Just wrap the cheese tightly with plastic wrap or store in airtight containers and refrigerate.
- When preparing your platter for serving, it's better to serve small quantities and then refill as needed. Otherwise, the flavor and texture of the cheeses will deteriorate and the cheeses may spoil.

Barbecue Muncher Mix

Looking for a twist on standard party mix?
My family enjoys this barbecue-seasoned snack at Christmas and throughout the year.
It also makes a nice addition to a holiday gift basket.
—Mrs. Dean Holmes, Altamont, Kansas

4 cups Corn Chex
4 cups Wheat Chex
2 cups cheese-flavored snack crackers
2 cups pretzel sticks
2 cups mixed nuts *or* dry roasted peanuts
1/2 cup butter *or* margarine
4 to 5 tablespoons barbecue sauce
1 tablespoon Worcestershire sauce
1 teaspoon seasoned salt

In a large roasting pan, combine the cereals, crackers, pretzels and nuts; set aside. In a small saucepan, melt butter; stir in the barbecue sauce, Worcestershire sauce and seasoned salt until blended. Pour over cereal mixture and stir to coat.

Bake, uncovered, at 250° for 1 hour, stirring every 15 minutes. Spread on waxed paper to cool completely. Store in airtight containers. **Yield:** 14 cups.

Tropical Winter Warmer

While raising our family, we lived in a chalet on a lake.
Winter mornings were cold and frosty, so I'd often prepare this warm beverage.
It's full of vitamins to give you energy on busy days.
—Patricia Slater, Baldwin, Ontario

1 quart apple cider *or* juice
1 to 1-1/4 cups packed brown sugar
1 cinnamon stick (3 inches)
12 whole cloves
2 cups grapefruit juice
2 cups orange juice

In a large saucepan, combine cider and brown sugar. Cook and stir over medium heat until sugar is dissolved. Add cinnamon and cloves; bring to a boil. Reduce heat; simmer, uncovered, for 5 minutes. Add grapefruit and orange juices; heat through (do not boil). Discard cinnamon and cloves before serving. **Yield:** 2 quarts.

Vegetable Wreath with Dip

(Pictured at right and on page 20)

Vegetables and dip are a mainstay at most holiday parties. I like to dress up this appetizer by cutting vegetables into festive shapes and arranging them as a wreath. It's a nice conversation piece.
—Edna Hoffman, Hebron, Indiana

  1 **package (8 ounces) cream cheese, softened**
1/4 **cup mayonnaise**
1/2 **teaspoon chili powder**
1/2 **teaspoon dill weed**
1/4 **teaspoon garlic powder**
1/4 **cup sliced green onions**
1/4 **cup chopped ripe olives, well drained**
  4 **cups broccoli florets**
  1 **medium green pepper, cut into strips**
  8 **cherry tomatoes**
  1 **medium jicama *or* turnip, peeled and sliced**
  1 **medium sweet red pepper**

In a small mixing bowl, combine the first five ingredients; mix well. Stir in onions and olives. Cover and refrigerate for at least 2 hours.

Transfer dip to a serving bowl; place in the center of a 12-in. round serving plate. Arrange broccoli, green pepper and tomatoes in a wreath shape around dip. Using a small star cookie cutter, cut out stars from jicama slices; place over wreath. Cut red pepper into five pieces that form the shape of a bow; position on wreath. **Yield:** 12 servings.

WHAT'S A JICAMA?

A JICAMA (HEE-kah-mah) is a root vegetable resembling a turnip that is also known as a Mexican potato. It has thin brown skin, white flesh, crunchy texture and a sweet, nutty flavor.

Look for firm, heavy jicamas with unblemished skin. Store whole jicamas in the refrigerator for up to 3 weeks. Wash, dry and peel before using.

Dijon Chicken Liver Pate

*I first served this chicken liver pate at a holiday party quite a few years ago,
and it was a real hit. The special flavoring comes from cream cheese,
mustard and pork sausage.*
—*Katherine Wells, Brodhead, Wisconsin*

1/2 **pound bulk pork sausage**
1 **small onion, chopped**
1/2 **pound chicken livers,
cut in half**
1/3 **cup milk**
2 **tablespoons Dijon mustard**
1 **package (8 ounces) cream
cheese, softened**
1/2 **teaspoon garlic powder**
1/4 **teaspoon *each* dried chives,
parsley flakes, tarragon and
marjoram**
Assorted crackers

In a large skillet over medium heat, cook sausage and onion until meat is no longer pink; remove with a slotted spoon and set aside. In the drippings, cook chicken livers over medium heat for 6-8 minutes or until no longer pink. Drain; cool for 10 minutes.

Place chicken livers, milk and mustard in a blender or food processor; cover and process. Add sausage mixture, cream cheese and seasonings; cover and process until nearly smooth. Pour into a 3-cup serving bowl. Cover and refrigerate for 6 hours or overnight. Serve with crackers. **Yield:** 3 cups.

Sesame Cheese Ball

*I came up with this cheese ball when I combined two favorite recipes. Unlike some cheese spreads
that can be somewhat bland, this has a little zest. I make it for occasions throughout the year.*
—*Brenda Baughman, Mansfield, Ohio*

2 **packages (8 ounces *each*)
cream cheese, softened**
1-1/2 **cups (6 ounces) finely
shredded cheddar cheese**
1/2 **cup finely chopped celery**
1/3 **cup finely chopped onion**
1/2 **teaspoon garlic salt**
1/2 **teaspoon seasoned salt**
1/2 **teaspoon hot pepper sauce**
1/3 **cup sesame seeds, toasted**
Assorted crackers

In a mixing bowl, combine the cream cheese, cheddar cheese, celery, onion, garlic salt, seasoned salt and hot pepper sauce; beat until well blended. Shape into a ball; roll in sesame seeds. Cover and refrigerate. Remove from the refrigerator 15 minutes before serving. Serve with crackers. **Yield:** 1 cheese ball (about 2-1/2 cups).

Marinated Shrimp

(Pictured at right)

My husband's aunt shared this recipe with me more than 20 years ago. Not only is it a Christmas Eve tradition in my home, but in the homes of our grown children as well.
—Delores Hill, Helena, Montana

2 **pounds uncooked jumbo shrimp, peeled and deveined**
1 **cup olive *or* vegetable oil**
2 **garlic cloves, minced**
4 **teaspoons dried rosemary, crushed**
2 **teaspoons dried oregano**
2 **bay leaves**
1 **cup dry white wine *or* chicken broth**
3/4 **teaspoon salt**
1/8 **teaspoon pepper**

In a bowl, combine the shrimp, oil, garlic, rosemary, oregano and bay leaves. Cover and refrigerate for 2-4 hours.

Pour shrimp and marinade into a large deep skillet. Add wine or broth, salt and pepper. Cover and cook over medium-low heat for 10-15 minutes or until shrimp turn pink, stirring occasionally. Discard bay leaves. Transfer with a slotted spoon to a serving dish. **Yield:** 4-6 servings.

Crab-Stuffed Celery

Convenient canned crab and flavored cream cheese combine to turn ordinary celery sticks into special appetizers. I keep this recipe's ingredients on hand for anytime snacking.
—Marian Platt, Sequim, Washington

1 **carton (8 ounces) whipped chive cream cheese**
1/2 **cup crabmeat, drained, flaked and cartilage removed *or* imitation crabmeat**
1 **tablespoon mayonnaise**
1/2 **teaspoon lemon juice**
1/8 **teaspoon onion salt**
1/8 **teaspoon garlic salt**
6 **celery ribs, cut into serving-size pieces**

In a bowl, combine the first six ingredients; mix well. Transfer to a small resealable plastic bag. Cut a small hole in the corner of the bag; pipe mixture into celery sticks. Store in the refrigerator. **Yield:** about 2 dozen appetizers.

Crispy Cheese Twists

My grown son enjoys these cheese twists so much that I'll often bake an extra
batch for his stocking stuffer. They make a great anytime snack.
—*Mary Maxeiner, Lakewood, Colorado*

6 tablespoons butter *or*
  margarine, softened
1 garlic clove, minced
1/8 teaspoon pepper
1 cup (4 ounces) shredded
  cheddar cheese
2 tablespoons milk
1 tablespoon minced fresh
  parsley
1 tablespoon snipped fresh dill
  or 1 teaspoon dill weed
1 cup all-purpose flour

In a mixing bowl, combine the butter, garlic and pepper; beat until light and fluffy. Stir in cheese, milk, parsley and dill. Gradually add flour, mixing thoroughly.

Divide dough into 20 pieces. Roll each piece into a 10-in. log; cut each in half and twist together. Place 1 in. apart on an ungreased baking sheet. Bake at 375° for 10-12 minutes or until golden brown. Remove to wire racks. **Yield:** 20 twists.

Pesto Cheese Ring

With garlic and red pepper flakes, this rich cheese spread has an irresistible zing.
It's perfect for parties because a little bit goes a long way.
—*Amy Cronwell, Stacy, Minnesota*

PARSLEY PESTO:
3 cups fresh parsley sprigs
1/2 cup coarsely chopped walnuts
1/2 cup grated Parmesan cheese
3 tablespoons vegetable oil
10 medium fresh basil leaves
8 garlic cloves
1/2 teaspoon crushed red pepper
  flakes
CHEESE RING:
4 packages (8 ounces *each*)
  cream cheese, softened
1/2 cup sour cream
1/4 cup mayonnaise
1/2 cup whipping cream
2 tablespoons sugar
1/4 cup finely chopped onion

2 to 3 tablespoons crushed red pepper flakes
Additional parsley sprigs and chopped walnuts, optional
Assorted crackers *or* fresh vegetables

In a food processor, combine the pesto ingredients; cover and process until smooth. Set aside. In a mixing bowl, beat cream cheese, sour cream and mayonnaise until smooth. Gradually add whipping cream and sugar. Stir in the onion and red pepper flakes.

Line a 6-cup ring mold with plastic wrap. Spread half of the cream cheese mixture into mold. Top with the pesto and remaining cheese mixture. Cover and refrigerate overnight.

Invert cheese ring onto a serving plate; remove plastic wrap. Smooth sides and top of ring with a wet knife. Garnish with parsley and nuts if desired. Serve with crackers or vegetables. **Yield:** 20-24 servings.

Hot Pink Punch

(Pictured at right)

With its rosy color, this beverage is perfect for any holiday gathering. Each delicious sip is sure to warm you up. Plus, it has a wonderful aroma that welcomes guests as they come through the door.
—Lucile Cline, Wichita, Kansas

1 package (12 ounces) fresh *or* frozen cranberries, thawed
11 to 12 cups water, *divided*
2-1/2 cups sugar
1/2 cup red-hot candies
10 whole cloves
1 cup orange juice
2/3 cup lemon juice

In a saucepan, combine the cranberries and 4 cups water. Cook over medium heat until berries pop, about 15 minutes. Cool slightly. Press through a strainer; discard skins. Set cranberry mixture aside.

In a large saucepan, combine the sugar, red-hots, cloves, orange juice, lemon juice and 4 cups water. Cook and stir until sugar is dissolved and red-hots are melted. Stir in cranberry mixture. Add enough remaining water to achieve desired concentration; heat through. Discard cloves before serving. **Yield:** about 3 quarts.

Asparagus Beef Roll-Ups

I first sampled this hearty appetizer at a dinner party. These roll-ups were the first thing to disappear from the table.
—Linda Senuta, Gettysburg, Pennsylvania

2 tablespoons whipping cream
2 tablespoons sour cream
2 to 4 teaspoons prepared horseradish
1/4 teaspoon grated lemon peel
1/4 teaspoon salt
Dash pepper
4 flour tortillas (7 inches)
4 thin slices cooked roast beef
4 fresh asparagus spears, cooked and drained

In a small mixing bowl, beat whipping cream until soft peaks form. Fold in sour cream, horseradish, lemon peel, salt and pepper. Spread about 2 teaspoons on each tortilla; top with a slice of beef. Spread with the remaining cream mixture. Place an asparagus spear at one end; roll up tightly. Wrap in plastic wrap. Refrigerate for at least 2 hours. Cut into 1/2-in. slices. **Yield:** about 4 dozen.

Oriental Pork Tenderloin

I first made this appetizer on Christmas Eve a few years ago, and it has since
become a tradition. Serve the pork slices alone or on small dinner rolls with
hot mustard sauce, ketchup or horseradish.
—Diana Beyer, Graham, Washington

1 cup soy sauce
1/2 cup packed brown sugar
2 tablespoons red wine vinegar
or cider vinegar
2 teaspoons red food coloring,
optional
1 garlic clove, minced
1 teaspoon ground ginger
1 teaspoon salt
1/2 teaspoon pepper
3 pork tenderloins
(about 1 pound *each*)
Sesame seeds, toasted

In a bowl, combine the first eight ingredients; mix well.
Remove 1/2 cup for basting; cover and refrigerate. Pour the
remaining marinade into a large resealable plastic bag; add
tenderloins. Seal bag and turn to coat; refrigerate overnight.

Drain and discard marinade. Place pork on a rack in a
shallow roasting pan. Bake, uncovered, at 350° for 55-60
minutes or until a meat thermometer reads 160°, brushing
with reserved marinade every 15 minutes.

Sprinkle with sesame seeds. Cool for 30 minutes. Refrigerate for 2 hours or overnight. Cut into thin slices. **Yield:**
8-10 servings.

Triple Cheese Spread

This simple cheese spread appeals to every palate, so I rely on it often. It's a no-fuss
favorite of mine because it can be made 2 days before your gathering and then refrigerated.
—Angie Meyers, Chambersburg, Pennsylvania

2 packages (8 ounces *each*)
cream cheese, softened
1/2 cup mayonnaise
2 tablespoons milk
1/2 teaspoon salt
1/4 teaspoon pepper
1/8 teaspoon hot pepper sauce
2 cups (8 ounces) shredded
cheddar cheese

1/4 cup grated Parmesan cheese
1/4 cup minced fresh parsley
Assorted crackers

In a mixing bowl, beat cream cheese, mayonnaise, milk, salt,
pepper and hot pepper sauce until smooth. Fold in cheeses
and parsley. Cover and refrigerate for at least 1 hour before serving. Serve with crackers. **Yield:** 3 cups.

Party Puffs

(Pictured at right)

For a substantial appetizer, you can't go wrong with mini sandwiches. Instead of serving egg or ham salad on ordinary bread, I like to present them on homemade puff pastry.
—*Karen Owen, Rising Sun, Indiana*

> 1 cup water
> 1/2 cup butter (no substitutes)
> 1 cup all-purpose flour
> 4 eggs

EGG SALAD FILLING:
> 6 hard-cooked eggs, chopped
> 1/3 cup mayonnaise
> 3 tablespoons chutney, finely chopped
> 2 green onions, finely chopped
> 1 teaspoon salt
> 1/2 teaspoon curry powder

HAM SALAD FILLING:
> 1 can (4-1/4 ounces) deviled ham
> 1 package (3 ounces) cream cheese, softened
> 2 tablespoons finely chopped green pepper
> 1-1/2 teaspoons prepared horseradish
> 1 teaspoon lemon juice

In a saucepan over medium heat, bring water and butter to a boil. Add flour all at once and stir until a smooth ball forms. Remove from the heat; let stand for 5 minutes. Add eggs, one at a time, beating well after each addition. Continue beating until mixture is smooth and shiny. Drop by teaspoonfuls 2 in. apart onto greased baking sheets.

Bake at 400° for 20-25 minutes or until lightly browned. Remove to wire racks. Immediately cut a slit in each puff to allow steam to escape; cool completely.

In separate bowls, combine the ingredients for egg salad filling and ham salad filling. Split puffs and remove soft dough from inside. Just before serving, spoon filling into puffs; replace tops. Refrigerate leftovers. **Yield:** 7-1/2 dozen.

Family Traditions

INSTEAD of sending letters to Santa, I burned them in our furnace! Dad said Santa's helpers, called "Brownies", waited at the top of the chimney, where they caught the smoke and took it to the North Pole. Since Santa brought most of the things I asked for, I never once doubted this story.
—*Ed Belcher, Valley Grove, West Virginia*

Mixed Fruit Cheese Ball

For a pretty holiday presentation, I like to place this cheese ball on a festive platter and surround it with wedges of unpeeled apples and assorted crackers. People are always pleasantly surprised by the combination of flavors in every bite.
—Pat Habiger, Spearville, Kansas

2 packages (8 ounces *each*) cream cheese, softened
1 cup (4 ounces) shredded cheddar cheese
1/4 cup sour cream
1 teaspoon ground coriander
1/4 cup raisins, diced
1/4 cup dried apricots, diced
1/4 cup dates, diced

1/4 cup prunes, diced
1 cup chopped pecans
Apple slices and assorted crackers

In a bowl, combine the cream cheese, cheddar cheese, sour cream and coriander; mix well. Stir in the fruit. Shape into a ball; roll in pecans. Wrap tightly in plastic wrap. Refrigerate until serving. Serve with apples and crackers. **Yield:** 20 servings.

Sticky Chicken Wings

You'll want to keep an extra stack of napkins nearby once people start reaching for these sweet and savory chicken wings. The brown sugar marinade makes every bite finger-lickin' good!
—Laura Mahaffey, Annapolis, Maryland

3-1/2 to 4 pounds whole chicken wings*
1 cup packed brown sugar
3/4 cup soy sauce
1/2 cup teriyaki sauce
1/2 cup butter *or* margarine, melted
1 tablespoon Creole seasoning
1 teaspoon ground mustard

Cut chicken wings into three sections; discard wing tips. In a large resealable plastic bag, combine the brown sugar, soy sauce, teriyaki sauce, butter, Creole seasoning and mustard; add chicken. Seal bag and turn to coat; refrigerate for 8 hours or overnight.

Drain and discard marinade. Place chicken in a greased 13-in. x 9-in. x 2-in. baking dish. Bake, uncovered, at 375° for 45-50 minutes or until chicken juices run clear. Transfer the wings to a rack on a broiler pan. Broil 4 in. from the heat for 2-3 minutes on each side or until crisp. **Yield:** 12-15 servings.

*Editor's Note: 3 pounds of uncooked chicken wing sections may be substituted for the whole chicken wings. Omit the first step of the recipe.

Zippy Curry Dip

It's easy to encourage everyone to eat their vegetables when this creamy dip is served alongside. The curry flavor gets stronger the longer this dip stands, so I like to make it in advance.
—Priscilla Steffke, Wausau, Wisconsin

1/2 cup sour cream
1/2 cup mayonnaise *or* salad dressing
1 tablespoon sugar
1 teaspoon prepared horseradish
1 teaspoon grated onion
1 teaspoon cider vinegar

1/2 to 1 teaspoon curry powder
1/2 teaspoon garlic salt
Assorted fresh vegetables *or* potato chips

In a bowl, combine the first eight ingredients; mix well. Refrigerate until serving. Serve with vegetables or chips. **Yield:** about 1 cup.

Setting Up a Buffet Table

(Pictured at right)

AT A BUFFET, the table filled with flavorful food is the main focus. An easy way to make the table especially attractive is to create risers in varying heights. You don't need special equipment to achieve this look...everyday items in your home work just fine.

Position the table in the room where you'll be serving the food. Place selected risers on the table to create different heights (see photo 1). For our risers, we used sturdy boxes, a phone book and a coffee can. Other ideas include hardcover books, inverted cake pans, clay pots and metal buckets. Make sure the risers are big enough so serving platters sit steadily.

Drape a tablecloth over the top and form around the risers so that the cloth won't pull when platters of food are set on top (see photo 2).

1.

2.

'Tis the Season

Home-Baked Holiday Breads

MOST FOLKS agree the holidays just wouldn't be the same without a sweet and savory assortment of home-baked breads, rolls and muffins.

Homemade goodies not only make great gifts from the kitchen, they also add flavorful variety to any holiday breakfast, lunch, dinner...or even snack.

Family, friends and neighbors will eagerly accept a basket brimming with Easy Batter Rolls, Pineapple Cherry Loaves and Cherry-Go-Round (shown at right).

From tasty quick breads and mouth-watering muffins to tender rolls and yummy yeast breads, you're sure to find an oven-fresh baked good fit for any occasion!

"FLOUR"ISHING FAVORITES
(Clockwise from top left)

Easy Batter Rolls (p. 40)

Pineapple Cherry Loaves (p. 41)

Cherry-Go-Round (p. 43)

Easy Batter Rolls

(Pictured on page 38)

The first thing my guests ask when they come for dinner is if I'm serving these dinner rolls.
The buns are so light, airy and delicious that I'm constantly asked for the recipe.
— Thomasina Brunner, Gloversville, New York

3 cups all-purpose flour
2 tablespoons sugar
1 package (1/4 ounce) active
  dry yeast
1 teaspoon salt
1 cup water
2 tablespoons butter *or*
  margarine
1 egg
Melted butter *or* margarine

In a mixing bowl, combine 2 cups flour, sugar, yeast and salt. In a saucepan, heat water and butter to 120°-130°. Add to dry ingredients; beat until blended. Add egg; beat on low speed for 30 seconds, then on high for 3 minutes. Stir in remaining flour (batter will be stiff). Do not knead. Cover and let rise in a warm place until doubled, about 30 minutes.

Stir dough down. Fill greased muffin cups half full. Cover and let rise until doubled, about 40 minutes.

Bake at 350° for 15-20 minutes or until golden brown. Cool for 1 minute before removing from pan to a wire rack. Brush tops with melted butter. **Yield:** 1 dozen.

Norwegian Christmas Bread

When my husband became the minister for a church in an area populated with Norwegians,
my father-in-law was delighted because I had easy access to recipes he enjoyed as a child.
This is a traditional Christmas bread, but I make it for any holiday we get together.
— Deborah Petersen, Princeton, New Jersey

1 package (1/4 ounce) active
  dry yeast
1 cup warm water
  (110° to 115°)
1/2 cup sugar
1 egg
1/4 cup butter *or* margarine,
  softened
1/2 teaspoon salt
1 teaspoon ground cardamom
3-3/4 to 4 cups all-purpose flour
1/2 cup raisins
1/2 cup diced citron *or* mixed
  candied fruit

In a mixing bowl, dissolve yeast in warm water. Add sugar, egg, butter, salt, cardamom and 2 cups flour; mix well. Stir in raisins, citron and enough remaining flour to form a soft dough.

Turn onto a floured surface; knead until smooth and elastic, about 6-8 minutes. Place in a greased bowl, turning once to grease top. Cover and let rise in a warm place until doubled, about 1 hour.

Punch dough down; divide in half. Shape each portion into a flattened ball. Place in two greased 9-in. round baking pans. Cover and let rise in a warm place until doubled, about 1 hour.

Bake at 350° for 30-35 minutes or until golden brown. Remove from pans to cool on wire racks. **Yield:** 2 loaves.

Pineapple Cherry Loaves

(Pictured at right and on page 39)

Pineapple adds a fun twist to this holiday quick bread, plus it makes each delicious bite nice and moist. My family prefers this to traditional fruitcake.
— Dolores Peltier, Warren, Michigan

1-3/4 cups butter *or* margarine,
    softened
  2 cups sugar
  8 eggs
  1 teaspoon vanilla extract
3-3/4 cups all-purpose flour
  1 teaspoon salt
  1 teaspoon baking powder
  2 cans (8 ounces *each*)
    pineapple chunks, drained
  1 jar (10 ounces) red
    maraschino cherries, drained
    and halved
  1 jar (10 ounces) green
    maraschino cherries, drained
    and halved
  2 cups chopped walnuts

In a mixing bowl, cream butter and sugar. Add eggs, one at a time, beating well after each addition. Beat in vanilla. Combine the flour, salt and baking powder; add to creamed mixture until well blended. Stir in pineapple, cherries and nuts. Pour into three greased and floured 8-in. x 4-in. x 2-in. loaf pans.

Bake at 325° for 1-1/4 hours or until a toothpick comes out clean. Cool for 10 minutes before removing from pans to wire racks. **Yield:** 3 loaves.

SHORT-TERM BREAD STORAGE

TO KEEP quick and yeast breads fresh and flavorful for a few days, it's important to store them properly. (For longer storage, see "Facts About Freezing Breads" on page 49.)

- Quick breads and muffins are often quite moist. To prevent them from spoiling, let cool completely, then wrap tightly in foil or plastic wrap and let stand overnight. Refrigerate any leftovers the next day.
- Yeast breads, too, should be cooled completely and placed in an airtight container or bag. Store at room temperature in a cool dry place for 2 to 3 days. Yeast breads made with cheese or meat should be refrigerated.

Banana Buttermilk Muffins

Like my father, I love to spend time in the kitchen inventing new recipes.
There are few pleasures greater than sampling one of these warm muffins on a winter day.
—Kimberly Kronenberg, New Lenox, Illinois

1/2 cup butter *or* margarine,
    softened
1 cup sugar
2 eggs
2 large ripe bananas, mashed
    (about 1 cup)
1 teaspoon vanilla extract
2 cups all-purpose flour
1 teaspoon salt
1 teaspoon baking powder
1/2 teaspoon baking soda
1 cup buttermilk
TOPPING:
1/4 cup all-purpose flour
1/4 cup packed brown sugar

1/4 cup quick-cooking oats
2 tablespoons cold butter *or* margarine

In a mixing bowl, cream butter and sugar. Add eggs, one at a time, beating well after each. Add bananas and vanilla; mix well. Combine the flour, salt, baking powder and baking soda; add to creamed mixture alternately with buttermilk.

Fill greased or paper-lined muffin cups two-thirds full. For the topping, combine the flour, brown sugar and oats. Cut in butter until crumbly. Sprinkle a rounded teaspoonful over each muffin.

Bake at 400° for 16-20 minutes or until a toothpick comes out clean. Cool for 5 minutes before removing from pans to wire racks. **Yield:** 15 muffins.

Poppy Seed Cranberry Bread

I make poppy seed bread about once a month. So one Christmas, I decided to make it a little more
festive by stirring in some cranberries. My family loved the colorful addition.
—Cindy Harmon, Stuarts Draft, Virginia

2-1/2 cups all-purpose flour
3/4 cup sugar
2 tablespoons poppy seeds
3 teaspoons baking powder
1/2 teaspoon salt
1 egg
1 cup milk
1/3 cup butter *or* margarine,
    melted
2 teaspoons vanilla extract
2 teaspoons grated lemon peel
1 cup fresh *or* frozen
    cranberries, thawed and
    chopped

ICING:
1/2 cup confectioners' sugar
2 teaspoons milk

In a mixing bowl, combine the flour, sugar, poppy seeds, baking powder and salt. Combine the egg, milk, butter, vanilla and lemon peel; add to dry ingredients, beating on low speed just until moistened. Fold in cranberries. Pour into a greased 8-in. x 4-in. x 2-in. loaf pan.

Bake at 350° for 55-60 minutes or until a toothpick comes out clean. Cool for 10 minutes before removing from pan to a wire rack. Combine icing ingredients; drizzle over cooled loaf. **Yield:** 1 loaf.

Cherry-Go-Round

(Pictured at right and on page 38)

This fancy coffee cake is surprisingly easy.
It makes a great gift.
—Kathy McCreary, Wichita, Kansas

    1 package (1/4 ounce) active
      dry yeast
  1/4 cup warm water (110° to 115°)
    1 cup warm milk (110° to 115°)
  1/2 cup sugar
  1/2 cup butter *or* margarine,
      softened
    1 teaspoon salt
    1 egg
4-1/2 to 5 cups all-purpose flour
FILLING:
    2 cans (16 ounces *each*) pitted
      tart cherries, well drained
  1/2 cup all-purpose flour
  1/2 cup packed brown sugar
  1/2 cup chopped pecans
ICING:
    1 cup confectioners' sugar
  1/4 teaspoon vanilla extract
    1 to 2 tablespoons milk

In a mixing bowl, dissolve yeast in warm water. Add warm milk, sugar, butter, salt, egg and 2 cups flour; beat until smooth. Stir in enough remaining flour to form a soft dough.

Turn onto a lightly floured surface; knead until smooth and elastic, about 6-8 minutes. Place in a greased bowl, turning once to grease top. Cover and refrigerate for at least 2 hours or overnight.

Line two baking sheets with foil and grease well; set aside. Punch dough down. Turn onto a lightly floured sur-face; divide in half. Roll each portion into a 14-in. x 7-in. rectangle. Spread cherries over dough to within 1/2 in. of edges. Combine the flour, brown sugar and pecans; sprinkle over cherries.

Roll up jelly-roll style, starting with a long side; pinch seams and tuck ends under. Place seam side down on prepared baking sheets; pinch ends together to form a ring. With kitchen scissors, cut from outside edge two-thirds of the way toward center of ring at 1-in. intervals. Separate strips slightly and twist to allow filling to show. Cover and let rise until doubled, about 1 hour.

Bake at 350° for 20-25 minutes or until golden brown. Remove from pans to wire racks. Combine icing ingredients; drizzle over warm coffee cakes. **Yield:** 2 coffee cakes.

SHAPING A COFFEE CAKE RING

1. With a scissors, make cuts two-thirds of the way through dough at 1-inch intervals.

2. Separate the strips slightly, twisting each individually to show the filling inside.

Country White Bread

Knowing how much I like to bake bread, an aunt shared this recipe with me.
I enjoy making it on rainy days and giving the house a warm, homey feeling.
—Nancy Perry, Sayre, Pennsylvania

  2 packages (1/4 ounce *each*)
    active dry yeast
  3 cups warm water
    (110° to 115°)
  1 egg
  3 tablespoons shortening
  3 tablespoons sugar
  1 tablespoon salt
  9 to 10 cups all-purpose flour
Melted butter *or* margarine

In a mixing bowl, dissolve yeast in warm water. Add the egg, shortening, sugar, salt and 5 cups flour; beat until smooth. Stir in enough remaining flour to form a stiff dough.

Turn onto a floured surface; knead until smooth and elastic, about 6-8 minutes. Place in a greased bowl, turning once to grease top. Cover and let rise in a warm place until doubled, about 1 hour.

Punch dough down. Turn onto a lightly floured surface; divide in half. Roll each portion into a 12-in. x 10-in. rectangle. Roll up jelly-roll style, starting with a long side; pinch seam to seal. Place seam side down on a greased baking sheet. Cover and let rise until doubled, about 30 minutes.

With a sharp knife, make five shallow diagonal slashes across the top of each loaf. Bake at 400° for 35-40 minutes or until golden brown. Remove from pans to wire racks. Brush with butter. **Yield:** 2 loaves.

Favorite Pull-Apart Rolls

I've been using this recipe for soft pull-apart rolls for over 20 years and have yet to tire of it.
This easy-to-make recipe yields wonderful results.
—Gay Nell Nicholas, Henderson, Texas

3/4 cup shortening
3/4 cup sugar
  1 cup boiling water
  2 packages (1/4 ounce *each*)
    active dry yeast
  1 cup warm water
    (110° to 115°)
  2 eggs
  1 teaspoon salt
  1 teaspoon baking powder
1/2 teaspoon baking soda
  6 to 7 cups all-purpose flour

In a mixing bowl, cream shortening and sugar. Add boiling water; mix well. Cool to 110°-115°. Dissolve yeast in warm water. Add yeast mixture and eggs to creamed mixture; mix well. Add salt, baking powder, baking soda and 5 cups flour; beat until smooth. Stir in enough remaining flour to form a soft dough.

Turn onto a floured surface; knead until smooth and elastic, about 6-8 minutes. Do not let rise. Divide into 32 pieces; shape each into a ball. Place in two greased 9-in. round baking pans. Cover and let rise in a warm place until doubled, about 1-1/2 hours.

Bake at 400° for 18-22 minutes or until golden brown. Remove from pans to wire racks. **Yield:** 32 rolls.

Cranberry Apple Muffins

(Pictured at right)

It's sometimes difficult to get our daughter to eat healthy foods, but she gobbles up these fruit-filled muffins. Although these are a "must" around the holidays, I keep cranberries in the freezer so I can whip up a batch any time of year.
—Esther Bowers, Westland, Michigan

2 cups shredded peeled apples
1-1/3 cups sugar
1 cup chopped fresh *or* frozen cranberries, thawed
1 cup shredded carrots
1 cup chopped nuts
2 eggs, lightly beaten
1/2 cup vegetable oil
2-1/2 cups all-purpose flour
3 teaspoons baking powder
2 teaspoons baking soda
2 teaspoons ground cinnamon
2 teaspoons ground coriander, optional
1/2 teaspoon salt

In a bowl, combine apples and sugar; let stand for 10 minutes. Add cranberries, carrots, nuts, eggs and oil; mix well. Combine the flour, baking powder, baking soda, cinnamon, coriander if desired and salt; stir into apple mixture just until moistened. Fill paper-lined muffin cups two-thirds full.

Bake at 375° for 25-30 minutes or until a toothpick comes out clean. Cool for 5 minutes before removing from pans to wire racks. **Yield:** 1-1/2 dozen.

BAKING POWDER AND SODA SHOULD BUBBLE

IF YOU don't seem to have much success with making baked goods, there may be a simple answer—your baking powder and/or baking soda may not be fresh. The shelf life for these products is about 6 months, but here's how to test for freshness to be sure:
- For baking powder, place 1 teaspoon baking powder in a cup and add 1/3 cup hot tap water.
- For baking soda, place 1/4 teaspoon baking soda in a cup and add 2 teaspoons vinegar.

If active bubbling occurs, the products are fine to use. If not, they should be replaced. When buying a new can, check for an expiration date.

Traditional Whole Wheat Bread

With all the sweet breads that get served during the holidays, it's nice to make this nutritious wheat bread. I use it for sandwiches and also enjoy it toasted and buttered.
—Carol Forcum, Marion, Illinois

3 cups whole wheat flour
1/2 cup toasted wheat germ
1/4 cup mashed potato flakes
1/4 cup nonfat dry milk powder
2 tablespoons sugar
2 packages (1/4 ounce *each*) active dry yeast
2 teaspoons salt
2 cups water
3 tablespoons vegetable oil
3 eggs
3 to 3-1/2 cups all-purpose flour

In a mixing bowl, combine the first seven ingredients. In a saucepan, heat water and oil to 120°-130°. Add to dry ingredients; beat until blended. Beat in eggs until smooth. Stir in enough all-purpose flour to form a soft dough.

Turn onto a floured surface; knead until smooth and elastic, about 8-10 minutes. Place in a greased bowl, turning once to grease top. Cover and let rise in a warm place until doubled, about 1 hour.

Punch dough down. Turn onto a lightly floured surface; divide in half. Shape into loaves. Place in two greased 9-in. x 5-in. x 3-in. loaf pans. Cover and let rise until doubled, about 45 minutes.

Bake at 375° for 35-40 minutes or until golden brown. Remove from pans to cool on wire racks. **Yield:** 2 loaves.

Orange Chocolate Muffins

No one can resist these muffins, which feature a pleasant pairing of orange and bittersweet chocolate. They're sensational for breakfast with a warm mug of coffee or tea.
—Anna Pidhirny, Gibsonia, Pennsylvania

1/2 cup butter *or* margarine, softened
1 cup sugar
2 eggs
1/2 cup sour cream
1/2 cup orange juice
2 to 3 tablespoons grated orange peel
2 cups all-purpose flour
1 teaspoon baking powder
1/2 teaspoon baking soda
3 squares (1 ounce *each*) bittersweet chocolate, grated

In a mixing bowl, cream butter and sugar. Add eggs, one at a time, beating well after each addition. Beat in the sour cream, orange juice and peel. Combine the flour, baking powder, baking soda and grated chocolate; stir into creamed mixture just until moistened. Fill paper-lined muffin cups three-fourths full.

Bake at 400° for 15-20 minutes or until a toothpick comes out clean. Cool for 5 minutes before removing from pans to wire racks. **Yield:** about 1-1/2 dozen.

Festive Biscuit Strips

(Pictured at right)

Many people—especially children—don't care for fruitcake, so I came up with this sweet biscuit recipe. A few years ago, these strips earned high honors in a recipe contest sponsored by a local newspaper.
— Tena Huckleby, Greeneville, Tennessee

    2 cups self-rising flour*
1-3/4 cups all-purpose flour
    1 teaspoon ground cinnamon
  3/4 cup cold butter (no
        substitutes)
1-1/4 cups milk
  1/4 cup chopped fresh *or* frozen
        cranberries
  1/4 cup chopped navel orange
  1/4 cup crushed pineapple,
        drained
  1/4 cup chopped red maraschino
        cherries
  1/4 cup chopped green
        maraschino cherries
ICING:
  1/2 cup confectioners' sugar
    3 to 4 teaspoons milk

In a bowl, combine flours and cinnamon. Cut in butter until mixture resembles coarse crumbs. Gradually add milk, stirring with a fork until mixture forms a soft dough. Fold in the cranberries, orange, pineapple and cherries.

Turn onto a lightly floured surface; knead 4-5 times. Pat into a 13-in. x 9-in. rectangle. Cut into 3-in. x 1-in. strips; place on greased baking sheets. Bake at 425° for 11-15 minutes or until golden brown. Combine icing ingredients; drizzle over strips. Serve warm. **Yield:** about 3 dozen.

*Editor's Note: As a substitute for *each* cup of self-rising flour, place 1-1/2 teaspoons baking powder and 1/2 teaspoon salt in a measuring cup. Add all-purpose flour to measure 1 cup.

Chocolate Yeast Bread

Your family will love this tender loaf of chocolate bread.
slices are excellent when toasted and spread with butter, cream cheese or peanut butter.
—Laura Cryts, Derry, New Hampshire

4-1/2 cups all-purpose flour
1/3 cup baking cocoa
2 tablespoons sugar
1 package (1/4 ounce) active dry yeast
1 teaspoon salt
1/4 teaspoon baking soda
1 cup water
1/2 cup milk
1/2 cup semisweet chocolate chips
2 tablespoons butter *or* margarine
1 egg

In a mixing bowl, combine 1-1/4 cups flour, cocoa, sugar, yeast, salt and baking soda. In a saucepan, heat the water, milk, chocolate chips and butter; stir until chocolate is melted. Cool to 120°-130°. Add to dry ingredients; beat on medium speed for 2 minutes. Add 1/2 cup flour and egg; beat on high for 2 minutes. Stir in enough remaining flour to form a stiff dough.

Turn onto a floured surface; knead until smooth and elastic, about 6-8 minutes. Place in a greased bowl, turning once to grease top. Cover and let rise in a warm place until doubled, about 1 hour.

Punch dough down. Turn onto a lightly floured surface; divide in half. Shape into loaves. Place in two greased 8-in. x 4-in. x 2-in. loaf pans. Cover and let rise until doubled, about 1 hour.

Bake at 375° for 25-30 minutes or until browned. Remove from pans to cool on wire racks. **Yield:** 2 loaves.

Pecan Graham Muffins

These unique muffins have a little heavier texture than other varieties, making them perfect for cool days. Although they were skeptical at first, my family now says these are their favorite muffins.
—Kim Franzen, San Bernardino, California

1-1/3 cups graham cracker crumbs (about 22 squares)
1-1/4 cups all-purpose flour
1/2 cup sugar
1 teaspoon baking powder
3/4 teaspoon baking soda
1/4 teaspoon salt
1 egg
1 cup milk
1/3 cup vegetable oil
1/2 cup chopped pecans

In a large bowl, combine the first six ingredients. In another bowl, beat the egg, milk and oil; stir into dry ingredients just until moistened. Fold in pecans. Fill greased or paper-lined muffin cups two-thirds full.

Bake at 375° for 18-22 minutes or until a toothpick comes out clean. Cool for 5 minutes before removing from pan to a wire rack. **Yield:** 1 dozen.

Editor's Note: Four dozen miniature muffin cups may be used; bake for 12-15 minutes.

Walnut Marmalade Mini Loaves

(Pictured at right)

The orange marmalade and fresh juice in this bread give it a citrusy aroma, moist texture and warm golden color. It's almost like giving friends a gift of home-baked sunshine!
—Michele Bragg, Palm City, Florida

2-1/2 cups all-purpose flour
  1/3 cup sugar
    1 tablespoon baking powder
    1 teaspoon salt
    1 jar (12 ounces) orange marmalade
    1 cup orange juice
    3 tablespoons vegetable oil
    1 egg
    1 cup chopped walnuts

In a mixing bowl, combine the flour, sugar, baking powder and salt. Combine the marmalade, orange juice, oil and egg; stir into dry ingredients just until moistened. Stir in walnuts. Pour into three greased 5-3/4-in. x 3-in. x 2-in. loaf pans.

Bake at 350° for 40-50 minutes or until a toothpick comes out clean. Cool for 10 minutes before removing from pans to wire racks. **Yield:** 3 loaves.

FACTS ABOUT FREEZING BREADS

DURING the hectic holiday season, it's nice to bake and freeze some breads, rolls and muffins a few weeks in advance.

After the baked goods have cooled completely, follow these steps to ensure they remain fresh and flavorful in the freezer.

- For best results, don't top bread with icing, frosting or glaze before freezing.
- Wrap baked goods tightly in freezer-safe plastic bags, airtight containers, heavy-duty aluminum foil or freezer paper. (Place coffee cakes and rolls on foil-wrapped cardboard before wrapping and freezing.)
- Make sure the temperature of your freezer is 0° or less.
- Most baked goods are fine to freeze for up to 1 month.
- To thaw, unwrap slightly and thaw at room temperature for 2 to 3 hours.
- The baked goods can be served at room temperature. Or to serve warm, wrap in foil and bake at 350° for 15 to 20 minutes.

Golden Pan Rolls

When I'm having company for dinner, I bake these rolls during the day. Then the house has a wonderful aroma when the guests arrive. The ranch dressing mix adds terrific flavor.
—*Kimm Avans, De Soto, Texas*

3-1/2 to 4 cups all-purpose flour
2 tablespoons sugar
1 envelope ranch salad dressing mix
2 packages (1/4 ounce *each*) active dry yeast
1 can (10-3/4 ounces) condensed cheddar cheese soup, undiluted
1/4 cup butter *or* margarine
1/4 cup milk
2 eggs
2 tablespoons cornmeal, *divided*

In a mixing bowl, combine 1-1/2 cups flour, sugar, dressing mix and yeast. In a saucepan, heat the soup, butter and milk to 120°-130°. Add to dry ingredients; beat until moistened. Add eggs; beat on medium speed for 3 minutes. Stir in enough remaining flour to form a stiff dough.

Turn onto a floured surface; knead until smooth and elastic, about 8-10 minutes. Place in a greased bowl, turning once to grease top. Cover and let rise in a warm place until doubled, about 1 hour.

Punch dough down. Turn onto a lightly floured surface. Divide into 24 pieces; shape each into a ball. Grease a 13-in. x 9-in. x 2-in. baking pan and sprinkle with 1 tablespoon cornmeal. Place rolls in pan; sprinkle with remaining cornmeal. Cover and let rise in a warm place until doubled, about 30 minutes.

Bake at 400° for 15-18 minutes or until golden brown. Remove from pan to wire racks. **Yield:** 2 dozen.

Potato Muffins

Come in from the cold to enjoy these moist parsley-flecked muffins. They're comforting and delicious with a steaming bowl of soup, a savory stew or a favorite casserole.
—*Marlene Loecke, Des Moines, Iowa*

1 egg
2/3 cup milk
1-1/2 cups all-purpose flour
2 tablespoons sugar
3 teaspoons baking powder
1 teaspoon salt
1-1/2 cups mashed potatoes (prepared with milk and butter)
1 tablespoon minced fresh parsley

In a bowl, beat egg and milk. Combine the flour, sugar, baking powder and salt; stir into egg mixture just until moistened. Fold in potatoes and parsley. Fill greased muffin cups two-thirds full.

Bake at 400° for 30-35 minutes or until a toothpick comes out clean. Cool for 5 minutes before removing from pan to a wire rack. Serve warm. **Yield:** 1 dozen.

Cardamom Braids

(Pictured at right)

This treasured recipe reflects my Norwegian heritage. The subtle hint of cardamom is undeniably good.
—Sally Nelsen, Tempe, Arizona

  2 packages (1/4 ounce *each*)
     active dry yeast
1/2 cup warm water
     (110° to 115°)
1-1/2 cups warm milk
     (110° to 115°)
1-1/2 cups sugar
1/2 cup butter *or* margarine,
     softened
  3 eggs
  2 teaspoons ground cardamom
1/2 teaspoon salt
  9 to 10 cups all-purpose flour
Additional sugar

In a mixing bowl, dissolve yeast in warm water. Add warm milk, sugar, butter, 2 eggs, cardamom, salt and 6 cups flour; beat until smooth. Stir in enough remaining flour to form a soft dough.

Turn onto a floured surface; knead until smooth and elastic, about 6-8 minutes. Place in a greased bowl, turning once to grease top. Cover and let rise in a warm place until doubled, about 1-1/4 hours.

Punch dough down; cover and let rest for 10 minutes. Divide into fourths. Divide each portion into thirds; shape each into a 12-in. rope. Place three ropes on a greased baking sheet and braid; pinch ends to seal and tuck under. Repeat with remaining dough. Cover and let rise in a warm place until nearly doubled, about 45 minutes.

Beat remaining egg; brush over loaves. Sprinkle with sugar. Bake at 375° for 20-25 minutes or until golden brown. Remove from pans to wire racks. **Yield:** 4 loaves.

BRAIDING BREAD

1. Place three ropes of dough almost touching on a baking sheet. Starting in the middle, loosely bring the left rope under the center rope. Bring the right rope under the new center rope and repeat until you reach the end.

2. Turn the pan and repeat braiding.

3. Press ends to seal; tuck under.

Dilly Bran Bread

My daughter, Deedee, used this recipe for her 4-H yeast bread project and received rave reviews.
This started out as a basic wheat recipe, but I eventually added dill to suit my family's tastes.
—Kathy Bock, Waterman, Illinois

3-1/2 to 4 cups all-purpose flour
1 cup whole wheat flour
1/2 cup bran cereal
2 tablespoons fresh dill *or* 2
   teaspoons dill weed
2 packages (1/4 ounce *each*)
   active dry yeast
2 teaspoons salt
1 cup warm buttermilk
   (120° to 130°)
1/2 cup warm water
   (120° to 130°)
1/2 cup honey
1/2 cup shortening
2 eggs
Additional butter *or* margarine,
   melted

In a mixing bowl, combine 1 cup all-purpose flour, whole wheat flour, cereal, dill, yeast and salt. Add the buttermilk, water, honey and shortening; beat until smooth. Add eggs; beat on medium speed for 3 minutes. Stir in enough remaining all-purpose flour to form a stiff dough.

Turn onto a floured surface; knead until smooth and elastic, about 5 minutes. Place in a greased bowl, turning once to grease top. Cover and let rise in a warm place until doubled, about 1 hour.

Punch dough down; divide in half. Shape into round loaves; place each in a greased 1-qt. baking dish. Cover and let rise until doubled, about 45 minutes.

Bake at 375° for 20-25 minutes or until golden brown. Remove from pans to wire racks. Brush with butter. **Yield:** 2 loaves.

Editor's Note: This recipe was tested with Post 100% Bran cereal. Warmed buttermilk will appear curdled.

Pecan Pumpkin Loaves

Pumpkin and a blend of spices make this quick bread a real holiday treat.
I can easily prepare three loaves to give to friends and neighbors as gifts.
—Leona Luecking, West Burlington, Iowa

3-1/3 cups all-purpose flour
3 cups sugar
2 teaspoons baking soda
1 teaspoon salt
1 teaspoon ground cinnamon
1/2 teaspoon ground ginger
1/4 teaspoon ground nutmeg
1/4 teaspoon ground cloves
2 cups cooked *or* canned
   pumpkin
4 eggs

1 cup vegetable oil
2/3 cup water
1/2 teaspoon vanilla extract
3/4 cup chopped pecans

In a mixing bowl, combine the first eight ingredients. Add pumpkin, eggs, oil, water and vanilla; mix well. Stir in pecans. Pour into three greased 8-in. x 4-in. x 2-in. loaf pans.

Bake at 350° for 1 hour or until a toothpick comes out clean. Cool for 10 minutes before removing from pans to wire racks. **Yield:** 3 loaves.

Creamy Chocolate Crescents

(Pictured at right)

"Homemade" chocolate-filled treats are easy when you start with convenient refrigerated crescent rolls. They're impressive yet easy to serve for breakfast or a midday snack.
— Bill Hughes, Dolores, Colorado

2 packages (3 ounces *each*)
  cream cheese, softened
1/4 cup butter (no substitutes),
  softened
1/2 cup confectioners' sugar
2 tablespoons cornstarch
2 cups (12 ounces) semisweet
  chocolate chips, melted
1/2 teaspoon vanilla extract
4 tubes (8 ounces *each*)
  refrigerated crescent rolls
GLAZE:
2 eggs
1 tablespoon butter (no
  substitutes), melted

1/2 teaspoon almond extract
Confectioners' sugar, optional

In a mixing bowl, beat cream cheese, butter and sugar. Add cornstarch, melted chocolate and vanilla; beat until smooth. Unroll crescent roll dough; separate into triangles.

In a small bowl, whisk together eggs, butter and extract. Brush some over dough. Drop rounded teaspoonfuls of chocolate mixture at the wide end of each triangle; roll up from the wide end. Place point side down on greased baking sheets; curve ends slightly. Brush with remaining glaze.

Bake at 350° for 10-15 minutes or until golden. Remove from pans to cool on wire racks. Dust with confectioners' sugar if desired. **Yield:** about 2-1/2 dozen.

FESTIVE WAYS TO SERVE BUTTER

INSTEAD of having a stick of butter in a dish, impress guests with fun and festive shapes.

- To create butter cutouts, cut a chilled stick of butter into 1/4-inch slices. Cut out shapes with small cookie cutters. Simple shapes like bells, Christmas trees and circles work best.
- To make balls of butter, dip a melon baller

in hot water and cut balls from a chilled 1-pound block of butter.

- Butter cutouts and balls can be made early in the day and refrigerated in an airtight container. Just before serving, arrange the cutouts or balls on a small lettuce-lined serving plate or on individual bread and butter plates.

'Tis the Season
Feast on Festive Entrees

WOULD YOU like to try a new and exciting entree for your next Christmas dinner but are worried your family will scoff?

With this chapter, you can set a new course with confidence. That's because these pages are packed with surefire beef, poultry, pork, seafood and game main dishes to suit casual get-togethers and formal sit-down dinners.

Each and every recipe is guaranteed to please because they've been taste-tested and approved by a finicky family just like yours.

So go ahead…present guests with impressive Stuffed Crown Roast of Pork, Roast Duck with Orange Glaze or Greek-Style Rib Eye Steaks (shown at right).

Then forever say farewell to skepticism—and ho-hum holiday dinners!

NEWFOUND
FAVORITES
(Top to bottom)

Stuffed Crown
Roast of Pork (p. 57)

Roast Duck with
Orange Glaze (p. 60)

Greek-Style
Rib Eye Steaks (p. 58)

Sage Chicken Cordon Bleu

It's nice to surprise the family with special meals like this during the week.
I usually double the recipe so we can enjoy leftovers the next day.
—*Martha Stine, Johnstown, Pennsylvania*

6 boneless skinless chicken
  breast halves
6 slices thinly sliced deli ham
6 strips mozzarella cheese
  (3 inches x 1-1/2 inches x 1/2
  inch)
1 medium tomato, seeded and
  chopped
3/4 teaspoon dried sage leaves
1/3 cup dry bread crumbs
2 tablespoons grated Parmesan
  cheese
2 tablespoons minced fresh
  parsley
1/4 cup butter *or* margarine,
  melted

Flatten chicken to 1/8-in. thickness. Place a ham slice, a mozzarella cheese strip, 1 tablespoon tomato and 1/8 teaspoon sage down the center of each chicken breast. Roll up and tuck in ends; secure with toothpicks.

In a shallow bowl, combine bread crumbs, Parmesan cheese and parsley. Dip chicken in butter, then roll in crumb mixture. Place in a greased 9-in. square baking dish. Drizzle with remaining butter.

Bake, uncovered, at 350° for 45 minutes or until chicken juices run clear. Discard toothpicks. **Yield:** 6 servings.

Holiday Pork Roast

This moist and tender pork roast always makes a statement when it appears
on the table. This is my husband's entree of choice for any occasion.
It's a no-fuss favorite because it marinates overnight.
—*Teri Lindquist, Gurnee, Illinois*

1/2 cup Dijon mustard
2 tablespoons soy sauce
1 tablespoon olive *or*
  vegetable oil
4 garlic cloves, minced
1 teaspoon dried thyme
1 boneless pork loin roast
  (about 4 pounds)
1 teaspoon salt
1/4 teaspoon pepper
1-1/2 cups white wine *or*
  chicken broth

In a bowl, combine the mustard, soy sauce, oil, garlic and thyme; rub over roast. Place in a large resealable bag. Seal bag; refrigerate overnight, turning occasionally.

Place roast on a rack in a shallow roasting pan. Sprinkle with salt and pepper; pour wine or broth into the pan. Bake, uncovered, at 325° for 2-1/2 hours until a meat thermometer reads 160°, basting with pan juices every 30 minutes. Let stand for 10 minutes before slicing. **Yield:** 12-15 servings.

Stuffed Crown Roast Of Pork

(Pictured at right and on page 55)

*I make this roast every Christmas, much
to the delight of family and friends.
The recipe was passed down from my
mother, so I've been using it for years.
The succulent stuffing is oh-so-tasty!*
—*Martha Forte, East Setauket, New York*

  3 tablespoons vegetable oil,
    divided
  1 pork crown roast
    (16 ribs and about 8 pounds)
1-1/4 pounds bulk Italian sausage
  3 cups finely chopped onions
  2 cups finely chopped carrots
  2 cups finely chopped celery
  2 garlic cloves, minced
  4 cups diced cooked peeled
    potatoes
1/3 cup minced fresh parsley
  1 teaspoon fennel seed, crushed
  1 teaspoon salt
1/8 teaspoon pepper
Decorative foil *or* paper frills,
  optional

Rub 1 tablespoon oil over entire roast; place on a rack in a
shallow roasting pan. Cover rib ends with aluminum foil.
Bake, uncovered, at 325° for 1-3/4 hours.

For stuffing, in a large skillet, cook sausage over medium heat until no longer pink; drain and set aside. In the
same skillet, saute the onions, carrots, celery and garlic in
remaining oil until tender. Stir in the potatoes, parsley, fennel, salt, pepper and reserved sausage. Carefully spoon into center of roast.

Bake 1 hour longer or until a meat thermometer reads
160° and meat juices run clear. Replace foil with decorative frills if desired. Remove stuffing to a serving bowl;
slice roast between ribs. **Yield:** 12-16 servings.

Greek-Style Rib Eye Steaks

(Pictured on page 54)

*Because our children are grown, I often cook for just my husband and me.
When I want to serve something special, this is the entree I usually reach for.
Seasonings, black olives and feta cheese give steak great flavor.*
—Ruby Williams, Bogalusa, Louisiana

1-1/2 teaspoons garlic powder
1-1/2 teaspoons dried oregano
1-1/2 teaspoons dried basil
   1/2 teaspoon salt
   1/8 teaspoon pepper
      2 beef rib eye steaks
         (1-1/2 inches thick)
      1 tablespoon olive *or*
         vegetable oil

1 tablespoon lemon juice
2 tablespoons crumbled feta *or* blue cheese
1 tablespoon sliced ripe olives

In a small bowl, combine the first five ingredients; press into both sides of steaks. In a large skillet, cook steaks in oil for 7-9 minutes on each side or until meat reaches desired doneness. Sprinkle with lemon juice, cheese and olives. Serve immediately. **Yield:** 2 servings.

HOLIDAY MENU SUGGESTIONS

DOES MEAL PLANNING around the holidays have you puzzled? Our Test Kitchen suggests five mouth-watering menus that are wonderful for both fancy get-togethers and casual gatherings. Each meal features an entree from this chapter and side dishes and desserts found in other chapters of this book.

- **Fine Dining.** Instead of traditional turkey, why not try succulent Holiday Pork Roast (page 56)? It makes for a festive meal when paired with Snowcapped Butternut Squash (page 73), green beans, a basket of rolls and Cranberry-Pistachio Ice Cream Cake (page 101).
- **Delightful Chicken Dinner.** Entertaining can be easy with the right foods. Honey-Glazed Chicken (page 64) is no-fuss fare because it bakes in the oven, while Broccoli with Ginger-Orange Butter (page 68) cooks in mere minutes. For a make-ahead dessert, turn to Pumpkin-Pecan Cake Roll (page 149).

- **Casual Cooking for Two.** Take a trip for two to the Mediterranean and sample Greek-Style Rib Eye Steaks (above). Dilly Bread Ring (page 139) and a simple green salad are perfect partners for this ethnic entree. Save leftovers of Chocolate Baklava (page 97) to impress folks at your next social engagement.
- **Convenient Casseroles.** Served alongside oven-baked Dilled Duchess Potatoes (page 77), Asparagus Chicken Divan (page 62) is one dish everyone will enjoy. Then enjoy indulging in decadent Chocolate Mousse Torte (page 94).
- **On the Lighter Side.** With all of the rich foods accompanying the holidays, it's nice to offer a little lighter fare. You'll reel in raves with Crispy Orange Roughy (page 60), Curried Rice Pilaf (page 71) and a tossed green salad. Then net compliments with cool and creamy Peppermint Stick Dessert (page 98).

Festive Meat Loaf Pinwheel

(Pictured at right)

Most people wouldn't think of serving meat loaf for a holiday gathering, but think again! It's wonderful for a crowd because its hearty, zesty flavor appeals to all.
— *Vera Sullivan, Amity, Oregon*

3 eggs
1 cup dry bread crumbs
1/2 cup finely chopped onion
1/2 cup finely chopped green pepper
1/4 cup ketchup
2 teaspoons minced fresh parsley
1 teaspoon dried basil
1 teaspoon dried oregano
1 garlic clove, minced
2 teaspoons salt
1/2 teaspoon pepper
5 pounds lean ground beef
3/4 pound thinly sliced deli ham
3/4 pound thinly sliced Swiss cheese

TOMATO PEPPER SAUCE:
1/2 cup finely chopped onion
2 celery ribs, cut into 1-1/2 inch-julienne strips
1/2 medium green pepper, cut into 1-1/2-inch julienne strips
1 garlic clove, minced
1 to 2 tablespoons olive *or* vegetable oil
2 cups chopped fresh tomatoes
1 cup beef broth
1 bay leaf
1 teaspoon sugar
1/4 teaspoon salt

1/4 teaspoon dried thyme
1 tablespoon cornstarch
2 tablespoons cold water

In a large bowl, combine the first 11 ingredients. Crumble beef over mixture and mix well. On a piece of heavy-duty foil, pat beef mixture into a 17-in. x 15-in. rectangle. Cover with ham and cheese slices to within 1/2 in. of edges. Roll up tightly jelly-roll style, starting with a short side. Place seam side down in a roasting pan. Bake, uncovered, at 350° for 1-1/4 to 1-1/2 hours or until a meat thermometer reads 160°.

In a saucepan, saute the onion, celery, green pepper and garlic in oil for 3-5 minutes or until tender. Add tomatoes, broth, bay leaf, sugar, salt and thyme. Simmer, uncovered, for 30 minutes. Discard bay leaf. Combine cornstarch and water until smooth; stir into sauce. Bring to a boil; cook and stir for 2 minutes or until thickened. Drain meat loaf; top with sauce. **Yield:** 15-20 servings.

Roast Duck with Orange Glaze

(Pictured on page 54)

This duck is a nice alternative for a festive dinner on holidays.
The meat remains moist and tender, thanks to the fruity glaze and simple stuffing.
—*Jeanne Koelsch, San Rafael, California*

1 domestic duckling
  (4 to 6 pounds)
1 teaspoon caraway seeds
4 cups crushed stuffing
1/2 medium green pepper,
  finely chopped
1 small onion, finely chopped
1 celery rib, finely chopped
1 tablespoon rubbed sage
1/2 teaspoon salt
1/8 teaspoon pepper
Pinch dried thyme
Pinch ground nutmeg
1/2 cup chicken broth
ORANGE GLAZE:
1/2 cup packed brown sugar
2 tablespoons plus 1-1/2
  teaspoons sugar
2 tablespoons cornstarch

Pinch salt
1 cup orange juice
1 tablespoon grated orange peel
1 drop hot pepper sauce

Sprinkle inside of duck with caraway seeds; prick skin well. In a bowl, combine stuffing, vegetables, seasonings and broth; mix lightly. Spoon into duck. Place breast side up on a rack in a large shallow roasting pan.

Bake, uncovered, at 350° for 2-1/2 to 3-1/4 hours or until a meat thermometer reads 180° for the duck and 165° for the stuffing (drain fat from pan as it accumulates). Cover and let stand for 20 minutes before removing stuffing and slicing.

Meanwhile, for glaze, combine the sugars, cornstarch and salt in a saucepan. Gradually stir in orange juice, peel and hot pepper sauce until blended. Bring to a boil; cook and stir for 2 minutes or until thickened. Serve with duck. **Yield:** 2-4 servings.

Crispy Orange Roughy

When you're looking for a main course on the lighter side, try this flavorful dish.
The crunchy topping nicely complements the tender fish.
—*Nancy Florian, St. Johnsville, New York*

1/3 cup lemon juice
1 tablespoon olive *or*
  vegetable oil
2 teaspoons dried oregano
1/4 teaspoon salt
1/4 teaspoon pepper
2 cups mashed potato flakes
4 orange roughy, cod *or*
  haddock fillets (6 ounces *each*)

Line a baking sheet with aluminum foil and spray with nonstick cooking spray; set aside. In a shallow bowl, whisk together the lemon juice, oil, oregano, salt and pepper. Place the potato flakes in another bowl.

Dip fillets in lemon juice mixture, then coat with potato flakes. Place on prepared pan. Bake at 500° for 10 minutes or until fish flakes easily with a fork and is golden brown. **Yield:** 4 servings.

Mushroom Pork Scallopini

(Pictured at right)

Tender pork has fantastic flavor when coated with a buttery sauce seasoned with garlic and herbs. This serves a lot, so I make it often for company.
—Carol Ebner, Fort Dodge, Iowa

     3 to 4 pork tenderloins
        (about 1 pound *each*), cut into
        1-inch slices
     1 cup all-purpose flour
   1/4 cup butter *or* margarine
   1/4 cup vegetable oil
     1 cup white wine *or*
        chicken broth
   1/2 cup water
     1 large onion, chopped
     1 to 2 garlic cloves, minced
   1/2 teaspoon salt
   1/2 teaspoon pepper
   1/2 teaspoon *each* dried thyme,
        oregano and rosemary,
        crushed
     1 pound fresh mushrooms,
        sliced
Hot cooked fettuccine

Dredge pork slices in flour. In a large skillet, heat butter and oil. Brown pork on both sides in batches; remove and keep warm. Stir wine or broth, water, onion, garlic and seasonings into drippings. Return pork to skillet, layering if necessary. Top with mushrooms.

Cover and cook over low heat for 15-20 minutes or until meat juices run clear. Serve over fettuccine. **Yield:** 8-10 servings.

Family Traditions

ACCORDING to German tradition, children would eagerly head to the tree on Christmas morning to search for the pickle ornament that their parents hid in the green boughs the night before. The children knew whoever found the blown-glass ornament first would receive an extra gift as a reward for being the most observant child.

Asparagus Chicken Divan

I first came across this recipe at a restaurant while living in New York City many years ago.
This makes a delectable dish for lunch or dinner served with a simple tossed salad.
—Jeanne Koelsch, San Rafael, California

1 **pound boneless skinless chicken breasts**
2 **pounds fresh asparagus, trimmed**
1 **can (10-3/4 ounces) condensed cream of chicken soup, undiluted**
1 **teaspoon Worcestershire sauce**
1/4 **teaspoon ground nutmeg**
1 **cup grated Parmesan cheese, *divided***
1/2 **cup whipping cream, whipped**
3/4 **cup mayonnaise***

Broil chicken 6 in. from the heat until juices run clear. Meanwhile, in a large skillet, bring 1/2 in. of water to a boil. Add asparagus. Reduce heat; cover and simmer for 3-5 minutes or until crisp-tender. Drain and place in a greased shallow 2-1/2-qt. baking dish. Cut chicken into thin slices.

In a bowl, combine the soup, Worcestershire sauce and nutmeg. Spread half over asparagus. Sprinkle with 1/3 cup Parmesan cheese. Top with chicken. Spread remaining soup mixture over chicken; sprinkle with 1/3 cup Parmesan cheese.

Bake, uncovered, at 400° for 20 minutes. Fold whipped cream into mayonnaise; spread over top. Sprinkle with remaining Parmesan cheese. Broil 4-6 in. from the heat for about 2 minutes or until golden brown. **Yield:** 6-8 servings.

*Editor's Note: Reduced-fat or fat-free mayonnaise may not be substituted for regular mayonnaise.

Grilled Rack of Lamb

Whenever my husband and I really want to impress guests, we make this rack of lamb. The
marinade keeps the meat juicy and tender while grilling.
—Gail Cawsey, Sequim, Washington

2 **cups apple cider *or* juice**
2/3 **cup cider vinegar**
2/3 **cup thinly sliced green onions**
1/2 **cup vegetable oil**
1/3 **cup honey**
1/4 **cup steak sauce**
2 **teaspoons dried tarragon**
2 **teaspoons salt**
1/2 **teaspoon pepper**
4 **racks of lamb (1-1/2 to 2 pounds *each*)**

In a saucepan, combine the first nine ingredients. Bring to a boil. Reduce heat; simmer, uncovered, for 20 minutes. Remove 1 cup for basting; cover and refrigerate. Pour the remaining marinade into a large resealable plastic bag; add lamb. Seal bag and turn to coat; refrigerate for 2-3 hours or overnight, turning once or twice.

Coat grill rack with nonstick cooking spray before starting the grill. Drain and discard the marinade. Cover rib ends of lamb with foil. Grill, covered, over medium heat for 15 minutes. Baste with reserved marinade. Grill 5-10 minutes longer, basting occasionally, or until meat reaches desired doneness (for rare, a meat thermometer should read 140°; for medium-well, 160°). **Yield:** 4-6 servings.

Shrimp Creole

(Pictured at right)

This seafood dish is perfect for casual holiday gatherings and will reel in rave reviews. I've been using this tried-and-true recipe for more than 30 years.
— Barbara Lindsey, Manvel, Texas

3 medium onions, chopped
1 large green pepper, chopped
2 celery ribs, chopped
6 tablespoons butter *or* margarine, *divided*
1 can (28 ounces) diced tomatoes, undrained
1 can (15 ounces) tomato sauce
1 cup picante sauce
1 tablespoon minced fresh parsley
3 tablespoons all-purpose flour
1 can (14-1/2 ounces) chicken broth
1/2 teaspoon salt
1/4 teaspoon pepper
2 bay leaves
3 pounds cooked medium shrimp, peeled and deveined
1 can (8 ounces) mushroom stems and pieces, drained
1/2 cup chopped stuffed olives
1/2 cup chopped green onions
Hot cooked rice

In a large skillet, saute onions, green pepper and celery in 5 tablespoons butter until tender. Add the tomatoes, tomato sauce, picante sauce and parsley. In a saucepan, melt the remaining butter; stir in flour until smooth. Gradually add the broth, salt, pepper and bay leaves. Stir into vegetable mixture. Bring to a boil. Reduce heat; cover and simmer for 30 minutes.

Add the shrimp, mushrooms, olives and green onions. Cover and cook 10 minutes longer or until heated through. Discard bay leaves. Serve over rice. **Yield:** 12-14 servings.

GREAT GARNISHES

INSTEAD of discarding the unused leaves when chopping celery for Shrimp Creole (pictured above), save them to use as an inexpensive garnish.

Other garnish ideas include a sprig of parsley or additional chopped stuffed olives or green onions. *Never* garnish with bay leaves...they pose a choking hazard.

Stuffed Flank Steak

Family and friends are always impressed when this entree appears on the table,
but it's actually quite easy. I sometimes assemble the steak roll in the morning and refrigerate
before browning. The rich tomato sauce tastes great over mashed potatoes.
—Nadeen Shrewsberry, Hickory, North Carolina

1 beef flank steak
    (about 1-1/2 pounds)
1/2 cup chopped onion, *divided*
2 tablespoons vegetable oil,
    divided
2 cups cubed seasoned stuffing
3/4 cup water, *divided*
1/2 teaspoon poultry seasoning
1/2 cup all-purpose flour
1/4 teaspoon salt
1/8 teaspoon pepper
1 can (28 ounces) diced
    tomatoes, undrained
2 tablespoons ketchup
1/4 cup chopped green pepper
1 jar (4-1/2 ounces) sliced
    mushrooms, drained

Flatten steak to 1/4-in. thickness. In a skillet, saute 1/4 cup onion in 1 tablespoon oil until golden brown. Add stuffing, 1/4 cup water and poultry seasoning; cook and stir until water is absorbed. Spoon over steak; roll up tightly jelly-roll style, starting with a long side. Secure with toothpicks or kitchen string.

Combine the flour, salt and pepper. Coat meat with flour mixture. In a Dutch oven, brown meat on all sides in remaining oil. Add the tomatoes, ketchup and remaining water and onion. Bring to a boil. Reduce heat; cover and simmer for 1-1/4 hours.

Add green pepper and mushrooms; cook 15 minutes longer or until meat reaches desired doneness. **Yield:** 4 servings.

Honey-Glazed Chicken

My family can't get enough of this finger-lickin'-good chicken, and I often double the recipe.
The sauce can also be used when grilling chicken.
—Harriet Lusch, Muncie, Indiana

2/3 cup soy sauce
2/3 cup sherry *or* apple juice
2/3 cup honey
1/2 cup water
1 small onion, chopped
2 garlic cloves, minced
1/4 teaspoon ground ginger
2 broiler/fryer chickens
    (3 to 4 pounds *each*), cut up

In a large resealable plastic bag, combine the first seven ingredients. Add chicken; seal and turn to coat. Refrigerate for 1-2 hours. Place chicken and marinade in two greased 13-in. x 9-in. x 2-in. baking dishes. Bake, uncovered, at 350° for 1 hour or until juices run clear. Drain marinade and serve with chicken. **Yield:** 8 servings.

Fish Fillets With Citrus-Herb Butter

(Pictured at right)

The staff in our Test Kitchen combined dried herbs to transform ordinary butter into a tasty topping for your favorite fish fillets. Served with wild rice, this is a simply elegant entree.

1 cup butter (no substitutes), softened
1/3 cup mixed dried herbs of your choice (chives, thyme, basil, dill weed)
2 tablespoons grated lemon peel
2 tablespoons grated orange peel
2 tablespoons lemon juice
2 tablespoons orange juice
4 teaspoons confectioners' sugar
1/2 teaspoon salt
1 pound orange roughy, cod *or* haddock fillets

In a small mixing bowl, combine the first eight ingredients; beat until blended. Shape half of the butter mixture into a log; wrap in plastic wrap and freeze. Place remaining mixture in a microwave-safe bowl; heat for 1-2 minutes or until melted.

Place fish fillets in an ungreased 13-in. x 9-in. x 2-in. baking dish. Drizzle with melted butter mixture. Bake, uncovered, at 375° for 10-15 minutes or until fish flakes easily with a fork. Cut butter log into slices; serve with fish. **Yield:** 4 servings.

Sparkling Yuletide Sides

IF YOUR FAMILY is like most, they expect your Christmas menu to include many of the same tried-and-true dishes from year to year.

But if you're looking to add a little variety to your table, why not offer one or two deliciously different side dishes alongside the old standbys?

Present holiday guests with the eye-catching color and appealing flavors of Cranberry Sweet Potato Bake, Swiss-Topped Cauliflower Soup, Broccoli with Ginger-Orange Butter, Curried Rice Pilaf and Cinnamon Gelatin Salad (shown at right).

Or turn the pages for even more mouth-watering vegetables, pasta, rice, soups and salads that are bound to become newfound favorites your family will ask for time and again!

TWISTS ON THE TRADITIONAL
(Clockwise from top right)

Cranberry Sweet Potato Bake (p. 69)

Swiss-Topped Cauliflower Soup (p. 72)

Broccoli with Ginger-Orange Butter (p. 68)

Curried Rice Pilaf (p. 71)

Cinnamon Gelatin Salad (p. 71)

Broccoli with Ginger-Orange Butter

(Pictured on page 66)

Instead of simply topping steamed broccoli with plain butter, the home economists in our Test Kitchen suggest you try serving it with an easy-to-prepare flavored butter. This is also a tasty topping for sugar snap peas, green beans and carrots.

1 pound fresh broccoli, cut into spears
2 tablespoons orange marmalade
1 tablespoon butter (no substitutes)
1/2 teaspoon cider vinegar
1/8 teaspoon ground ginger

Add 1 in. of water to a large saucepan; add broccoli. Bring to a boil. Reduce heat; cover and simmer for 5-8 minutes or until crisp-tender. Meanwhile, in a small saucepan, combine the marmalade, butter, vinegar and ginger. Cook until marmalade and butter are melted. Drain broccoli; drizzle with butter mixture. **Yield:** 6 servings.

Cheddar Cauliflower Quiche

A dear friend shared this recipe one year when we both had an abundance of cauliflower from our gardens. My husband and I enjoy this so much that I make it for breakfast, lunch and dinner!
— *Tracy Watson, Hobson, Montana*

1 cup all-purpose flour
1/4 teaspoon salt
1/3 cup shortening
3 tablespoons cold milk
4 cups chopped fresh cauliflower, cooked
1/2 cup slivered almonds, toasted
2 eggs
1/2 cup milk
1/2 cup mayonnaise*
1-1/2 cups (6 ounces) shredded cheddar cheese, *divided*
1/8 teaspoon ground nutmeg
1/8 teaspoon pepper

In a bowl, combine flour and salt. Cut in shortening until mixture resembles coarse crumbs. Stir in milk until mixture forms a ball. Wrap in plastic wrap; refrigerate for 30 minutes. Unwrap dough. On a floured surface, roll out to fit a 9-in. pie plate. Place in pie plate; flute edges. Line unpricked pastry with a double thickness of foil. Bake at 450° for 5 minutes. Remove foil; bake 5 minutes longer.

Spoon cauliflower into crust; top with almonds. In a blender, combine eggs, milk, mayonnaise, 1-1/4 cups cheese, nutmeg and pepper; cover and process until smooth. Pour over almonds; sprinkle with remaining cheese. Bake at 350° for 30-35 minutes or until a knife inserted near the center comes out clean. Let stand for 10 minutes before cutting. **Yield:** 6-8 servings.

*Editor's Note: Reduced-fat or fat-free mayonnaise may not be substituted for regular mayonnaise.

Cranberry Sweet Potato Bake

(Pictured at right and on page 67)

Instead of serving sweet potatoes alone at Christmas, I like to pair them with cranberries. Each bite offers a delicious contrast of sweet and tart flavors.
—Linda Boot
Fort St. John, British Columbia

3-1/2 pounds sweet potatoes
   2 large onions, peeled and halved
   2 teaspoons olive *or* vegetable oil
   2 cups halved fresh *or* frozen cranberries
2/3 cup packed brown sugar
1/2 cup orange juice
   2 tablespoons butter *or* margarine, melted
   1 tablespoon grated orange peel
1/2 teaspoon *each* salt, ground ginger, cinnamon and nutmeg

Place sweet potatoes and onions on a baking sheet; brush onions with oil. Bake, uncovered, at 400° for 50-60 minutes or just until tender. When cool enough to handle, peel and cube potatoes and dice onions; place in a large bowl.

Combine the remaining ingredients; mix well. Gently stir into potato mixture. Transfer to a greased 13-in. x 9-in. x 2-in. baking dish. Bake, uncovered, at 350° for 25-30 minutes or until heated through, stirring once. **Yield:** 12-14 servings.

DRESSING UP EVERYDAY VEGETABLES

A SIDE DISH doesn't have to be elaborate. In fact, when serving a variety of flavorful foods, it's nice to include a basic vegetable that's been simply seasoned. Try these tasty toppings for hot cooked vegetables.

- Combine 1/4 cup plain dry bread crumbs, 1-1/2 teaspoons melted butter *or* margarine, 1/2 teaspoon dried parsley flakes and a dash of salt. Sprinkle over cooked vegetables.

- Melt 1/4 cup butter *or* margarine over low heat; stir in 1/2 teaspoon garlic powder, 2 tablespoons lemon juice, 1 tablespoon slivered toasted almonds, 1 tablespoon minced chives *or* 1 tablespoon grated Parmesan cheese. Drizzle over cooked vegetables.
- For extra ease, prepare a packaged white, hollandaise or bernaise sauce mix as directed and serve over your vegetable of choice.

Hearty Meatball Soup

A little bit of this thick and hearty soup goes a long way, so it's terrific to take to potlucks.
My husband, Patrick, and I enjoy this on cold winter nights.
—Janice Thompson, Lansing, Michigan

2 eggs
1 cup soft bread crumbs
1 teaspoon salt
1/2 teaspoon pepper
1 pound lean ground beef
1 pound ground pork
1/2 pound ground turkey
4 cups beef broth
1 can (46 ounces) tomato juice
2 cans (14-1/2 ounces *each*) stewed tomatoes
8 cups shredded cabbage
1 cup thinly sliced celery
1 cup thinly sliced carrots
8 green onions, sliced
3/4 cup uncooked long grain rice
2 teaspoons dried basil
3 tablespoons minced fresh parsley
2 tablespoons soy sauce

In a bowl, combine the eggs, bread crumbs, salt and pepper. Crumble meat over mixture and mix well. Shape into 1-in. balls. In a soup kettle, bring broth to a boil. Carefully add the meatballs. Add the tomato juice, tomatoes, vegetables, rice and basil. Cover and simmer for 30 minutes.

Add the parsley and soy sauce. Simmer, uncovered, for 10 minutes or until meatballs are no longer pink and vegetables are tender. **Yield:** 22-24 servings (5-3/4 quarts).

Supreme Scalloped Potatoes

For a true down-home dinner, serve these creamy potatoes alongside your favorite roast beef.
When I know I have a full day ahead, I'll assemble this casserole the night before.
—Erla Burkholder, Ewing, Illinois

8 medium potatoes (about 3 pounds), peeled
1-1/2 cups (6 ounces) shredded cheddar cheese, *divided*
1/3 cup chopped onion
1 can (10-3/4 ounces) condensed cream of chicken soup, undiluted
1 cup (8 ounces) sour cream
3/4 cup milk
2 tablespoons butter *or* margarine, melted
1/2 teaspoon salt
1/2 teaspoon pepper

In a Dutch oven or large kettle, cook potatoes in boiling salted water until tender. Cool completely; shred and place in a large bowl. Add 1 cup cheese and onion. Combine remaining ingredients; pour over potato mixture.

Transfer to a greased 2-1/2-qt. baking dish. Sprinkle with remaining cheese. Bake, uncovered, at 350° for 35-40 minutes or until bubbly. **Yield:** 12-14 servings.

Cinnamon Gelatin Salad

(Pictured at right and on page 67)

Crunchy apples and pecans contrast nicely with smooth gelatin in this pretty salad.
— Denita DeValcourt
Lawrenceburg, Tennessee

1/4 cup red-hot candies
1/4 cup water
1 package (6 ounces) raspberry *or* cherry gelatin
1-3/4 cups boiling water
1/2 to 1 teaspoon ground cinnamon
1-3/4 cups cold water
1 medium tart apple, peeled and chopped
1/4 cup chopped pecans

In a heavy saucepan, cook and stir candies and water until candies are melted. In a bowl, dissolve gelatin in boiling water. Stir in candy mixture and cinnamon. Stir in cold water. Cover and refrigerate until partially set. Fold in apple and pecans. Pour into a 1-1/2-qt. serving bowl. Refrigerate until set. **Yield:** 6 servings.

Curried Rice Pilaf

(Pictured on page 66)

In this baked rice dish, green onions give great color, raisins bring a touch of sweetness and almonds add crunch. I think you'll agree the mild curry flavor pleases all palates.
— Lee Bremson, Kansas City, Missouri

1/2 cup chopped green onions, *divided*
2 garlic cloves, minced
1/4 cup butter *or* margarine
1-1/2 cups uncooked long grain rice
1/2 teaspoon curry powder
3 cups chicken broth
1/2 teaspoon salt
1/2 cup golden raisins
1/2 cup chopped almonds, toasted

In a skillet, saute 1/4 cup onions and garlic in butter until tender. Stir in rice and curry. Saute for 2-3 minutes or until rice is lightly browned.

In a saucepan, heat broth and salt. Pour over rice mixture; stir. Cover and simmer for 35-40 minutes or until rice is tender. Remove from the heat; stir in raisins, almonds and remaining onions. **Yield:** 4-6 servings.

Swiss-Topped Cauliflower Soup

(Pictured on page 67)

Since I came across this recipe a few years ago, it's become my husband's favorite soup.
With fresh bread, we enjoy this as a hearty supper in winter.
—*C.C. McKie, Chicago, Illinois*

2 medium onions
4 whole cloves
4 cups water
2 cans (10-1/2 ounces *each*)
  condensed chicken broth,
  undiluted
3 medium leeks (white portion
  only), sliced
3 medium carrots, sliced
1 teaspoon salt
1 teaspoon dried marjoram
1/2 teaspoon celery seed
1/2 teaspoon ground nutmeg
1/4 teaspoon white pepper
1 medium head cauliflower,
  broken into florets and thinly
  sliced (about 6 cups)
1 tablespoon cornstarch
1/2 cup whipping cream
2 egg yolks, beaten
1/2 pound sliced Swiss cheese,
  cut into 4-inch x 1/2-inch
  strips

Quarter one onion; stuff the cloves into the second onion. In a large saucepan, combine water and broth; add onions, leeks, carrots and seasonings. Bring to a boil. Reduce heat; cover and simmer for 15 minutes. Add cauliflower; simmer, uncovered, for 30 minutes or until vegetables are tender. Remove from the heat.

In a bowl, combine cornstarch and cream until smooth. Stir in egg yolks. Stir a small amount of hot soup into cream mixture; return all to the pan, stirring constantly. Simmer, uncov-

ered, for 15 minutes. Discard the whole onion.

Ladle soup into individual ramekins. Top with cheese strips. Broil 4-6 in. from the heat for 3-5 minutes or until cheese is bubbly. Serve immediately. **Yield:** 6-8 servings.

SELECTING SUCCESSFUL SIDE DISHES

TRYING to decide which side dishes to serve for your holiday dinner can be overwhelming. Here are some suggestions to help simplify your selection.

- Variety is key to pleasing all of your guests. So have an assortment of hot and cold foods and offer vegetables along with grains and pasta. For kids and older guests, provide at least one simple, lightly seasoned side dish.
- The entree and side dishes should complement one another. If your entree has intense flavor, pair it with more mild-flavored side dishes and vice versa. If your entree has lots of garlic, onion or nuts, stay away from a side dish that's loaded with any of those same ingredients.
- For ease of preparation, look for an oven-baked side dish that cooks at the same temperature as your oven entree.
- If your oven will be full with the entree and other side dishes, choose another side dish that can be prepared on the stovetop or in a slow cooker. Or for a refreshing break from the hot foods, turn to a tossed salad, an assortment of fresh fruit or a tried-and-true relish tray.
- Recipes that can be prepared ahead (like gelatin salads and overnight casseroles) are a real boon to busy cooks.

Snowcapped Butternut Squash

(Pictured at right)

I first prepared this side dish in my high school home economics class. The cool sour cream sauce makes it irresistible, even to those people who usually don't care for squash.
—*Karen Peterson-Johnson*
Salt Lake City, Utah

2 pounds butternut squash, peeled, seeded and cubed (about 4 cups)
1 medium onion, halved and thinly sliced
2 tablespoons butter *or* margarine
1 cup (8 ounces) sour cream
1/2 teaspoon salt
1/2 teaspoon dill weed
Dash pepper
Additional dill weed, optional

Place squash in a large saucepan and cover with water; bring to a boil. Reduce heat; cover and simmer for 20-30 minutes or until tender.

In a skillet, saute onion in butter until tender. Remove from the heat. Stir in sour cream, salt, dill and pepper. Drain squash and transfer to a serving bowl; top with sauce. Sprinkle with additional dill if desired. **Yield:** 4-6 servings.

Paprika Mushrooms

I use paprika in much of my cooking. . .it gives food a nice, mild flavor and adds pretty color. These mushrooms are great alongside chicken or beef entrees.
—*Rosemarie Kondrk, Old Bridge, New Jersey*

2 medium onions, chopped
2 tablespoons vegetable oil
1 tablespoon paprika
1 pound fresh mushrooms, halved
1 cup chicken broth

In a large skillet, saute onions in oil until tender. Stir in paprika. Add mushrooms and broth; bring to a boil. Reduce heat; cover and simmer for 5-10 minutes or until mushrooms are tender. **Yield:** 4 servings.

Slow-Cooked Vegetable Soup

You just have to try this hearty soup for its unique blend of flavors and beautiful appearance. With all the rich foods served during the holidays, it's nice to serve this soup loaded with fiber and vitamins.
—*Christina Till, South Haven, Michigan*

3/4 cup chopped onion
1/2 cup chopped celery
1/2 cup chopped green pepper
2 tablespoons olive *or* vegetable oil
1 large potato, peeled and diced
1 medium sweet potato, peeled and diced
1 to 2 garlic cloves, minced
3 cups chicken broth *or* water
2 medium fresh tomatoes, chopped
1 can (16 ounces) kidney beans, rinsed and drained
1 can (15 ounces) garbanzo beans *or* chickpeas, rinsed and drained

2 teaspoons soy sauce
1 teaspoon paprika
1/2 teaspoon dried basil
1/4 teaspoon salt
1/4 teaspoon ground turmeric
1 bay leaf
Dash cayenne pepper

In a large skillet, saute onion, celery and green pepper in oil until crisp-tender. Add potato, sweet potato and garlic; saute 3-5 minutes longer. Transfer to a 5-qt. slow cooker. Stir in the remaining ingredients. Cover and cook on low for 9-10 hours or until vegetables are tender. Discard bay leaf before serving. **Yield:** 12 servings (about 3 quarts).

Walnut Broccoli Bake

A friend shared this recipe with me years ago and it instantly became a family favorite. When I make it for potluck luncheons, there are no leftovers.
—*Carolyn Bosetti, LaSalle, Ontario*

3 packages (10 ounces *each*) frozen chopped broccoli
1/2 cup butter *or* margarine, *divided*
1/4 cup all-purpose flour
4-1/2 teaspoons chicken bouillon granules
2 cups milk
1/2 cup water
4 cups seasoned stuffing croutons
1/2 cup chopped walnuts

Cook broccoli according to package directions; drain and transfer to a greased 3-qt. baking dish. In a saucepan, melt 1/4 cup butter. Stir in flour and bouillon. Gradually add milk. Bring to a boil; cook and stir for 2 minutes or until thickened and bubbly. Pour over broccoli.

In a large saucepan, melt the remaining butter. Add the water, stuffing and walnuts; mix well. Spoon over the broccoli. Bake, uncovered, at 375° for 20-25 minutes or until stuffing is lightly browned. **Yield:** 12 servings.

Chicken Wild Rice Soup

(Pictured at right)

I'm originally from Minnesota, where wild rice grows in abundance and is very popular in recipes. This soup has been part of our Christmas Eve menu for years. To save time, I cook the chicken and wild rice and cut up the vegetables the day before.
—Virginia Montmarquet
Riverside, California

2 quarts chicken broth
1/2 pound fresh mushrooms, chopped
1 cup finely chopped celery
1 cup shredded carrots
1/2 cup finely chopped onion
1 teaspoon chicken bouillon granules
1 teaspoon dried parsley flakes
1/4 teaspoon garlic powder
1/4 teaspoon dried thyme
1/4 cup butter *or* margarine
1/4 cup all-purpose flour
1 can (10-3/4 ounces) condensed cream of mushroom soup, undiluted
1/2 cup dry white wine *or* additional chicken broth
3 cups cooked wild rice
2 cups cubed cooked chicken

In a large saucepan, combine the first nine ingredients. Bring to a boil. Reduce heat; cover and simmer for 30 minutes.

In a soup kettle or Dutch oven, melt butter. Stir in flour until smooth. Gradually whisk in broth mixture. Bring to a boil; cook and stir for 2 minutes or until thickened. Whisk in soup and wine or broth. Add rice and chicken; heat through. **Yield:** 14 servings (3-1/2 quarts).

Family Traditions

WHEN I was growing up in Minnesota, Mom would open our home to many friends and family on Christmas Eve. After having our fill of her steaming Chicken Wild Rice Soup (recipe this page), crusty bakery rolls and a sweet assortment of cookies, we'd bundle up and head out for Christmas caroling before attending midnight Mass. The memories of that magical night continue to warm my heart.
—Virginia Montmarquet, Riverside, California

Eggnog Fruit Fluff

I regularly fit a blend of apples, blueberries and other fruit into my December menus.
The eggnog in the dressing suits this sweet salad for Christmas.
— Tami Harrington, West Chicago, Illinois

1 cup eggnog,* chilled
1 envelope whipped topping mix
1/4 teaspoon ground nutmeg
1 can (20 ounces) pineapple tidbits, drained
1 can (16 ounces) sliced peaches, drained
2 medium tart apples, chopped
1 cup fresh blueberries
3/4 cup halved maraschino cherries
3/4 cup chopped walnuts

In a mixing bowl, beat eggnog, whipped topping mix and nutmeg on high speed until soft peaks form. Combine the remaining ingredients; fold into eggnog mixture. Cover and refrigerate. Gently stir just before serving. **Yield:** 10-12 servings.

*Editor's Note: This recipe was tested with commercially prepared eggnog.

Spinach Noodle Casserole

We enjoyed a similar casserole at a friend's house many years ago. She didn't have a recipe but
told me the basic ingredients. I eventually came up with my own version and have shared
the recipe many times since. It goes great with ham but also is filling by itself.
— Doris Tschorn, Levittown, New York

4 cups uncooked egg noodles
1/4 cup butter *or* margarine
1/4 cup all-purpose flour
1 teaspoon salt
1/8 teaspoon pepper
2 cups milk
2 packages (10 ounces *each*) frozen chopped spinach, thawed and drained
2 cups (8 ounces) shredded Swiss cheese
2 cups (8 ounces) shredded mozzarella cheese
1/4 cup grated Parmesan cheese
Paprika, optional

Cook noodles according to package directions; drain and rinse in cold water. In a saucepan, melt butter over medium heat. Stir in flour, salt and pepper until smooth. Gradually add milk. Bring to a boil; cook and stir for 2 minutes or until thickened.

Arrange half of the noodles in an ungreased 11-in. x 7-in. x 2-in. baking dish; cover with half of the spinach and half of the Swiss cheese. Spread with half of the white sauce. Repeat layers. Top with mozzarella and Parmesan cheeses. Sprinkle with paprika if desired.

Cover and bake at 350° for 20 minutes. Uncover; bake 20 minutes longer. Let stand for 15 minutes before cutting. **Yield:** 12-14 servings.

Dilled Duchess Potatoes

(Pictured at right)

When you want to impress dinner guests with a splendid side dish, these eye-catching potatoes from our Test Kitchen fill the bill. The appealing flavor of dill really shines through.

9 **medium baking potatoes (about 3 pounds), peeled and quartered**
3 **eggs**
3/4 **cup butter *or* margarine, softened, *divided***
2 **tablespoons snipped fresh dill *or* 2 teaspoons dill weed**
1-1/2 **teaspoons salt**
1/4 **teaspoon pepper**
3 **to 6 tablespoons milk**

Place potatoes in a Dutch oven or large kettle and cover with water; bring to a boil. Reduce heat; cover and simmer for 20-25 minutes or until tender. Drain. In a large mixing bowl, mash potatoes. Beat in the eggs, 6 tablespoons of butter, dill, salt, pepper and enough milk to achieve a light fluffy consistency.

Using a pastry bag or heavy-duty resealable plastic bag and a large star tip, pipe potatoes into 12 mounds on two greased baking sheets. Melt remaining butter; drizzle over potatoes. Bake at 400° for 20 minutes or until golden brown. **Yield:** 12 servings.

Hot Fruit Soup

Some fruit soups call for soaking dried fruit overnight. But my fast version conveniently uses canned fruits. This makes a unique ham dinner side dish.
—Rose Kammerling, Sun City, Arizona

1 **can (21 ounces) cherry pie filling**
1 **can (20 ounces) pineapple tidbits, drained**
1 **can (15-1/4 ounces) apricot halves, drained and halved**
1 **can (15 ounces) sliced peaches, drained**

1 **can (15 ounces) sliced pears, drained**
1 **can (11 ounces) mandarin oranges, drained**
1 **cup golden raisins**

In a large bowl, combine all ingredients; mix well. Pour into an ungreased 2-1/2-qt. baking dish. Bake, uncovered, at 350° for 25-30 minutes or until bubbly. **Yield:** 16-18 servings.

Creamy Vegetable Medley

With its rich, cheesy sauce and golden onion topping, this casserole has broad appeal.
Because of that—and the fact that it's quick to prepare—I frequently prepare it for many functions.
—Pat Waymire, Yellow Springs, Ohio

1 package (16 ounces) frozen broccoli, carrot and cauliflower blend
1 can (10-3/4 ounces) condensed cream of mushroom soup, undiluted
1 cup (4 ounces) shredded Swiss cheese, *divided*
1/3 cup sour cream
1 jar (2 ounces) diced pimientos, drained
1/4 teaspoon salt
1/4 teaspoon pepper
1 can (2.8 ounces) french-fried onions, *divided*

In a bowl, combine the vegetables, soup, 1/2 cup cheese, sour cream, pimientos, salt, pepper and half of the onions. Pour into a greased 1-1/2-qt. baking dish. Cover and bake at 350° for 30-40 minutes or until the edges are browned. Uncover; sprinkle with the remaining cheese and onions. Bake 5 minutes longer or until the cheese is melted. **Yield:** 8 servings.

Slow-Cooked Chowder

The hectic holidays often leave little time for cooking. That's why this slow cooker recipe
is a favorite. I just combine the ingredients, flip a switch and forget it!
—Pam Leonard, Aberdeen, South Dakota

5 cups water
5 teaspoons chicken bouillon granules
8 medium potatoes, cubed
2 medium onions, chopped
1 medium carrot, thinly sliced
1 celery rib, thinly sliced
1/4 cup butter *or* margarine, cubed
1 teaspoon salt
1/4 teaspoon pepper
1 can (12 ounces) evaporated milk
1 tablespoon minced fresh parsley

In a 5-qt. slow cooker, combine the nine ingredients. Cover and cook on high for 1 hour. Reduce heat to low; cover and cook for 5-6 hours or until vegetables are tender. Stir in milk and parsley; heat through. **Yield:** 12 servings (about 3 quarts).

SIMPLE SOUP GARNISHES

ADDING A GARNISH to soup before serving gives color and adds to the flavor and texture. Easy ideas include: finely chopped green onions or chives, minced fresh parsley, shredded cheddar cheese, grated or shredded Parmesan cheese, a dollop of sour cream and plain or seasoned croutons.

Cauliflower Zucchini Toss

(Pictured at right)

I appreciate make-ahead recipes like this that keep me out of the kitchen.
—Paula Marchesi
Lenhartsville, Pennsylvania

2 cups cauliflowerets
2 cups sliced zucchini
1/2 cup sliced green onions
1/2 cup halved pitted ripe olives
1/3 cup vegetable oil
1/4 cup orange juice
2 tablespoons white wine
   vinegar *or* cider vinegar
1 teaspoon dried tarragon
1 teaspoon grated orange peel
1/2 teaspoon salt
1/4 to 1/2 teaspoon pepper
8 cups torn salad greens

Add 1 in. of water to a saucepan; add cauliflower. Bring to a boil. Reduce heat; cover and simmer for 5-8 minutes or until crisp-tender. Rinse in cold water; drain and place in a large bowl. Add zucchini, onions and olives; toss.

In a jar with a tight-fitting lid, combine the oil, orange juice, vinegar, tarragon, orange peel, salt and pepper; shake well. Pour over cauliflower mixture and toss to coat. Cover and refrigerate for 2 hours. Just before serving, toss with salad greens. **Yield:** 14-16 servings.

Bacon Wild Rice Bake

This casserole is very special to me. I found the recipe when visiting a friend in Canada, and now my daughter sends me wild rice from Wisconsin. I like to serve this with Cornish game hens.
—Nancy Schlinger, Middleport, New York

2 cups uncooked wild rice
2 small green peppers, chopped
1 large onion, chopped
2 tablespoons butter *or*
   margarine
2 jars (4-1/2 ounces *each*) sliced
   mushrooms, drained
1 teaspoon salt
4 to 6 bacon strips, cooked and
   crumbled

In a large saucepan, cook wild rice according to package directions. Meanwhile, in a skillet, saute green peppers and onion in butter until tender. Add mushrooms and salt; heat through. Stir into wild rice; add bacon.

Transfer to a greased 13-in. x 9-in. x 2-in. baking dish. Cover and bake at 350° for 30 minutes. Uncover; bake 5-10 minutes longer or until heated through. **Yield:** 12-14 servings.

Tangy Red Cabbage

I often make Christmas dinners for the elderly ladies of our church who live alone.
Many are of German descent and look forward to this traditional cabbage dish.
—Joan Solberg, Ashland, Wisconsin

1 medium head red cabbage, shredded
10 bacon strips, diced
1 cup white vinegar
6 tablespoons sugar
2 teaspoons dill seed
2 teaspoons salt
Minced fresh parsley *or* parsley sprigs, optional

Place cabbage in a large bowl; cover with boiling water. Let stand for 5 minutes; drain. In a Dutch oven, cook bacon over medium heat until crisp. Drain, reserving 1/4 cup drippings; set bacon aside. Stir vinegar, sugar, dill seed and salt into drippings until sugar is dissolved.

Stir in cabbage; bring to a boil. Reduce heat; cover and simmer for 1 to 1-1/2 hours or until cabbage is tender. Stir in bacon. Garnish with parsley if desired. **Yield:** 10 servings.

Creamed Pearl Onions

When our children were small, we always celebrated Christmas at our house. This was one of many recipes I relied on that can be prepared a day in advance, which gave me more time to spend with guests. Everyone expected to see this vegetable dish on the table every year.
—Barbara Caserman, Lake Havasu City, Arizona

50 pearl onions
1/4 cup butter *or* margarine
1/4 cup all-purpose flour
1/2 teaspoon salt
Dash pepper
1 cup chicken broth
1 cup half-and-half cream
1/4 cup minced fresh parsley
3 tablespoons grated Parmesan cheese
Pimiento strips, optional

In a Dutch oven or large kettle, bring 6 cups water to a boil. Add pearl onions; boil for 10-15 minutes or until tender. Drain and rinse in cold water; peel and set aside.

In a saucepan, melt butter. Stir in flour, salt and pepper until smooth. Gradually add broth and cream, stirring constantly. Bring to a boil; cook and stir for 2 minutes or until thickened and bubbly. Stir in parsley, cheese and onions.

Pour into an ungreased 1-qt. baking dish. Cover and refrigerate overnight. Remove from the refrigerator 30 minutes before baking. Cover and bake at 350° for 15 minutes; stir. Top with pimientos if desired. Bake, uncovered, 10 minutes longer or until bubbly and heated through. **Yield:** 4-6 servings.

Colorful Veggie Casserole

(Pictured at right)

When I retired from the U.S. Army a few years ago, I began tinkering in the kitchen and now work in there regularly. This casserole is chock-full of vegetables and flavor and couldn't be easier to prepare.
—Marion White
La Center, Washington

1 cup chopped green onions
1 large carrot, shredded
2 celery ribs, chopped
1 small green pepper, chopped
1 small sweet red pepper, chopped
6 garlic cloves, minced
2 tablespoons vegetable oil
3 pounds frozen cubed hash brown potatoes, thawed
2 cans (10-3/4 ounces *each*) condensed cream of chicken soup, undiluted
1-1/2 cups (6 ounces) shredded cheddar cheese, *divided*
1-1/2 cups (6 ounces) shredded mozzarella cheese, *divided*

2 tablespoons minced fresh parsley *or* 2 teaspoons dried parsley flakes
1 teaspoon salt
Paprika

In a large skillet, saute onions, carrot, celery, peppers and garlic in oil until crisp-tender. Transfer to a large bowl; add hash browns, soup, 1 cup cheddar cheese, 1 cup mozzarella cheese, parsley and salt; mix well.

Pour into a greased 3-qt. baking dish. Sprinkle with remaining cheeses and paprika. Bake, uncovered, at 350° for 1 hour or until golden brown. **Yield:** 12-16 servings.

'TIS THE *Season*

Come for Cheesecake & Coffee!

THE HOLIDAYS are hectic and there's often not a moment to spare. So if time doesn't allow you to plan an entire sit-down dinner party, consider a simple, elegant get-together featuring cheesecakes and coffee.

Although cheesecakes do take some time to prepare, they're conveniently made the day before and simply served on party day. Best of all, cheesecakes will surely impress all of your guests!

For a superb assortment of flavorful crusts, creamy fillings and tasty toppings, you can rely on Chocolate Macadamia Cheesecake, Cranberry Cheesecake and Apricot Swirl Cheesecake (shown at right).

To round out your dazzling dessert party, see our suggestions for setting up an unforgettable coffee service.

CHEERS FOR
CHEESECAKE
(Left to right)

Chocolate Macadamia
Cheesecake (p. 84)

Cranberry
Cheesecake (p. 86)

Apricot Swirl
Cheesecake (p. 85)

Chocolate Macadamia Cheesecake

(Pictured on page 82)

When one of my co-workers turned 50, I created this recipe for her birthday.
There wasn't a crumb left on the platter when I left for home that day!
—*Bob Weaver, University Place, Washington*

1-1/4 cups chocolate wafer crumbs
   (about 25 wafers)
 1/4 cup ground macadamia nuts
   2 tablespoons sugar
   3 tablespoons butter *or*
   margarine, melted
 1/8 teaspoon almond extract
FILLING:
   8 squares (1 ounce *each*) white
   baking chocolate
   4 packages (8 ounces *each*)
   cream cheese, softened
 3/4 cup sugar
   3 tablespoons all-purpose flour
   5 eggs
   1 teaspoon vanilla extract
 1/3 cup milk chocolate chips
TOPPING:
   8 squares (1 ounce *each*)
   semisweet chocolate
   7 tablespoons whipping cream
White chocolate shavings and
   chopped macadamia nuts

In a bowl, combine wafer crumbs, nuts and sugar; stir in butter and almond extract. Press onto the bottom of a greased 10-in. springform pan. Bake at 350° for 10 minutes. Cool on a wire rack. Reduce heat to 325°.

In a saucepan over low heat, melt white chocolate, stirring frequently until smooth. Cool. In a mixing bowl, beat cream cheese and sugar until smooth. Add flour; mix well. Add eggs and vanilla; beat on low speed just until combined. Remove 1 cup and set aside. Stir melted white chocolate into remaining cream cheese mixture; beat just until combined. Pour over crust.

Melt chocolate chips; cool slightly. Stir in reserved cream cheese mixture; drop by spoonfuls over filling. Cut through filling with a knife to swirl chocolate mixture.

Place pan on a baking sheet. Bake at 325° for 55-60 minutes or until center is almost set. Cool on a wire rack for 10 minutes. Carefully run a knife around edge of pan to loosen. Cool 1 hour longer.

In a saucepan over low heat, melt semisweet chocolate with cream; stir until smooth. Cool slightly. Spread over cheesecake. Refrigerate for 4 hours or overnight. Remove sides of pan. Garnish with chocolate shavings and macadamia nuts. **Yield:** 12 servings.

PREVENTING CRACKED CHEESECAKES

SOMETIMES a "cracked" cheesecake is unavoidable. But these steps can help prevent the top from slitting open.
- Let cream cheese and eggs stand at room temperature for 30 minutes before mixing.
- After adding the eggs, beat mixture on low speed. (If too much air is beaten into the mixture, it will puff during baking, then collapse and split when cooled.)
- Grease the sides of the pan so the cake easily pulls away as it cools.
- Prevent drafts by opening the oven door as seldom as possible during baking.
- Don't use a knife to test for doneness because it may create a crack. The center of the cheesecake (about the size of a walnut) should not be completely set and will jiggle slightly.

Apricot Swirl Cheesecake

(Pictured at right and on page 83)

I've always loved to cook and try new dishes. But there are just some recipes—like this fancy cheesecake—that I turn to time after time. This is a favorite of family and friends.
—Ardyth Voss, Rosholt, South Dakota

1/2 cup finely ground almonds
1 cup dried apricots
1 cup water
1 tablespoon grated lemon peel
3 packages (8 ounces *each*)
   cream cheese, softened
1 cup sugar
2 tablespoons all-purpose flour
4 eggs
1/2 cup whipping cream
1 cup apricot preserves
Whipped cream and toasted sliced
  almonds

Grease the bottom and sides of a 10-in. springform pan; sprinkle with ground almonds and set aside. In a saucepan over medium heat, cook apricots and water for 15 minutes or until the water is nearly absorbed and apricots are tender, stirring occasionally. Stir in lemon peel. Cool slightly; pour into a blender. Cover and process until smooth; set aside.

In a mixing bowl, beat cream cheese and sugar until smooth. Add flour; mix well. Add eggs; beat on low speed just until combined. Beat in cream just until blended. Stir 1 cup into pureed apricots; set aside. Pour remaining mixture into prepared pan. Drop apricot mixture by 1/2 teaspoonfuls over filling. Cut through filling with a knife to swirl apricot mixture.

Place pan on a baking sheet. Bake at 350° for 50-55 minutes or until center is almost set. Cool on a wire rack for 10 minutes. Carefully run a knife around edge of pan to loosen. Cool 1 hour longer.

In a small saucepan, heat preserves. Press through a strainer (discard pulp). Spread over cheesecake. Refrigerate overnight. Remove sides of pan. Garnish with whipped cream and sliced almonds. **Yield:** 12 servings.

Cranberry Cheesecake

(Pictured at right and on page 82)

Refreshing cranberries, lemon juice and orange peel complement the cheesecake's sweet filling. This is my favorite Christmas dessert to make as gifts. It really appeals to people who don't care for chocolate.
—Joy Monn, Stockbridge, Georgia

1-1/2 cups cinnamon graham
  cracker crumbs (about 24
  squares)
 1/4 cup sugar
 1/3 cup butter *or* margarine,
  melted
FILLING:
  4 packages (8 ounces *each*)
   cream cheese, softened
  1 can (14 ounces) sweetened
   condensed milk
 1/4 cup lemon juice
  4 eggs
1-1/2 cups chopped fresh *or* frozen
  cranberries
  1 teaspoon grated orange peel
Sugared cranberries and orange
 peel strips, optional

In a bowl, combine cracker crumbs and sugar; stir in butter. Press onto the bottom of a greased 9-in. springform pan; set aside.

In a mixing bowl, beat cream cheese and milk until smooth. Beat in lemon juice until smooth. Add eggs; beat on low speed just until combined. Fold in cranberries and orange peel. Pour over the crust. Place pan on a baking sheet.

Bake at 325° for 60-70 minutes or until center is almost set. Cool on a wire rack for 10 minutes.

Carefully run a knife around edge of pan to loosen. Cool 1 hour longer. Refrigerate for at least 6 hours or overnight. Remove sides of pan. Garnish with sugared cranberries and orange peel if desired. **Yield:** 12 servings.

FUN WITH FRUIT

TO MAKE the sugared cranberries and orange peel garnishing the Cranberry Cheesecake, combine several orange peel strips, 1/3 cup fresh cranberries and 1/2 cup sugar. Stir gently to combine. Cover and refrigerate  for 1 hour. Arrange orange peel strips and cranberries on top of the cheesecake just before serving.

Chocolate Chip Cookie Cheesecake

(Pictured at right)

Our daughter first astounded us with her cooking talents when she made this cheesecake at 13 years of age. With a unique cookie crumb crust and extra-creamy filling, people think this dessert was made by a gourmet baker!
—Kathleen Gualano, Cary, Illinois

2 cups chocolate chip cookie crumbs (about 28 cookies)
3 tablespoons sugar
5 tablespoons butter *or* margarine, melted

FILLING:
5 packages (8 ounces *each*) cream cheese, softened
1-1/4 cups sugar
3 tablespoons all-purpose flour
5 eggs
2 egg yolks
1/4 cup sour cream
1 teaspoon grated orange peel
1/2 teaspoon vanilla extract
1 cup miniature semisweet chocolate chips

TOPPING:
1 cup (8 ounces) sour cream
2 tablespoons sugar
1 teaspoon vanilla extract
1 tablespoon chocolate chip cookie crumbs

In a bowl, combine cookie crumbs and sugar; stir in butter. Press onto the bottom and 2 in. up the sides of a greased 9-in. springform pan; set aside.

In a mixing bowl, beat cream cheese and sugar until smooth. Add flour; mix well. Add eggs and egg yolks; beat on low speed just until combined. Beat in sour cream, orange peel and vanilla just until combined. Stir in chocolate chips. Pour over crust. Place pan on a baking sheet.

Bake at 325° for 65-75 minutes or until center is almost set. Remove from the oven; let stand for 5 minutes. Combine the sour cream, sugar and vanilla; spread over filling. Return to the oven for 8 minutes. Cool on a wire rack for 10 minutes. Carefully run a knife around edge of pan to loosen. Cool 1 hour longer. Refrigerate overnight. Remove sides of pan. Garnish with cookie crumbs. **Yield:** 12-14 servings.

Caramel Cashew Cheesecake

When a friend served this luscious cheesecake at a birthday party, I left with the recipe.
Every time I make it, rave reviews and recipe requests come my way.
—Pat Price, Bucyrus, Ohio

1/4 cup cold butter *or* margarine
1/2 cup all-purpose flour
3/4 cup chopped unsalted
    cashews
2 tablespoons confectioners'
    sugar
Pinch salt
FILLING:
4 packages (8 ounces *each*)
    cream cheese, softened
1-1/4 cups sugar
1 tablespoon vanilla extract
5 eggs
2 tablespoons whipping cream
TOPPING:
1 cup sugar
3 tablespoons water
3/4 cup whipping cream
1 cup coarsely chopped
    unsalted cashews

In a bowl, cut butter into flour until mixture resembles coarse crumbs. Stir in cashews, confectioners' sugar and salt. Press onto the bottom and 1/2 in. up the sides of a greased 9-in. springform pan. Bake at 350° for 15 minutes. Cool on a wire rack. Reduce heat to 325°.

In a mixing bowl, beat cream cheese, sugar and vanilla until smooth. Add eggs and cream; beat on low speed just until combined. Pour over crust. Place pan on a baking sheet. Bake at 325° for 55-60 minutes or until center is almost set. Cool on a wire rack for 10 minutes. Carefully run a knife around edge of pan to loosen. Cool 1 hour longer.

In a saucepan, combine sugar and water. Cook over medium-low heat until sugar is dissolved. Bring to a boil over medium-high heat; cover and boil for 2 minutes. Uncover; boil until mixture is golden brown and a candy thermometer reads 300° (hard-crack stage), about 8 minutes.

Remove from the heat. Stir in cream until smooth, about 5 minutes (mixture will appear lumpy at first). Add cashews; cool to lukewarm. Carefully spoon over cheesecake. Refrigerate overnight. Remove sides of pan. **Yield:** 12 servings.

Company Cheesecake

This plain cheesecake is anything but ordinary! The marvelously rich filling is terrific with
the pecan-laden crust. My brother gave me the recipe.
—Donna Bucher, Tirane, Albania

3/4 cup all-purpose flour
1/4 cup sugar
1/4 cup finely chopped pecans
1 teaspoon grated lemon peel
6 tablespoons cold butter
    (no substitutes)
1 egg yolk
1/2 teaspoon vanilla extract

FILLING:
5 packages (8 ounces *each*) cream cheese, softened
1-3/4 cups sugar
3 tablespoons all-purpose flour
1 teaspoon vanilla extract
1/4 teaspoon salt
4 eggs
2 egg yolks
1/4 cup whipping cream

In a bowl, combine the flour, sugar, pecans and lemon peel; cut in butter until crumbly. Combine egg yolk and vanilla; stir into flour mixture. Press onto the bottom of a greased 10-in. springform pan. Bake at 400° for 9-11 minutes or until edges are lightly browned. Cool on a wire rack.

Fill a 13-in. x 9-in. x 2-in. baking dish with 8 cups water; place on lowest oven rack. Reduce heat to 325°.

In a mixing bowl, beat cream cheese until smooth. Gradually beat in sugar. Add the flour, vanilla and salt. Combine eggs and egg yolks; add to cream cheese mixture just until combined. Beat in cream just until combined. Pour over crust.

Bake on middle rack at 325° for 70-75 minutes or until center is almost set (top of cheesecake will crack). Cool on a wire rack for 10 minutes. Carefully run a knife around edge of pan to loosen. Cool 1 hour longer. Refrigerate overnight. Remove sides of pan. **Yield:** 12 servings.

Setting Up A Coffee Service

(Pictured at right)

WHEN OFFERING an assortment of rich desserts—like the cheesecakes in this chapter—it's nice to serve guests a hot beverage. Here are hints for successfully serving coffee.

• For guests to dress up individual cups of coffee, set out bowls of cream, sugar cubes, red-hot candies, cinnamon sticks, purchased chocolate stirrers, vanilla and almond extracts and ground cinnamon, nutmeg or ginger.

Other stir-in ideas include grated chocolate, whipped cream, cocoa powder, chocolate syrup or orange and peppermint extracts.

• To flavor an entire pot of coffee, sprinkle coffee grounds with orange or lemon peel or ground cinnamon, nutmeg and ginger before brewing.

• The flavor of coffee begins to diminish within an hour after it's made, and leaving coffee on the heating element accelerates the problem. To keep coffee fresh and hot, transfer it to a

carafe or thermos that's been preheated with hot water.

• Only make as much coffee as needed and avoid reheating coffee, which can make it bitter. For 12 people, you need about 1/4 pound of coffee and 3 quarts water. For 25 people, you need about 1/2 pound of coffee and 1-1/2 gallons water. For best flavor, start with cold, fresh tap water. If your tap water has an off-taste, use bottled water instead.

Dazzling Desserts

WHEN it comes to choosing a favorite dessert, people's tastes run the gamut, from elegant to casual...rich and creamy to light and luscious...chocolate-laden to fruit-filled.

To be sure you'll satisfy every sweet tooth during the holiday season, turn to this chapter's sweet assortment of cakes, pies and desserts, including Chocolate Mousse Torte, Black Forest Cake and Orange-Cranberry Upside-Down Cake (shown at right).

Whether you're looking for a creative conclusion to a special holiday meal, a quick-and-easy ending to a festive family dinner or simply a sweet treat to snack on in front of the tree, finding a fitting finale to suit your time and taste is as easy as pie!

Orange-Cranberry Upside-Down Cake

(Pictured on page 90)

I'm lucky enough to have my great-grandmother's cookbook. In it are numerous tried-and-true recipes that she and my grandmother served our family through the years.
—Carrie Zuhlke, Fostoria, Michigan

1 cup packed brown sugar
2 tablespoons butter
  (no substitutes), melted
2 cups fresh cranberries, halved
2 medium naval oranges, peeled
  and chopped
BATTER:
  3/4 cup shortening
1-1/4 cups sugar
  2 eggs
  2 teaspoons grated orange peel
  2 cups all-purpose flour
  2 teaspoons baking powder
1/2 teaspoon salt
1/4 teaspoon baking soda

1/2 cup evaporated milk
1/2 cup orange juice

Combine the brown sugar and butter; spread evenly into a greased 13-in. x 9-in. x 2-in. baking dish. Sprinkle with cranberries and oranges; set aside.

In a mixing bowl, cream shortening and sugar. Beat in eggs and orange peel. Combine the flour, baking powder, salt and baking soda; add to creamed mixture alternately with milk and orange juice. Spread over cranberry mixture.

Bake at 375° for 35-40 minutes or until a toothpick inserted into the cake comes out clean. Run a knife around edges of pan; immediately invert onto a serving plate. Serve warm. **Yield:** 12-15 servings.

Coconut Walnut Tart

My mother and aunt perfected this recipe and then handed it down to me.
The flavor is similar to pecan pie. My family requests this delicious dessert every Christmas.
—Cindy DeRoos, Iroquois, Ontario

Pastry for a single-crust pie
  2 eggs
1-1/2 cups packed brown sugar
1/2 cup butter *or* margarine,
    melted
  3 tablespoons milk
1-1/2 teaspoons vanilla extract
1-1/2 cups flaked coconut
1/3 cup chopped walnuts

Place pastry in a 9-in. fluted tart pan with a removable bottom; set aside. In a mixing bowl, beat eggs for 1 minute. Add brown sugar, butter, milk and vanilla; mix well. Stir in coconut and walnuts. Pour into crust. Bake at 450° for 8 minutes. Reduce heat to 350°; bake 20-25 minutes longer or until puffed and golden brown. **Yield:** 12-14 servings.

Editor's Note: Even a tight-fitting tart pan may leak. To prevent drips, place the filled tart pan on a baking sheet in the oven.

Black Forest Cake

(Pictured at right and on page 91)

One taste and you'll agree this spectacular dessert is worth the effort!
— Patricia Roylance
U.S. Navy, Stationed in Spain

2 squares (1 ounce *each*)
   unsweetened chocolate
1/3 cup vegetable oil
2 eggs, *separated*
1-1/2 cups sugar, *divided*
1-3/4 cups cake flour
1 teaspoon salt
3/4 teaspoon baking soda
1 cup milk
CREAM FILLING:
   6 tablespoons butter
     (no substitutes), softened
   4 cups confectioners' sugar,
     divided
1-1/2 teaspoons vanilla extract
   4 to 5 tablespoons half-and-half
     cream
CHERRY FILLING:
   1 can (14-1/2 ounces) pitted tart
     cherries
   2 tablespoons cornstarch
3/4 cup sugar
1/4 teaspoon almond extract
   6 drops red food coloring
CHOCOLATE FILLING:
   1 cup whipping cream
1/4 cup chocolate syrup
   1 teaspoon vanilla extract
FROSTING:
   2 cups whipping cream
   2 tablespoons sugar
   1 teaspoon vanilla extract
Chocolate curls, maraschino
   cherries and fresh mint

In a microwave-safe bowl, melt chocolate; stir until smooth. Cool slightly. In a large mixing bowl, combine the oil, egg yolks, 1 cup sugar and melted chocolate; beat well. Combine flour, salt and baking soda; add to chocolate mixture alternately with milk. In a small mixing bowl, beat egg whites until soft peaks form. Beat in remaining sugar, 1 tablespoon at a time, until stiff. Fold into batter.

Pour into two greased and waxed paper-lined 9-in. round baking pans. Bake at 350° for 30-35 minutes or until a toothpick inserted near the center comes out clean. Cool for 10 minutes before removing from pans to wire racks.

In a mixing bowl, beat cream filling ingredients; cover and refrigerate. For cherry filling, drain cherries, reserving juice. In a saucepan, combine cornstarch, sugar and cherry juice until smooth. Add cherries. Bring to a boil; cook and stir for 2 minutes or until thickened. Stir in extract and food coloring. Cool completely. In a mixing bowl, beat chocolate filling ingredients until soft peaks form. Cover and refrigerate. For frosting, in a mixing bowl, beat cream, sugar and vanilla until soft peaks form. Cover and refrigerate.

To assemble, split each cake into two horizontal layers. Place bottom layer on a serving plate; top with 1/2 cup cream filling. Place 1 cup cream filling in a heavy-duty resealable plastic bag; cut a 1/2-in. triangle in one corner of bag. Make a rim of filling 3/4 in. high around outer edge of cake.

Make a second rim 2 in. from edge. Spoon cherry filling between rings. Refrigerate for 30 minutes. Spread chocolate filling over second cake layer; place over cherry filling. Spread remaining cream filling over third layer; place over chocolate filling. Top with fourth layer. Spread frosting over top and sides of cake. Garnish with chocolate curls, cherries and mint. Store in the refrigerator. **Yield:** 16 servings.

Chocolate Mousse Torte

(Pictured at right and on page 90)

Although this mousse torte created by our Test Kitchen is very rich, people just can't seem to get enough of it. Decorated with melted chocolate and Chocolate Almond Pinecones, this is an impressive dessert.

1-1/4 cups chocolate wafer crumbs
    (about 25 wafers)
1/4 cup sugar
1/4 cup butter *or* margarine,
    melted
FILLING:
    4 squares (1 ounce *each*)
      bittersweet chocolate
1/2 cup plus 2 tablespoons milk
    chocolate chips
    4 squares (1 ounce *each*) white
      baking chocolate
    1 tablespoon unflavored gelatin
1/4 cup water
    5 egg yolks
1/4 cup sugar
    1 cup half-and-half cream,
      warmed
1-3/4 cups whipping cream
Semisweet chocolate chips, melted
    and Chocolate Almond Pinecones
    (recipe on opposite page), optional

Combine the first three ingredients; press onto the bottom of a greased 9-in. springform pan. Bake at 375° for 8-10 minutes. Cool. Place each flavor of chocolate in a separate bowl; set aside. In another bowl, sprinkle gelatin over water; let stand for 1 minute or until softened.

In a small mixing bowl, beat egg yolks on high speed for 3 minutes or until light and fluffy. Gradually add sugar, beating until thick and lemon-colored. Gradually whisk in half-and-half. Transfer to a saucepan; cook and stir over medium heat until a thermometer reads 160° and mixture has thickened, about 3 minutes.

Remove from the heat; stir in gelatin until dissolved. Immediately pour a third of the egg mixture over each flavor of chocolate; quickly stir each until melted. Cool for 10 minutes.

In a mixing bowl, beat whipping cream until stiff peaks form. Fold a third of the whipped cream into each bowl. Pour bittersweet chocolate mixture into prepared pan. Freeze until firm, about 15 minutes. Repeat with milk chocolate mixture, then white chocolate mixture.

To serve, carefully run a sharp knife around edge of pan to loosen. Remove sides of pan. Garnish if desired by drizzling with melted chocolate to create pine boughs and topping with Chocolate Almond Pinecones. **Yield:** 16 servings.

Editor's Note: Torte can be prepared 2 days in advance. Cover with plastic wrap and store in the refrigerator.

Chocolate Almond Pinecones

(Pictured at right)

Our Test Kitchen suggests this clever way of dressing up any winter dessert. Make these "pinecones" when you have some time, then use—and reuse—them on a variety of desserts...or even on a pretty plate piled with candies.

1 tube (7 ounces) almond paste
4 ounces sliced almonds
1-1/4 cups semisweet chocolate chips
1 tablespoon shortening

Divide almond paste into six equal portions. Form each into a cone shape, about 1-1/2 in. tall and 1 in. in diameter. Beginning at the base, insert pointed end of almonds into paste to resemble a pinecone.

In a microwave-safe bowl, melt chocolate chips and shortening; stir until smooth. Insert a toothpick into bottom of each cone. Holding over bowl, spoon melted chocolate over almonds (if needed, use another toothpick to spread the chocolate to completely cover almonds). Place on a wire rack over waxed paper; let stand until firm. **Yield:** 6 pinecones.

MAKING CHOCOLATE ALMOND PINECONES

1. Shape almond paste into six cone shapes. Insert pointed end of almonds into paste to resemble a pinecone.

2. Insert a toothpick into bottom of each cone. Holding over a bowl, spoon melted chocolate over almonds.

3. Use another toothpick to spread the chocolate to completely cover almonds. Let stand until firm.

Layered Icebox Dessert

This creamy make-ahead dessert has delicious old-fashioned flavor.
German chocolate cake mix makes for an irresistible, interesting crust.
—Edie DeSpain, Logan, Utah

CRUST:
- 1 package (18-1/4 ounces) German chocolate cake mix
- 1 egg
- 1/2 cup butter *or* margarine, melted
- 1/2 cup chopped pecans

FILLING/TOPPING:
- 1 package (8 ounces) cream cheese, softened
- 1 cup sugar
- 1 carton (12 ounces) frozen whipped topping, thawed, *divided*
- 3 cups cold milk
- 2 packages (3.4 ounces *each*) instant French vanilla pudding mix
- 1/4 teaspoon ground nutmeg
- 1/4 teaspoon rum extract
- 2 tablespoons chopped pecans, toasted

In a mixing bowl, combine dry cake mix, egg, butter and pecans. Press into a greased 13-in. x 9-in. x 2-in. baking dish. Bake at 350° for 15-20 minutes or until a toothpick inserted near the center comes out clean. Cool completely (as crust cools, it will fall in the center to form a shell).

In a mixing bowl, beat cream cheese and sugar for 2 minutes. Fold in 1 cup whipped topping. Spread over crust. Refrigerate for 10 minutes.

In a mixing bowl, beat milk and pudding mix on low speed for 2 minutes. Beat in nutmeg and extract. Spread over cream cheese layer. Top with remaining whipped topping. Sprinkle with pecans. Refrigerate for at least 2 hours. **Yield:** 16-20 servings.

Sugarplum Cake

Family and friends are surprised to hear this simple cake gets its moist flavor
from a jar of baby food. It's a nice, light dessert.
—Denita DeValcourt, Lawrenceburg, Tennessee

- 2 cups sugar
- 1 cup vegetable oil
- 3 eggs
- 2 cups self-rising flour*
- 3 teaspoons ground cinnamon
- 1 jar (6 ounces) plums with apples baby food
- 1/2 cup chopped walnuts
- Confectioners' sugar, optional

In a large mixing bowl, combine sugar and oil. Beat in eggs, one at a time, until well blended. Combine flour and cinnamon; add to egg mixture. Beat in baby food; stir in nuts. Transfer to a greased and floured 10-in. fluted tube pan.

Bake at 350° for 35-45 minutes or until a toothpick inserted near the center comes out clean. Cool for 10 minutes before inverting onto a wire rack to cool completely. Dust with confectioners' sugar if desired. **Yield:** 12 servings.

*Editor's Note: As a substitute for *each* cup of self-rising flour, place 1-1/2 teaspoons baking powder and 1/2 teaspoon salt in a measuring cup. Add all-purpose flour to measure 1 cup.

Chocolate Baklava

(Pictured at right)

I've been cooking for years, and baklava remains a favorite. Most folks find one piece of this rich dessert very satisfying, so this recipe feeds many people.
—Cindy Schumacher, Kenvil, New Jersey

   1 package (16 ounces) frozen
      phyllo dough, thawed
1-1/4 cups butter (no substitutes),
      melted
   1 pound finely chopped walnuts
   1 package (12 ounces)
      miniature semisweet
      chocolate chips
   3/4 cup sugar
1-1/2 teaspoons ground cinnamon
   1 teaspoon grated lemon peel
SYRUP:
   3/4 cup orange juice
   1/2 cup sugar
   1/2 cup water
   1/2 cup honey
   2 tablespoons lemon juice

Butter a 15-in. x 10-in. x 1-in. baking pan. Layer eight sheets of phyllo dough in pan, brushing each with butter. In a bowl, combine nuts, chocolate chips, sugar, cinnamon and lemon peel. Sprinkle 2 cups over top layer of phyllo.

Layer and brush four sheets of dough with butter. Top with 2 more cups nut mixture. Layer and brush four more sheets of dough with butter; top with remaining nut mixture. Top with the remaining dough, brushing each sheet with butter. Drizzle any remaining butter over top.

Using a sharp knife, cut baklava into 1-1/2-in. diamonds. Bake at 325° for 50-60 minutes or until golden brown. Meanwhile, combine the syrup ingredients in a saucepan; bring to a boil over medium heat, stirring occasionally. Reduce heat; simmer, uncovered, for 20 minutes. Pour over warm baklava. Cool completely in pan on a wire rack. **Yield:** 50 pieces.

MAKING AN ORANGE ROSE

TO ADD COLOR to any dessert platter, try your hand at the easy yet impressive orange rose shown on Chocolate Baklava (above). Just follow these steps:
- Cut a very thin slice from bottom of orange and discard. Starting at the top of the orange, with a vegetable peeler, cut a continuous narrow strip of peel in a spiral fashion around the entire orange.
- Starting at the end of the strip where you started, wrap the strip around itself to form a coil. Insert one or two toothpicks horizontally into the base to secure.

Peppermint Stick Dessert

With every spoonful of this cool and creamy concoction, my family goes back in time to when our Grandma Dagmar made it each Christmas. The minty, refreshing flavor can't be topped.

—Dianne Oertel, Racine, Wisconsin

8 ounces peppermint candy, crushed
1/2 cup half-and-half cream
1-1/4 teaspoons unflavored gelatin
1 tablespoon cold water
1-1/2 cups whipping cream, whipped
27 chocolate wafers

In a small saucepan, combine crushed candy and half-and-half cream. Cook over low heat until candy is melted, stirring occasionally. In a small bowl, sprinkle gelatin over water; let stand for 1 minute. Stir into hot peppermint mixture until dissolved. Refrigerate for 20 minutes or until mixture begins to set. Fold in whipped cream.

Crush three chocolate wafers; set aside for garnish. Line a 1-1/2-qt. serving bowl with 12 wafers. Top with half of the peppermint mixture. Repeat layers. Sprinkle with chocolate crumbs. Refrigerate for at least 8 hours. **Yield:** 9-12 servings.

CRUSHING PEPPERMINT CANDY

TO EASILY CRUSH peppermint candy, put candy in a heavy-duty resealable plastic bag; seal. Using a hammer or flat side of a meat mallet, pound the candy on a sturdy countertop until crushed.

Frozen Coconut Caramel Pie

I received this recipe from a dear friend, who was a great cook and often tried new recipes. This pretty pie is just right for those with a sweet tooth.

—Lois Triplet, Springhill, Louisiana

2 tablespoons butter *or* margarine
1 cup flaked coconut
1/4 cup chopped pecans
1 package (8 ounces) cream cheese, softened
1 can (14 ounces) sweetened condensed milk
1 carton (16 ounces) frozen whipped topping, thawed
2 graham cracker crusts (9 inches *each*)
1 jar (12 ounces) caramel ice cream topping

In a skillet, melt butter; add coconut and pecans. Cook and stir over medium heat for 10 minutes or until golden brown and toasted; set aside.

In a mixing bowl, beat cream cheese and milk until smooth. Fold in whipped topping. Pour into crusts. Drizzle with caramel topping; sprinkle with coconut mixture. Cover and freeze for 8 hours or overnight or until firm. Remove from the freezer 5 minutes before slicing. **Yield:** 2 pies (6-8 servings each).

Cinnamon Candied Apples

(Pictured at right)

For years, we enjoyed baked cinnamon apples at Christmas when my great-grandmother made them. When she passed away, no one could find the recipe. I eventually came across this stovetop version and have continued her tradition.
—Angie Marquart, Mt. Gilead, Ohio

2 cups water
1 cup sugar
1 cup red-hot candies
6 medium tart apples, peeled, cored and halved
Fresh mint, optional

In a large saucepan over medium heat, bring water, sugar and candies to a boil, stirring constantly until sugar and candies are dissolved. Reduce heat; carefully add apples. Cook, uncovered, until apples are tender, about 8 minutes.

With a slotted spoon, transfer apples to a serving dish; pour syrup over apples. Serve warm or chilled. Garnish with mint if desired. **Yield:** 6 servings.

Chocolate Crunch Pie

This rich, fudgy pie came from an aunt of a good friend. The recipe makes two pies, which seem to quickly disappear at holiday gatherings.
—Jo Ellen Greenhaw, Athens, Alabama

2 unbaked pastry shells (9 inches)
4 eggs
2 cups sugar
1 cup butter *or* margarine, cut into 8 pieces
1 cup (6 ounces) semisweet chocolate chips
1 cup chopped pecans
1 cup flaked coconut
1 teaspoon vanilla extract

Line unpricked pastry shells with a double thickness of heavy-duty foil. Bake at 450° for 8 minutes. Remove from oven and set aside; remove foil. Reduce heat to 350°.

In a saucepan, beat eggs and sugar until thickened, about 2 minutes. Add butter and chocolate chips. Cook over low heat until melted and smooth, stirring constantly. Stir in pecans, coconut and vanilla. Pour into pie shells. Cover edges of pastry with foil. Bake at 350° for 20-25 minutes or until puffed. **Yield:** 2 pies (6-8 servings each).

Gingerbread Yule Log

Nicely seasoned gingerbread holds a sweet creamy filling. This dessert is surprisingly light, so it's easy to indulge in a generous slice after a hearty meal.
—Bernadette Colvin, Lexington, Kentucky

3 eggs, *separated*
1/2 cup molasses
1 tablespoon butter *or* margarine, melted
1/4 teaspoon cream of tartar
1/3 cup sugar
1 cup all-purpose flour
1/4 teaspoon baking soda
1/2 teaspoon *each* ground cinnamon, cloves and ginger
1/8 teaspoon salt
FILLING/FROSTING:
1-1/2 cups whipping cream
1/3 cup confectioners' sugar
1 teaspoon ground cinnamon
1 teaspoon vanilla extract
1/4 teaspoon ground cloves

Line a greased 15-in. x 10-in. x 1-in. baking pan with waxed paper and grease the paper; set aside. In a mixing bowl, beat egg yolks, molasses and butter until thickened, about 3 minutes. In another mixing bowl, beat egg whites and cream of tartar until soft peaks form. Gradually add sugar, 1 tablespoon at a time, beating until stiff peaks form. Fold into egg yolk mixture. Combine the flour, baking soda, spices and salt; fold into egg mixture until well combined.

Spread batter into prepared pan. Bake at 350° for 12-15 minutes or until cake springs back when lightly touched. Cool for 5 minutes. Turn cake onto a kitchen towel dusted with confectioners' sugar. Gently peel off waxed paper. Roll up cake in the towel jelly-roll style, starting with a short side. Cool completely on a wire rack.

In a mixing bowl, combine the cream, confectioners' sugar, cinnamon, vanilla and cloves; beat until soft peaks form. Unroll cake; spread half of the filling evenly over cake to within 1/2 in. of edges. Roll up again. Place seam side down on serving plate. Frost with remaining filling. Cover and refrigerate until serving. **Yield:** 12 servings.

Custard Sauce

This recipe has been in the family for generations. I'm not surprised at its popularity, because it can be used in a variety of ways. We especially like it served over pound cake and gingerbread or simply topped with fresh strawberries.
—Lou Tippett, Fayetteville, North Carolina

8 cups milk
2 cups sugar
6 eggs, beaten
2 tablespoons vanilla extract

In a heavy saucepan over low heat, cook and stir milk and sugar until sugar is dissolved. Remove from the heat.

Stir a small amount of hot milk mixture into eggs; return all to the pan, stirring constantly. Cook and stir until mixture reaches 160° or is thick enough to coat a metal spoon.

Remove from the heat; stir in vanilla. Cool to room temperature, stirring several times. Transfer to a bowl; press a piece of waxed paper or plastic wrap on top of custard. Refrigerate. Serve over gingerbread or pound cake. **Yield:** about 8-1/2 cups.

Cranberry-Pistachio Ice Cream Cake

(Pictured at right)

Red cranberries and green pistachios in this ice cream cake delightfully showcase the colors of the season. My family prefers this refreshing homemade ice cream cake to store-bought desserts.
—Quadelle Rose, Springbrook, Alberta

1-1/2 cups crushed chocolate cream-filled cookies
1/4 cup butter *or* margarine, melted
1-1/2 cups fresh *or* frozen cranberries, thawed
1/2 cup light corn syrup
1/3 cup sugar
1/3 cup water
6 cups vanilla ice cream, softened, *divided*
1/2 cup chopped pistachios, *divided*

Combine crushed cookies and butter; press onto the bottom of a greased 9-in. springform pan. Freeze for 1 hour or until firm.

In a saucepan, combine the cranberries, corn syrup, sugar and water. Bring to a boil; cook over medium heat until the berries pop, about 10 minutes. Transfer to a blender; cover and process until smooth. Pour into a bowl. Refrigerate for 30 minutes or until cooled, stirring occasionally.

Remove crust from freezer. Spread with half of the ice cream. Set aside 1/4 cup cranberry puree. Pour remaining puree over ice cream. Set aside 1 tablespoon nuts; sprinkle remaining nuts over puree. Freeze for 30 minutes or until firm.

Layer with remaining ice cream, puree and nuts. Cover with plastic wrap; freeze for 6 hours or until firm. Remove from freezer 15 minutes before serving. **Yield:** 8-12 servings.

Coconut Pound Cake

This proven pound cake turns out perfectly moist every time. It doesn't need any frosting,
just a dusting of confectioners' sugar over the top.
—*Lazetta Bruce, Minatare, Nebraska*

1/2 cup butter (no substitutes),
    softened
1/2 cup shortening
  1 package (8 ounces) cream
    cheese, softened
  3 cups sugar
  6 eggs
  1 teaspoon vanilla extract
  1 teaspoon coconut extract
  3 cups all-purpose flour
1/4 teaspoon baking soda
1/4 teaspoon salt
2-1/4 cups flaked coconut
Confectioners' sugar

In a mixing bowl, cream butter, shortening, cream cheese and sugar until light and fluffy. Add eggs, one at a time, beating well after each. Beat in extracts. Combine the flour, baking soda and salt; add to creamed mixture. Fold in coconut. Transfer to a greased and floured 10-in. tube pan.

Bake at 325° for 1-1/2 hours or until a toothpick inserted near the center comes out clean. Cool for 10 minutes before removing from pan to a wire rack to cool completely. Dust with confectioners' sugar. **Yield:** 12-16 servings.

Snowball Cake

Whipped topping and coconut blanket a layered angel food cake and gelatin dessert.
My husband's grandmother really liked this cool treat and requested that I make it every Christmas.
—*Judith Guthrie, Charleston, West Virginia*

  2 tablespoons unflavored
    gelatin
1/4 cup cold water
  1 cup boiling water
  1 cup sugar
  1 tablespoon lemon juice
  1 can (20 ounces) crushed
    pineapple, drained
  1 carton (16 ounces) frozen
    whipped topping, thawed,
    divided
  1 prepared angel food cake
    (8 inches), cut into cubes
1-1/2 cups flaked coconut

In a bowl, sprinkle gelatin over cold water; let stand for 1 minute. Add boiling water; stir until gelatin is dissolved. Stir in sugar and lemon juice until sugar is dissolved. Add pineapple. Refrigerate until partially thickened, about 20 minutes. Fold in 4 cups whipped topping.

Line a 3-qt. round bowl with plastic wrap. Spoon about 2 cups pineapple mixture into bowl. Layer with half of the cake cubes and half of the remaining pineapple mixture. Repeat layers. Refrigerate for at least 4 hours.

Unmold onto a serving plate. Spread remaining whipped topping over cake. Sprinkle with coconut. **Yield:** 16 servings.

Pecan Date Fruitcake

(Pictured at right)

My husband grew up in Louisiana and has fond memories of his mother's fruitcake. I make this for him every year to remind him of special times. Pretty slices are an attractive addition to the dessert table.

— *Dolores Brewster*
Milwaukee, Wisconsin

2 **pounds pitted dates, quartered**
1 **pound pecan halves (4 cups)**
1 **pound candied cherries, halved (2-1/4 cups)**
1 **cup all-purpose flour**
1 **cup sugar**
1/2 **teaspoon baking powder**
1/2 **teaspoon salt**
4 **eggs**
2 **teaspoons vanilla extract**

Grease and line three 8-in. x 4-in. x 2-in. loaf pans with waxed paper; set aside. In a large bowl, combine dates, nuts and cherries. Combine the flour, sugar, baking powder and salt; stir into fruit mixture until well coated. In a mixing bowl, beat eggs and vanilla until foamy. Fold into fruit mixture and mix well. Pour into prepared pans.

Bake at 300° for 1 hour or until a toothpick inserted near the center comes out clean. Cool for 10 minutes before removing from pans to wire racks. Remove waxed paper. Cool completely before slicing. Wrap and store in a cool dry place. **Yield:** 3 loaves.

LINING A PAN WITH WAXED PAPER

PLACE the pan on a large piece of waxed paper. Trace the shape of the outside of the pan (for a tube pan, also trace the inner circle); cut out. Grease the pan; place the waxed paper in the pan and grease it. Remove the paper as soon as the baked cake is removed to a wire rack to cool.

'TIS THE Season

Sweet Treats for Santa

KIDS of all ages quickly get into a festive frame of mind when they see a merry array of fresh-baked cookies and rich candies adorning pretty platters.

For most cooks, the jolly job of creating these confections begins weeks in advance. Families can't wait for the wonderful aroma of homemade cookies and candies to fill the house, signaling the start of the holiday season.

You'll create sweet memories in your kitchen with a magical assortment of fresh-baked cookies and dandy candies like Nutty Popcorn Party Mix, Viennese Fudge, Caramel-Filled Chocolate Cookies and Buttery Spritz Cookies (shown at right).

Santa (and all the "elves" in your family) will appreciate each mouth-watering morsel!

Nutty Popcorn Party Mix

(Pictured on page 105)

Whoever receives this crunchy concoction is guaranteed merry munching. The snapped-up-in-seconds party mix features a combination of sweet and savory flavors.
—Zita Wilensky, North Miami Beach, Florida

3 quarts popped popcorn
1 cup unsalted dry roasted peanuts
1 jar (3-1/2 ounces) macadamia nuts, halved
1/2 cup slivered almonds
1/4 cup flaked coconut
3/4 cup butter (no substitutes)
1 cup sugar
1/2 cup packed brown sugar
1/4 cup light corn syrup
1/4 cup strong brewed coffee
1/8 teaspoon ground cinnamon
2 teaspoons vanilla extract

In a large bowl, combine popcorn, nuts and coconut. In a saucepan, combine the butter, sugars, corn syrup, coffee and cinnamon. Bring to a boil over medium heat; boil and stir for 5 minutes. Remove from the heat; stir in vanilla. Pour over popcorn mixture and stir until coated.

Transfer to two greased 15-in. x 10-in. x 1-in. baking pans. Bake, uncovered, at 250° for 45-55 minutes or until golden brown, stirring every 15 minutes. Spread onto waxed paper; cool completely. Store in an airtight container. **Yield:** about 12 cups.

Viennese Fudge

(Pictured on page 105)

This fudge recipe from my mother combines two ingredients commonly found in Viennese desserts—semisweet chocolate and hazelnuts. It's a staple in my home at the holidays.
—Loranne Weir, San Ramon, California

1 teaspoon plus 3 tablespoons butter (no substitutes), *divided*
2 cups sugar
1 cup evaporated milk
1/2 teaspoon salt
1 cup miniature marshmallows
1-1/2 cups semisweet chocolate chips
2 teaspoons vanilla extract
1-1/2 cups ground hazelnuts, toasted

Line an 8-in. square pan with foil and butter the foil with 1 teaspoon butter; set aside. In a large saucepan, combine the sugar, milk, salt and remaining butter. Bring to a boil over medium heat, stirring constantly. Boil and stir for 6 minutes.

Remove from the heat; stir in marshmallows until melted. Add chocolate chips and stir until melted. Stir in vanilla and nuts. Pour into prepared pan. Let stand at room temperature until cool.

Using foil, lift fudge out of pan; cut into 1-in. squares. Store in an airtight container in the refrigerator. **Yield:** 2 pounds.

Buttery Spritz Cookies

(Pictured at right and on page 104)

These tender little cookies are very eye-catching on my Christmas cookie tray. The dough is easy to work with, so it's fun to make these into a variety of festive shapes.
—Beverly Launius, Sandwich, Illinois

1 cup butter (no substitutes),
   softened
1-1/4 cups confectioners' sugar
1 egg
1 teaspoon vanilla extract
1/2 teaspoon almond extract
2-1/2 cups all-purpose flour
1/2 teaspoon salt
Food coloring, optional

In a mixing bowl, cream butter and sugar until smooth. Beat in egg and extracts. Combine the flour and salt; gradually add to creamed mixture. Tint with food coloring if desired.

Using a cookie press fitted with the disk of your choice, press dough 2 in. apart onto ungreased baking sheets. Bake at 375° for 6-8 minutes or until set (do not brown). Remove to wire racks to cool. **Yield:** 7-1/2 dozen.

Almond Potato Candy

When my mother was a child, my grandmother would make this as a substitute for expensive store-bought marzipan. I've since added the melted chocolate, which gives it more richness.
—Betty Hartigan, Calgary, Alberta

1/2 cup mashed potatoes
   (prepared without milk and
   butter)
2 cups whole blanched almonds,
   finely ground
2 cups confectioners' sugar
1 tablespoon baking cocoa
1 teaspoon almond extract

2/3 cup semisweet chocolate chips, melted
Additional confectioners' sugar *or* ground almonds

In a bowl, combine the mashed potatoes, almonds, sugar, cocoa and almond extract; mix well. Add melted chips and stir well. Cover and refrigerate for several hours. Shape teaspoonfuls into balls; roll in sugar or almonds. **Yield:** about 5 dozen.

Cherry Bonbon Cookies

This is a very old recipe from my grandma.
The sweet cherry filling surprises folks trying them for the first time.
—Pat Habiger, Spearville, Kansas

1/2 cup butter (no substitutes), softened
3/4 cup confectioners' sugar
2 tablespoons milk
1 teaspoon vanilla extract
1-1/2 cups all-purpose flour
1/8 teaspoon salt
24 maraschino cherries
GLAZE:
1 cup confectioners' sugar
1 tablespoon butter, melted
2 tablespoons maraschino cherry juice
Additional confectioners' sugar

In a mixing bowl, cream butter and sugar. Add milk and vanilla. Combine the flour and salt; gradually add to the creamed mixture. Divide dough into 24 portions; shape each portion around a cherry, forming a ball. Place on ungreased baking sheets. Bake at 350° for 18-20 minutes or until lightly browned. Cool on wire racks.

For glaze, combine the sugar, butter and cherry juice until smooth. Drizzle over cookies. Dust with confectioners' sugar. **Yield:** 2 dozen.

Sugarcoated Meltaways

I have fond memories of my parents spending days in the kitchen baking Christmas cookies.
It's a tradition that my husband and I now happily carry on.
—Charlotte Wright, Lebanon, Connecticut

1/2 cup orange juice
1 tablespoon grated orange peel
3/4 cup butter (no substitutes), softened
1/4 cup sugar
1 tablespoon cold water
1 teaspoon vanilla extract
1-3/4 cups all-purpose flour
1/8 teaspoon salt
1 cup miniature semisweet chocolate chips
1 cup finely chopped walnuts
Additional sugar

In a small bowl, combine orange juice and peel; set aside. In a mixing bowl, cream butter and sugar. Beat in water and vanilla. Combine flour and salt; gradually add to creamed mixture. Stir in chocolate chips and walnuts.

Roll into 1-in. balls. Place 1 in. apart on ungreased baking sheets. Bake at 325° for 12-15 minutes or until lightly browned. Remove to wire racks to cool.

Strain reserved orange juice. Dip cookies in juice, then roll in additional sugar. Let dry. Store in an airtight container. **Yield:** 3-1/2 dozen.

Caramel-Filled Chocolate Cookies

(Pictured at right and on page 104)

These yummy chocolate cookies have a tasty caramel surprise inside. With pecans on top and a contrasting white chocolate drizzle, they're almost too pretty to eat!
—Deb Walsh, Cabery, Illinois

1 cup butter (no substitutes), softened
1 cup plus 1 tablespoon sugar, *divided*
1 cup packed brown sugar
2 eggs
1 teaspoon vanilla extract
2-1/2 cups all-purpose flour
3/4 cup baking cocoa
1 teaspoon baking soda
1-1/4 cups chopped pecans, *divided*
1 package (13 ounces) Rolo candies
4 squares (1 ounce *each*) white baking chocolate, melted

In a mixing bowl, cream butter, 1 cup sugar and brown sugar. Add the eggs, one at a time, beating well after each addition. Beat in vanilla. Combine the flour, cocoa and baking soda; gradually add to the creamed mixture, beating just until combined. Stir in 1/2 cup pecans.

Shape a tablespoonful of dough around each candy, forming a ball. In a small bowl, combine the remaining sugar and pecans; dip each cookie halfway. Place nut side up 2 in. apart on greased baking sheets.

Bake at 375° for 7-10 minutes or until tops are slightly cracked. Cool for 3 minutes before removing to wire racks to cool completely. Drizzle with melted white chocolate. **Yield:** about 5 dozen.

FREEZING HOLIDAY COOKIES

TO PREPARE for holiday mania, begin your cookie-baking marathon a few weeks before Christmas. Store cooled, baked cookies in an airtight container at room temperature for about 3 days. To freeze cookies for up to 3 months, wrap the cookies in plastic, stack in an airtight container, seal and freeze. Thaw wrapped cookies at room temperature before serving.

Pecan Clusters

Toasting the pecans before stirring in the chocolate adds to the richness of this easy-to-make candy. I usually make four batches each Christmas and never have leftovers.
—*Collette Reynolds, Raleigh, North Carolina*

3 tablespoons butter *or* margarine, melted
3 cups chopped pecans
12 ounces chocolate candy coating, melted

In a 15-in. x 10-in. x 1-in. baking pan, combine butter and pecans. Bake at 250° for 20-30 minutes, stirring every 10 minutes. Remove from the oven; transfer to a bowl. Add candy coating and stir until evenly coated. Drop by rounded teaspoonfuls onto waxed paper. Cool completely. Store in an airtight container. **Yield:** about 4 dozen.

PACKING COOKIES FOR SHIPPING

NOTHING WARMS the hearts of out-of-town relatives and friends at holiday time like receiving a package from home. And when the parcel contains a pretty tin packed with home-baked cookies, their delight is undeniable. To ensure the mouth-watering morsels are at their best upon arrival, review these packing pointers.

- Bake and completely cool cookies just before packing and shipping so they're as fresh as possible.
- Determine which cookies to mail based on their fragility. Many bars, brownies and drop, refrigerator and sandwich cookies are fairly sturdy and travel well. Some cutouts and shaped varieties are a little more delicate and more likely to break. Cookies requiring refrigeration are poor choices to ship because they'll spoil.
- To help the cookies stay fresh and intact, wrap them in bundles of two (for drop cookies, place their bottoms together) with plastic wrap. It's best to wrap bars individually.
- Pack crisp and soft cookies in separate tins. If they're packed together, the moisture from the soft cookies will seep into the crisp cookies, making them lose their crunch. Consider shipping soft cookies by express mail so they'll be moist upon arrival.
- To help retain the best flavor, don't put strong-flavored cookies (like gingersnaps) and mild-flavored ones (like sugar cookies) in the same tin.
- Line a festive tin or box with crumpled waxed paper to help cushion the cookies. Snugly pack the cookies to within 1 inch of the top. Use crumpled waxed paper or bubble wrap to fill any gaps between the cookies. Add more waxed paper or bubble wrap over the last layer to cushion the cookies and prevent them from shifting during shipping. Close the tin or box.
- Place a layer of crumpled paper, bubble wrap or foam shipping peanuts in the bottom of a cardboard box that is slightly larger than your cookie tin. Set the tin on top, then add more paper, bubble wrap or shipping peanuts.
- Seal the box tightly with tape, label the top and sides of the package "Fragile and Perishable" and adhere a mailing label.

Sugar Cookie Cutouts

(Pictured at right)

I must have over 100 different cookie cutters and have had fun putting them to use with this recipe over the years. Each Christmas, my brother, sister and I would eagerly wait for Grandpa and Grandma to arrive with these cookies in tow.

—*Elizabeth Walters, Waterloo, Iowa*

1 cup butter (no substitutes),
  softened
1 cup sugar
2 eggs
1/4 cup half-and-half cream
3 cups all-purpose flour
2 teaspoons baking powder
1 teaspoon baking soda
1/2 teaspoon salt
FROSTING:
1/2 cup butter, softened
4 cups confectioners' sugar
1 teaspoon vanilla extract
2 to 4 tablespoons half-and-half
  cream
Food coloring and colored sugar,
  optional

In a mixing bowl, cream butter and sugar. Add eggs, one at a time, beating well after each addition. Beat in cream. Combine the flour, baking powder, baking soda and salt; gradually add to creamed mixture. Cover and refrigerate for 3 hours or until easy to handle.

On a lightly floured surface, roll out dough to 1/8-in. thickness. Cut with 2-1/2-in. cookie cutters dipped in flour. Place 1 in. apart on ungreased baking sheets. Bake at 325° for 6-8 minutes or until edges are lightly browned. Remove to wire racks to cool.

In a mixing bowl, cream butter, sugar, vanilla and enough cream to achieve desired frosting consistency. Add food coloring if desired. Frost cookies. Sprinkle with colored sugar if desired. **Yield:** 8 dozen.

White Chocolate Holiday Cookies

At first glance, these look a bit like traditional chocolate chip cookies.
But one bite quickly reveals white chocolate chunks plus spicy dashes of ginger and cinnamon.
—Bonnie Baumgardner, Sylva, North Carolina

1/2 cup butter *or* margarine, softened
1/2 cup shortening
3/4 cup packed brown sugar
1/2 cup sugar
  1 egg
1/2 teaspoon almond extract
  2 cups all-purpose flour
  1 teaspoon baking soda
1/4 teaspoon salt
1/4 teaspoon ground cinnamon
1/4 teaspoon ground ginger
  6 squares (1 ounce *each*) white baking chocolate, chopped
1-1/2 cups chopped pecans

In a mixing bowl, cream the butter, shortening and sugars. Add egg and almond extract; mix well. Combine the dry ingredients; add to creamed mixture. Stir in white chocolate and pecans. Drop by rounded teaspoonfuls 2 in. apart onto greased baking sheets. Bake at 350° for 8-10 minutes or until lightly browned. Remove to wire racks to cool. **Yield:** 10 dozen.

Caramel Snack Mix

Instead of the usual savory cereal snack mix, this version gets just the
right amount of sweetness from brown sugar and corn syrup.
—Barbara Strohbehn, Gladbrook, Iowa

  6 cups Rice Chex
  6 cups Corn Chex
  6 cups Crispix
  1 cup butter (no substitutes)
  1 cup packed brown sugar
1/2 cup corn syrup
  1 teaspoon vanilla extract

Grease three 15-in. x 10-in. x 1-in. baking pans; set aside. In a large heatproof bowl, combine the cereals; set aside.

In a heavy saucepan over medium heat, bring butter, brown sugar and corn syrup to a boil, stirring constantly. Reduce heat. Simmer, uncovered, for 5 minutes, stirring occasionally. Remove from the heat; stir in vanilla. Pour over cereal and stir until well coated.

Transfer to prepared pans. Bake, uncovered, at 200° for 1 hour, stirring every 15 minutes. Cool completely. Break apart and store in airtight containers. **Yield:** 4-1/2 quarts.

Triple-Nut Diamonds

(Pictured at right)

My dad has always been crazy about nuts, so when I came upon this recipe, I knew I had to try it. The diamond shape is a nice addition to the Christmas cookie tray.
—*Darlene King, Estevan, Saskatchewan*

1 cup all-purpose flour
1/2 cup sugar
1/2 cup cold butter (no
    substitutes), *divided*
1/2 cup packed brown sugar
2 tablespoons honey
1/4 cup whipping cream
2/3 cup *each* chopped pecans,
    walnuts and almonds

Line a greased 9-in. square baking pan with foil; grease the foil and set aside. In a bowl, combine the flour and sugar. Cut in 1/4 cup butter until mixture resembles coarse crumbs; press into prepared pan. Bake at 350° for 10 minutes.

In a saucepan, heat the brown sugar, honey and remaining butter until bubbly. Boil for 1 minute. Remove from the heat; stir in cream and nuts. Pour over crust. Bake at 350° for 16-20 minutes or until surface is bubbly. Cool on a wire rack.

Refrigerate for 30 minutes. Using foil, lift bars out of the pan; cut into 1-in. diamonds. Store in an airtight container. **Yield:** 4 dozen.

Orange Walnut Candy

A friend shared the recipe for these tangy goodies. Whenever I need a guaranteed crowd-pleaser, I roll them out by the dozens.
—*Betty Hostetler, Ocean Park, Washington*

3-3/4 cups (1 pound) confectioners'
    sugar
1 package (12 ounces) vanilla
    wafers, crushed
1 can (6 ounces) frozen orange
    juice concentrate, thawed

1/2 cup butter *or* margarine, melted
1-1/2 to 2 cups ground walnuts

In a bowl, combine the sugar, wafer crumbs, orange juice concentrate and butter; mix well. Shape into 3/4-in. balls; roll in walnuts. Cover and refrigerate in an airtight container for at least 24 hours before serving. **Yield:** 8 dozen.

Peanut Oat Cookies

I'm not surprised when people say these are the best cookies they've ever had...I agree!
Oats make them hearty and more delicious than traditional peanut butter cookies.
—Stacia McLimore, Indianapolis, Indiana

1-1/4 cups butter-flavored
    shortening
1-1/4 cups chunky peanut butter
1-1/2 cups packed brown sugar
   1 cup sugar
   3 eggs
4-1/2 cups old-fashioned oats
   2 teaspoons baking soda
   1 package (11-1/2 ounces) milk
    chocolate chips
   1 cup chopped peanuts

In a mixing bowl, cream shortening, peanut butter and sugars. Add eggs, one at a time, beating well after each addition. Combine oats and baking soda; gradually add to creamed mixture. Stir in chocolate chips and peanuts. Drop by tablespoonfuls 2 in. apart onto greased baking sheets. Bake at 350° for 10-12 minutes or until golden brown. Remove to wire racks to cool. **Yield:** about 8 dozen.

Mamie Eisenhower's Fudge

My mother came across this recipe in a newspaper some 40 years ago.
One taste and you'll see why it doesn't take long for a big batch to disappear.
—Linda First, Hinsdale, Illinois

   1 tablespoon plus 1/2 cup
    butter (no substitutes), *divided*
   3 milk chocolate candy bars
    (two 7 ounces, one 1.55
    ounces), broken into pieces
   4 cups (24 ounces) semisweet
    chocolate chips
   1 jar (7 ounces) marshmallow
    creme
   1 can (12 ounces) evaporated
    milk
4-1/2 cups sugar
   2 cups chopped walnuts

Line a 13-in. x 9-in. x 2-in. pan with foil and butter the foil with 1 tablespoon butter; set aside. In a large heatproof bowl, combine the candy bars, chocolate chips and marshmallow creme; set aside.

In a large heavy saucepan over medium-low heat, combine the milk, sugar and remaining butter. Bring to a boil, stirring constantly. Boil and stir for 4-1/2 minutes. Pour over chocolate mixture; stir until chocolate is melted and mixture is smooth and creamy. Stir in walnuts. Pour into prepared pan. Cover and refrigerate until firm.

Using foil, lift fudge out of pan; cut into 1-in. squares. Store in an airtight container in the refrigerator. **Yield:** about 6 pounds.

Date-Filled Sandwich Cookies

(Pictured at right)

Of all the cookies I've baked over the years, these have remained one of my all-time favorites. The dough is very easy to work with, and the result is eye-catching.
— Debbie Rode, Oxbow, Saskatchewan

1 cup butter (no substitutes), softened
2 cups packed brown sugar
2 eggs
2 teaspoons vanilla extract
3-1/2 cups all-purpose flour
1 teaspoon baking powder
1 teaspoon baking soda
FILLING:
2 cups chopped dates
3/4 cup sugar
3/4 cup water

In a mixing bowl, cream butter and brown sugar. Add eggs, one at a time, beating well after each addition. Beat in vanilla. Combine the flour, baking powder and baking soda; gradually add to creamed mixture. Refrigerate for 1 hour or until easy to handle.

On a lightly floured surface, roll out dough to 1/8-in. thickness. Cut with a 2-1/2-in. cookie cutter dipped in flour. Place 1 in. apart on greased baking sheets. Bake at 350° for 10-12 minutes or until edges are lightly browned. Remove to wire racks to cool.

In a saucepan, combine filling ingredients. Cook over medium heat for 3 minutes or until thickened and bubbly. Cool to room temperature. Spread on the bottom of half of the cookies; top with remaining cookies. **Yield:** 3 dozen.

German Chocolate Caramel Bars

I get at least one recipe request every time I take these cookies to a church potluck.
The caramel and cream cheese filling is a winner.
— Hazel Baldner, Austin, Minnesota

1 package (18-1/4 ounces)
  German sweet chocolate
  cake mix
1 cup quick-cooking oats
6 tablespoons cold butter
  (no substitutes)
1 egg, beaten
FILLING:
1 package (8 ounces) cream
  cheese, softened
1/2 cup caramel ice cream topping
1 egg
TOPPING:
1/2 cup chopped pecans
1/4 cup packed brown sugar
1/4 cup quick-cooking oats
2 tablespoons butter

In a bowl, combine cake mix and oats; cut in butter until crumbly. Set aside 1 cup. Stir the egg into remaining oat mixture (mixture will be crumbly). Press into a greased 13-in. x 9-in. x 2-in. baking pan. Bake at 350° for 12 minutes or until almost set. Cool on a wire rack for 10 minutes.

Combine filling ingredients; spread over crust. For topping, combine the pecans, brown sugar, oats, butter and reserved oat mixture until crumbly. Sprinkle over filling. Bake 15 minutes longer. Cool on a wire rack. Refrigerate until firm before cutting. **Yield:** 3 dozen.

Hazelnut Crescents

My mom and I make these delicate cookies every Christmas.
Hazelnuts give a little different flavor from the usual pecans.
— Beverly Launius, Sandwich, Illinois

1 cup butter (no substitutes),
  softened
1/4 cup sugar
1 teaspoon vanilla extract
2 cups all-purpose flour
1 cup whole hazelnuts, ground
Confectioners' sugar

In a mixing bowl, cream butter, sugar and vanilla. Gradually add the flour and nuts. Cover and refrigerate for 2 hours or until easy to handle.

Shape dough by teaspoonfuls into 2-in. rolls. Form into crescents. Place 2 in. apart on ungreased baking sheets. Bake at 350° for 12 minutes or until lightly browned. Cool for 2 minutes before removing from pans to wire racks. Dust with confectioners' sugar. **Yield:** about 10 dozen.

Toasted Almond Caramels

(Pictured at right)

Preparing these caramels never fails to put me in the holiday spirit. Later, when I'm passing them around, that cheerful feeling becomes contagious.
—Mae Ondracek, Pahrump, Nevada

1 teaspoon plus 1/4 cup butter
   (no substitutes), *divided*
2 cups sugar
1 cup light corn syrup
1/4 teaspoon salt
1 cup whipping cream
1 teaspoon vanilla extract
1 cup chopped almonds, toasted

Line an 8-in. square pan with foil and butter the foil with 1 teaspoon butter; set aside. In a heavy saucepan, combine the sugar, corn syrup, salt and remaining butter. Bring to a boil over medium heat, stirring constantly. Reduce heat to medium-low; boil gently without stirring for 4 minutes.

Remove from the heat; slowly stir in cream. Return to the heat; cook, without stirring, over medium-low heat until a candy thermometer reads 245° (firm-ball stage). Remove from the heat; stir in vanilla and almonds. Pour into prepared pan (do not scrape sides of saucepan). Cool completely.

Cut into squares. Wrap individually in waxed paper or foil; twist ends. **Yield:** about 4 dozen.

CANDY MAKING TIPS

IT'S ACTUALLY quite easy to make candy from scratch if you keep in mind these pointers.

- Make sure that you test your candy thermometer before each use by bringing water to a boil; the thermometer should read 212°. Adjust your recipe temperature up or down based on your test.
- Measure and assemble all ingredients for a recipe before beginning. Do not substitute or alter the basic ingredients.
- Use heavy-gauge saucepans that are deep enough to allow candy mixtures to boil freely without boiling over.
- For safe stirring when preparing recipes with hot boiling sugar, use wooden spoons with long handles.
- Humid weather affects results when making candy that is cooked to a specific temperature or that contains egg whites. For best results, make candy on days when the humidity is less than 60%.
- Store homemade candies in tightly covered containers unless otherwise directed. Don't store more than one kind of candy in a single container.

Truffle Topiary Centerpiece

(Pictured on opposite page)

This impressive, edible centerpiece from our Test Kitchen takes truffles to new heights! Set out the extras on plates or package them for guests to take home.

Gold spray paint
5-inch clay pot
Floral foam to fit inside pot
New small flat paintbrush
5-inch Styrofoam ball
Milk chocolate candy coating, melted (about 1/2 cup)
12-inch length of 3/8-inch wooden dowel
Double-sided transparent tape
2-1/3 yards of gold metallic cord
Craft scissors
White (tacky) glue
18-inch square of gold-flecked tulle netting
Craft wire
Two large wire-edged bows
Toothpicks
60 to 70 Coconut Truffles (recipe on opposite page)
60 to 70 paper *or* foil candy cups

Spray-paint clay pot gold. When dry, fill pot with floral foam.

Use paintbrush to cover Styrofoam ball with melted chocolate. Let harden.

With a pencil, mark dowel about 1-1/2 inches from one end and 4-1/2 inches from the other end. Place several pieces of double-sided tape on dowel between markings. Wrap gold metallic cord around dowel between markings. Cut away excess cord and glue ends to secure.

Insert long unwrapped end of dowel straight up and down into center of floral foam. Place pot in center of tulle netting. Bring up netting on all sides to cover pot. Use craft wire to secure net-ting to dowel just above top of pot. Arrange netting to cover wire, trimming excess netting as desired. Attach bows to opposite sides of top of pot. Trim ribbon ends as desired.

Use a pencil to make a hole in chocolate-covered Styrofoam ball, centering hole inside ball. Push ball onto end of dowel until wood on dowel is covered, making sure ball and dowel are centered and straight.

Insert a toothpick into top center of ball, leaving about a third of the toothpick exposed. Set a truffle into a candy cup; carefully push truffle and cup onto exposed end of toothpick. Repeat until ball is completely covered with truffles.

MAKING A TRUFFLE TOPIARY

1. Insert long unwrapped end of dowel into center of floral foam in painted clay pot.
2. Center clay pot on top of tulle netting. Bring net-ting up around sides of clay pot to cover.

3. Push chocolate-covered ball onto end of dowel until wood on dowel is covered.
4. Insert toothpicks into ball, leaving about a third of toothpick exposed. Set truffles into candy cups and push onto ends of toothpicks.

Coconut Truffles

(Pictured at right)

These chocolate-covered coconut truffles can be flavored with a variety of extracts with delicious results. Making candy is a favorite pastime of mine.
—Janelle Johnson, Muncy, Pennsylvania

1-1/2 cups butter (no substitutes)
    6 cups confectioners' sugar
   3/4 cup whipping cream
    6 cups flaked coconut
   1/2 teaspoon almond extract
   1/2 teaspoon rum extract
   1/2 teaspoon peppermint extract
    1 teaspoon cherry extract
    2 pounds milk chocolate candy
     coating, melted
   1/2 cup ground almonds
    4 ounces white candy coating,
     melted
Red and green candy coating
  disks,* melted

In a Dutch oven, heat butter over medium heat until golden brown, about 7 minutes. Remove from the heat; stir in confectioners' sugar, cream and coconut. Divide mixture between four bowls; stir a different flavor extract into each bowl. Cover and refrigerate for 45 minutes or until easy to handle.

Shape chilled mixtures into 1-in. balls; place on four separate waxed paper-lined baking sheets. Chill for 1-2 hours or until firm.

Dip the almond-flavored balls in milk chocolate coating; sprinkle with ground almonds. Place on waxed paper to harden.

Dip remaining balls in milk chocolate coating; place on waxed paper to harden. Drizzle white coating over rum truffles, red coating over cherry truffles and green coating over mint truffles. **Yield:** about 9 dozen.

*Editor's Note: Colored candy coating disks can be obtained by mail from Wilton Industries Inc., 2240 W. 75th St., Woodridge IL 60517. To order, call 1-800/794-5866 (fax 1-888/824-9520). Or visit their Web site at *www.wilton.com*.

In Canada, contact Wilton Industries, Canada Ltd., 98 Carrier Dr., Etobicoke ON Canada M9W 5R1. Phone 1-416/679-0798.

TIME-SAVING TRUFFLES

YOU CAN make the coconut centers for these truffles and freeze them in airtight containers for up to 2 months. Thaw in the refrigerator; dip in chocolate and decorate as directed.

Soft Chocolate Mint Cookies

If you don't care for crisp cookies that crumble when you take a bite, give this soft variety a try.
No one can resist the fudgy, minty flavor.
—*Kristin Vincent, Orem, Utah*

1/2 cup butter (no substitutes)
3 squares (1 ounce *each*) unsweetened chocolate
1/2 cup sugar
1/2 cup packed brown sugar
1 egg
1/4 cup buttermilk
1 teaspoon peppermint extract
1-3/4 cups all-purpose flour
1/2 teaspoon baking powder
1/4 teaspoon baking soda
1/4 teaspoon salt

In a microwave or heavy saucepan, melt butter and chocolate; stir until smooth. In a mixing bowl, beat sugars and egg; add buttermilk and peppermint extract. Beat in chocolate mixture. Combine the flour, baking powder, baking soda and salt; gradually add to sugar mixture. Let stand for 15 minutes or until dough becomes firmer.

Drop by tablespoonfuls 3 in. apart onto ungreased baking sheets. Bake at 350° for 8-10 minutes or until edges are firm. Cool for 2 minutes before removing from pans to wire racks. **Yield:** about 3 dozen.

Brown Sugar Pecan Candies

These sweet candies are similar to those served at Mexican restaurants in our area.
The recipe comes from a cookbook put together by the staff of the school where I teach.
—*Barbara Windham, Houston, Texas*

1-1/2 cups sugar
1/2 cup packed brown sugar
1/2 cup evaporated milk
3 tablespoons light corn syrup
4 large marshmallows, cut into quarters
2 tablespoons butter *or* margarine
2 cups coarsely chopped pecans
1/2 teaspoon vanilla extract

In a large heavy saucepan, combine the sugars, milk and corn syrup. Cook over medium-low heat, stirring occasionally, until a candy thermometer reads 238° (soft-ball stage).

Remove from the heat; stir in marshmallows and butter until melted. Add pecans and vanilla; stir only until mixture begins to thicken. Quickly drop by tablespoonfuls onto waxed paper. Cool until set. Store in an airtight container at room temperature. **Yield:** 5 dozen.

Editor's Note: If mixture begins to thicken, stir in hot water, a teaspoon at a time. We recommend that you test your candy thermometer before each use by bringing water to a boil; the thermometer should read 212°. Adjust your recipe temperature up or down based on your test.

Snowmen Cookies

(Pictured at right)

These cute snowmen cookies make great treats for children's parties. Kids are always willing to chip in and help decorate them.
—Sherri Johnson, Burns, Tennessee

- **1 package (16 ounces) Nutter Butter cookies**
- **1-1/4 pounds white candy coating, melted**
- **Miniature chocolate chips**
- **M&M miniature baking bits**
- **Pretzel sticks, halved**
- **Orange and red decorating gel *or* frosting**

Using tongs, dip cookies in candy coating; shake off excess. Place on waxed paper. Place two chocolate chips on one end of cookies for eyes. Place baking bits down middle for buttons. For arms, dip ends of two pretzel stick halves into coating; attach one to each side. Let stand until hardened. Pipe nose and scarf with gel or frosting. **Yield:** 32 cookies.

Popcorn Christmas Trees

(Pictured above)

The kids in my family like these popcorn trees instead of traditional popcorn balls. You can substitute red-hot candies for the M&M's if you like.
—Nicole Clayton, Las Vegas, Nevada

- **6 cups popped popcorn**
- **1/2 cup sugar**
- **1/2 cup light corn syrup**
- **1/4 cup creamy peanut butter**
- **10 to 12 drops green food coloring**
- **2 to 3 tablespoons red M&M miniature baking bits**

Place popcorn in a large bowl; set aside. In a heavy saucepan over medium heat, bring sugar and corn syrup to a boil, stirring occasionally. Boil and stir for 1 minute. Remove from the heat; stir in peanut butter and food coloring until blended. Pour over popcorn and stir to coat.

With wet hands, shape mixture by 3/4 cupfuls into evergreen tree shapes. While warm, press a few baking bits into each tree. Place on a greased baking sheet; let stand until firm, about 30 minutes. **Yield:** 8 servings.

Spiced Pecans

(Pictured at right)

The combination of spices on these nuts seems to warm everyone on cold winter days. I make this recipe several times over the holidays.
— Tammi Simpson
Greensburg, Kentucky

  2 cups pecan halves
1/4 cup butter *or* margarine
1/4 cup sugar
  1 teaspoon ground cinnamon
1/4 teaspoon ground nutmeg
1/4 teaspoon ground cloves

In a skillet over low heat, toast pecans in butter for 15 minutes or until lightly browned, stirring often. Drain on paper towels. In a bowl, combine the sugar and spices. Add pecans and toss to coat. Spread on a foil-lined baking sheet. Bake at 325° for 10 minutes. Cool. Store in an airtight container. **Yield:** 2 cups.

Sugar-Topped Walnut Bars

If I haven't set out these nutty treats at a holiday gathering, family and friends are sure to notice—and to ask where my bars are! They travel well to potluck dinners.
—Gloria Siddiqui, Houston, Texas

2-1/4 cups all-purpose flour
  1 cup sugar
  1 cup butter (no substitutes), softened
  2 egg yolks
FILLING:
  4 eggs
  2 cups finely ground walnuts
1-1/3 cups sugar

  1 teaspoon vanilla extract
Confectioners' sugar

In a mixing bowl, combine flour and sugar. Beat in butter and egg yolks. Press into an ungreased 15-in. x 10-in. x 1-in. baking pan. For filling, in a bowl, beat eggs. Stir in the walnuts, sugar and vanilla. Pour over crust. Bake at 300° for 55-60 minutes or until lightly browned. Cool completely on a wire rack. Dust with confectioners' sugar. Cut into bars. **Yield:** 6 dozen.

Wrap Up Cookies and Candies as Gifts

YOU DON'T have to spend a fortune or valuable time at the mall in search of perfect Christmas gifts. Quite often the most priceless treasures are your own homemade cookies and candies presented in decorative tins or in one of the pretty packages suggested below and shown at right.

• You'll have a handle on decorating gifts from the kitchen if you rely on baskets. They come in a variety of styles, shapes and sizes and are commonly found on sale at craft and variety stores—so be on the lookout for them throughout the year. And save any baskets you've acquired either from a gift you've received or from a purchase you've made for yourself.

Line the basket with white or colored tissue paper, then top with cookies that have been bundled in plastic wrap. Place the basket on a large piece of clear, colored or patterned cellophane; bring the edges of the cellophane up and tie with a ribbon. Add a decorative bow if desired.

• At Christmastime, craft and variety stores sell a variety of papier-mache boxes perfect for gift giving. In the photo (above right), we stacked star-shaped sugar cookies in a star-shaped papier-mache box that's been lined with wax-coated tissue paper. (Wax-coated tissue paper can be found at specialty cooking stores. It's sturdier than regular tissue paper and won't ab-

sorb the cookie's flavor and oils.) If you care to show your creativity, spray-paint the box and/or stamp it with festive designs. Let the box dry completely before adding tissue paper and cookies.

• Little dressing up is needed when you fill inexpensive clear jars with colorful snack mixes and individually wrapped candies. Simply tie a festive ribbon and some tiny ornaments around the top for an easy-to-prepare present.

Don't limit your creativity to the suggestions shown above. Consider these other ideas:

• Decorative tins, plates and candy dishes can often be found at bargain prices throughout the year at stores and rummage sales and at after-Christmas sales. Keep them on hand for last-minute gifts.

• Stack cookies in a wide-mouth canning jar, cover the lid with fabric and screw on the band. You may also want to include the recipe for the cookies.

• Instead of discarding potato chip cans, coffee tins or shortening cans, wash them, decorate the outside with wrapping paper or Con-Tact paper and fill with cookies or candies. Attach a bow to the lid and close.

• Wrap cookies in plastic wrap, place a bow on top and tuck inside a pretty coffee mug or teacup.

GIVING *Thanks*

For a twist on the traditional this Thanksgiving, turn
to the mouth-watering meal, succulent side dishes and
delectable desserts showcased on the following pages.
Every recipe offers a cornucopia of the season's finest
flavors...from pumpkin, cranberries and squash to
sweet potatoes, apples and more. Your family is
certain to fall for these tried-and-true dishes
and offer up thanks to the hostess.

Traditional Turkey Dinner

"IF IT'S NOT broken, don't fix it." That's the popular motto Edie DeSpain lives by in her Logan, Utah kitchen.

So it's no wonder that each Thanksgiving Day, this mother of three and grandmother of seven relies on the tried-and-true menu of Turkey with Apple Stuffing, Maple-Glazed Carrots, Peachy Sweet Potato Bake and Pumpkin Shortbread Dessert.

Other staples in this special dinner include brussels sprouts, a cranberry gelatin salad, mashed potatoes and fresh-baked rolls.

"A few years ago, I tried to start a new tradition of having my daughters make a recipe they like. But they both ended up bringing the same dishes I was already making!" she laughs.

Why not try one of Edie's delicious recipes and start a new tradition in your home this holiday season?

ALL THE FIXINGS
(Clockwise from top left)

**Turkey with
Apple Stuffing** (p. 129)

Maple-Glazed Carrots (p. 130)

Peachy Sweet Potato Bake (p. 128)

**Pumpkin Shortbread
Dessert** (p. 130)

Peachy Sweet Potato Bake

(Pictured on page 127)

With canned sweet potatoes and peaches, this side dish can be put together in a hurry.

1/2 cup packed brown sugar
 3 tablespoons all-purpose flour
1/2 teaspoon ground nutmeg
 2 tablespoons cold butter *or* margarine
1/2 cup chopped pecans
 4 cans (17 ounces *each*) cut-up sweet potatoes, drained
 2 cans (16 ounces *each*) sliced peaches, drained
 1 to 1-1/2 cups miniature marshmallows

In a bowl, combine brown sugar, flour and nutmeg; cut in butter until the mixture resembles coarse crumbs. Stir in pecans. Place sweet potatoes and peaches in a shallow 2-qt. broiler-proof baking dish. Sprinkle with pecan mixture.

Bake, uncovered, at 350° for 35 minutes. Sprinkle with marshmallows. Broil 4-6 in. from the heat until marshmallows are golden brown. **Yield:** 10-12 servings.

THANKSGIVING DAY DINNER TIMELINE

A Few Weeks Before:

- Make Harvest Centerpiece on page 131.
- Prepare two grocery lists—one for non-perishable items to purchase now, and one for perishable items to purchase a few days before Thanksgiving.
- Order a fresh turkey or buy and freeze a frozen turkey.

Four to Five Days Before:

- Thaw frozen turkey in a pan in the re-frigerator. (Allow 24 hours of thawing for every 5 pounds.)

Two Days Before:

- Buy remaining grocery items, including the fresh turkey if you ordered one.

The Day Before:

- Set the table.
- Prepare and refrigerate the Pumpkin Shortbread Dessert.
- For the Apple Stuffing, chop onion and celery; refrigerate in an airtight con-tainer. Cube bread; store in an airtight container.

Thanksgiving Day:

- Make stuffing, stuff turkey and bake.
- Make the Peachy Sweet Potato Bake and Maple-Glazed Carrots.
- Let cooked turkey stand for 20 minutes. Meanwhile, make the gravy. Remove the stuffing and carve the turkey.
- Serve Pumpkin Shortbread Dessert.

Turkey with Apple Stuffing

(Pictured at right and on page 126)

*The accompanying foolproof gravy recipe
is one I created in an attempt to
copy my mom's own rich gravy.*

4 cups chopped peeled tart
apples
3 cups sliced almonds
1-1/2 cups chopped onion
1-1/2 cups chopped celery
1/2 cup butter *or* margarine
2 teaspoons salt
2 teaspoons ground cinnamon
2 teaspoons poultry seasoning
12 cups cubed whole wheat bread
2 cups raisins
1 cup apple cider *or* juice
1/2 cup egg substitute
1 turkey (15 to 20 pounds)
1-1/2 cups water

GRAVY:

2 teaspoons chicken bouillon granules
1/2 teaspoon poultry seasoning
1/4 teaspoon pepper
1/2 cup all-purpose flour
1 cup milk

In a large skillet, saute apples, almonds, onion and celery in butter for 5 minutes. Remove from the heat. Stir in salt, cinnamon and poultry seasoning. In a large bowl, combine bread cubes, raisins and apple mixture. Add cider and egg substitute; toss to mix.

Just before baking, loosely stuff turkey with half of the stuffing. Place remaining stuffing in a greased 2-qt. baking dish; refrigerate until ready to bake. Skewer turkey opening; tie drumsticks together. Place breast side up on a rack in a roasting pan. Pour water into pan.

Bake, uncovered, at 325° for 4-1/2 to 5 hours or until a meat thermometer reads 180° for the turkey and 165° for the stuffing, basting occasionally with pan drippings. (Cover loosely with foil if turkey browns too quickly.)

Bake additional stuffing, covered, for 30-40 minutes. Uncover; bake 10 minutes longer or until lightly browned. Cover turkey and let stand for 20 minutes before removing stuffing and carving.

For gravy, pour pan drippings into a 4-cup measuring cup; skim off fat. Add enough water to measure 4 cups. Pour into a saucepan. Stir in bouillon, poultry seasoning and pepper. Bring to a boil. In a bowl, combine flour and milk until smooth; whisk into boiling broth. Cook and stir for 2 minutes or until thickened and bubbly. Serve with turkey and stuffing. **Yield:** 15-18 servings (12 cups stuffing and 3 cups gravy).

BASIC BRUSSELS SPROUTS

TO MAKE boiled buttered brussels sprouts as shown on page 127, remove any yellow outer leaves from the sprouts and trim stem ends.

Add 1 inch of water to saucepan; add brussels sprouts. Bring to a boil. Reduce heat; cover and simmer for 10 to 12 minutes or until crisp-tender. Drain. Top with melted butter.

Pumpkin Shortbread Dessert
(Pictured on page 126)

My family prefers this to traditional pumpkin pie, which is just fine with me.
It feeds a crowd, so I only need to make one dessert instead of several pies.

1-3/4 cups sugar, *divided*
1-1/2 cups all-purpose flour
1/2 cup cold butter *or* margarine
4 eggs, lightly beaten
1 can (29 ounces) solid-pack
   pumpkin
1 teaspoon salt
1 teaspoon ground cinnamon
1 teaspoon ground ginger
1/2 teaspoon ground cloves
2 cans (12 ounces *each*)
   evaporated milk
Whipped cream and additional
   ground cinnamon, optional

In a bowl, combine 1/4 cup sugar and flour; cut in butter until the mixture resembles coarse crumbs. Press into an ungreased 13-in. x 9-in. x 2-in. baking pan. In a bowl, combine the eggs, pumpkin, salt, spices and remaining sugar. Stir in milk. Pour over crust.

Bake at 425° for 15 minutes. Reduce heat to 350°; bake 50-55 minutes longer or until filling is set. Cool on a wire rack. Cover and refrigerate overnight.

Cut into squares. Top with whipped cream and sprinkle with cinnamon if desired. **Yield:** 15-18 servings.

Maple-Glazed Carrots
(Pictured on page 126)

Carrots are my favorite vegetable, so I'm always searching for different ways to prepare them. This festive dish is quick to make and nicely complements the turkey.

12 medium carrots, peeled and
   julienned*
2 tablespoons cornstarch
2/3 cup orange juice
5 tablespoons maple syrup
5 tablespoons butter *or*
   margarine, melted
1 tablespoon grated orange peel
3/4 teaspoon ground nutmeg
1/2 teaspoon salt

Add 1 in. of water to a large saucepan; add carrots. Bring to a boil. Reduce heat; cover and simmer for 3-5 minutes or until crisp-tender.

Meanwhile, in another saucepan, combine the cornstarch and orange juice until smooth. Stir in the remaining ingredients. Bring to a boil; cook and stir for 2 minutes or until thickened and heated through.

Drain carrots; top with glaze and toss to coat. **Yield:** 6-8 servings.

Editor's Note: Two 10-ounce packages of shredded carrots can be substituted for julienned carrots.

Harvest Centerpiece

(Pictured at right)

There's no need to call your local florist and order a centerpiece for this autumn gathering. With a few easy-to-find and inexpensive items—like a simple basket, rustic candles and seasonal natural materials—you can quickly create your own festive table decoration that captures the warm and rustic feel of fall.

Divided container such as a cutlery tray *or* drawer divider
Candles of various sizes, shapes and colors
Jute string, optional
Assorted natural materials such as Indian corn kernels, dried apple slices, bark *or* small stones, strawflowers and small pinecones

Select a divided container to coordinate with your tableware and linens (we used a rattan drawer divider). Place candles into compartments as desired, varying the height for added interest. (If needed, place smaller candles on a sturdy base to add height.) Tie jute string around the larger candles if desired. Fill remaining partitions with a variety of natural materials.

MAKING THE HARVEST CENTERPIECE

1. Place candles of different shapes and heights into selected compartments of a divided container.

2. Fill compartments with assorted natural materials.

GIVING Thanks

A Bounty of Side Dishes

THANKSGIVING dinner with all the fixings is often the year's most memorable meal for families—and one they eagerly look forward to. In addition to the traditional succulent turkey, a variety of side dishes round out this special feast.

From delectable dressings and seasonal vegetables to fresh tossed salads and sweet sauces or fruits, this harvest of holiday dishes provides many mouth-watering options you can take to your Thanksgiving table year after year.

For a surefire way to receive a bushel of compliments, you'll want to try Oat 'n' Rye Bread Dressing, Tangy Baked Apples and Roasted Root Vegetables (shown at right).

CORNUCOPIA!
(Clockwise from top left)

Oat 'n' Rye
Bread Dressing (p. 134)

Tangy Baked Apples (p. 135)

Roasted Root
Vegetables (p. 137)

Oat 'n' Rye Bread Dressing

(Pictured on page 132)

Two kinds of bread, spinach, green pepper and cranberries make this an outstanding dressing for special occasions. The flavor of sage really shines through.
—Judith Toubes, Tamarac, Florida

3 cups cubed day-old oatmeal
  bread
3 cups cubed day-old rye bread
1 cup chopped fresh spinach
1 cup chopped green pepper
1 cup dried cranberries
2 tablespoons chopped onion
2 teaspoons rubbed sage
1 cup chicken broth
2 eggs, lightly beaten *or* 1/2 cup
  egg substitute

In a large bowl, combine the bread cubes, spinach, green pepper, cranberries, onion and sage. Stir in broth and eggs until well combined. Spoon into a greased 2-qt. baking dish. Cover and bake at 350° for 45 minutes. Uncover; bake 10-15 minutes longer or until lightly browned. **Yield:** 6 servings.

Editor's Note: This recipe makes enough to stuff a 6-pound roasting chicken. It can easily be doubled for a 12-pound turkey.

TURKEY AND STUFFING TIPS

ANY DRESSING can be used to stuff a turkey. For food safety reasons, review these pointers before cooking your Thanksgiving turkey and stuffing.

- Use egg substitute in place of eggs for dressing that is stuffed into the turkey.
- Stuff the turkey just before baking—not beforehand. Loosely spoon the stuffing into the neck and body cavities to allow for expansion as it cooks.
- To be sure the stuffing is done, a meat thermometer at the center of the stuffing inside the bird should reach 165°.
- Always remove all of the stuffing before carving the bird. Never leave stuffing in cooked turkey when storing in the refrigerator.
- Don't let cooked turkey and stuffing stand at room temperature longer than 2 hours.

Maple Cranberry Sauce

My mother insists I bring this simple cranberry sauce every Thanksgiving.
Maple syrup adds a pleasant sweetness people don't expect.
—Mathilda Navias, Tiffin, Ohio

1 package (12 ounces) fresh *or*
  frozen cranberries
1-1/2 cups maple syrup
1/3 cup water

In a large saucepan, combine all ingredients. Bring to a boil. Reduce heat; simmer, uncovered, for 20 minutes, stirring occasionally. Cool. Cover and refrigerate until ready to serve. **Yield:** 2-1/2 cups.

Tangy Baked Apples

(Pictured at right and on page 133)

When the weather turns cooler in fall, these baked apples from my mom are sure to warm you up. Our family enjoys them with turkey, pork...even meat loaf. My husband and I like to add a bit more horseradish for extra zip.
—*Dee Poppie, Gilman, Illinois*

3 medium tart apples, cored
2 teaspoons lemon juice, *divided*
1/3 cup packed brown sugar
1/3 cup ketchup
2 tablespoons butter *or* margarine, softened
2 tablespoons prepared horseradish
1/4 cup water

Cut apples in half; brush with 1 teaspoon lemon juice. Place in an ungreased 11-in. x 7-in. x 2-in. baking dish. Combine the brown sugar, ketchup, butter, horseradish and remaining lemon juice. Top each apple half with 2 tablespoons ketchup mixture. Pour water around apples.

Bake, uncovered, at 325° for 30 minutes or until apples are tender. Serve warm. **Yield:** 6 servings.

Sausage Potato Dressing

Mashed potatoes and sausage are the deliciously different ingredients in this moist dressing. I've been using this recipe since the 1960s with no complaints from my family.
—*Germaine Stank, Pound, Wisconsin*

1 large onion, chopped
1/2 cup butter *or* margarine, melted
3 cups hot mashed potatoes (prepared with milk and butter)
8 slices bread, toasted and cubed
1/2 pound bulk pork sausage, cooked and drained
2 eggs, lightly beaten *or* 1/2 cup egg substitute

1 teaspoon rubbed sage
1/2 teaspoon salt
1/2 teaspoon pepper

In a large skillet, saute onion in butter until tender. Remove from the heat. Add the remaining ingredients; mix well. Transfer to a greased 2-1/2-qt. baking dish. Cover and bake at 325° for 35 minutes. Uncover; bake 10 minutes longer or until golden brown. **Yield:** 8-10 servings.

Editor's Note: This recipe makes enough to stuff a 10- to 12-pound turkey.

Two-Cheese Spinach Bake

*My family will eat spinach on Thanksgiving and throughout the year if it's in
this rich, cheesy side dish loaded with flavor. It also makes
a great meatless meal with a tossed salad.*
—Chris Barila, Pisgah Forest, North Carolina

1 cup all-purpose flour
2 eggs, lightly beaten
1 cup milk
1/4 cup butter *or* margarine,
    melted
1/2 small onion, chopped
2 tablespoons grated Parmesan
    cheese
2 garlic cloves, minced
1/2 teaspoon salt
1/8 teaspoon cayenne pepper

1 package (10 ounces) frozen chopped spinach,
    thawed and squeezed dry
2 cups (8 ounces) shredded Monterey Jack cheese

In a large bowl, whisk the flour, eggs, milk, butter, onion,
Parmesan cheese, garlic, salt and cayenne until combined.
Fold in spinach and Monterey Jack cheese. Transfer to a
greased 1-1/2-qt. baking dish.

    Bake, uncovered, at 350° for 40-45 minutes or until a
knife inserted near the center comes out clean. Serve immediately. **Yield:** 6 servings.

Artichoke-Red Pepper Tossed Salad

*During college, I lived in France, where I learned to make vinaigrette.
My host family served the dressing with artichoke hearts. That inspired me to add
them to my basic tossed salad when I returned home.*
—Rachel Hinz, St. James, Minnesota

1 head iceberg lettuce, torn
1 bunch romaine, torn
1 can (14 ounces) water-packed
    artichoke hearts, drained and
    chopped
2 medium sweet red peppers,
    julienned
1/2 cup thinly sliced red onion
1/2 cup olive *or* vegetable oil
1/2 cup red wine vinegar *or*
    cider vinegar

2 tablespoons Dijon mustard
2 teaspoons sugar
1 teaspoon seasoned salt
1/2 cup shredded Parmesan cheese

In a large bowl, combine the first five ingredients. In a jar
with a tight-fitting lid, combine oil, vinegar, mustard, sugar
and seasoned salt; shake well. Drizzle over salad and toss to
coat. Sprinkle with Parmesan cheese. **Yield:** 20-25 servings.

Roasted Root Vegetables

(Pictured at right and on page 132)

This dish's pretty harvest colors make it an eye-catching addition to the Thanksgiving table. It's a fix-it-and-forget-it favorite of mine.
—Cathryn White, Newark, Delaware

2 cups pearl onions
2 pounds red potatoes, cut into 1/2-inch pieces
1 large rutabaga, peeled and cut into 1/2-inch pieces
1 pound parsnips, peeled and cut into 1/2-inch pieces
1 pound carrots, cut into 1/2-inch pieces
3 tablespoons butter *or* margarine, melted
3 tablespoons olive *or* vegetable oil
4-1/2 teaspoons dried thyme
1-1/2 teaspoons salt
3/4 teaspoon coarsely ground pepper
2 packages (10 ounces *each*) frozen brussels sprouts, thawed
3 to 4 garlic cloves, minced

In a Dutch oven or large kettle, bring 6 cups water to a boil. Add the pearl onions; boil for 3 minutes. Drain and rinse with cold water; peel.

In a large roasting pan, combine the onions, potatoes, rutabaga, parsnips and carrots. Drizzle with butter and oil. Sprinkle with thyme, salt and pepper; toss to coat.

Cover and bake at 425° for 30 minutes. Uncover; stir in brussels sprouts and garlic. Bake, uncovered, for 50-60 minutes or until vegetables are tender and begin to brown, stirring occasionally. **Yield:** 16-18 servings.

Family Traditions

INSTEAD of simply saying grace at our Thanksgiving dinner, each person around the table takes a turn to state what they're thankful for. Even the little ones pipe in and express their appreciation for something they cherish. More often than not, our eyes fill with tears as we take the time to remember what's truly important in life. We hope the kids carry on this touching tradition.
—*Suzanne Davidsz, Oak Creek, Wisconsin*

Sweet Potato Casserole

Pineapple, sugar and marshmallows lend a super sweetness to sweet potatoes.
I've been making this casserole for years, both for special occasions at home and for casual dinners.
—*Ruth Leach, Shreveport, Louisiana*

6 medium sweet potatoes
1/2 cup butter *or* margarine, cubed
3/4 cup sugar
1 can (20 ounces) crushed pineapple, drained
2 eggs, beaten
1 teaspoon vanilla extract
1/2 teaspoon ground nutmeg
1/2 teaspoon salt
15 large marshmallows

Place sweet potatoes in a large kettle and cover with water; bring to a boil. Boil gently until potatoes can easily be pierced with the tip of a sharp knife, about 30-45 minutes. Drain; cool slightly. Peel potatoes and place in a large bowl; mash. Stir in butter and sugar until butter is melted. Add pineapple, eggs, vanilla, nutmeg and salt.

Spoon into a greased 2-qt. baking dish. Top with marshmallows. Bake, uncovered, at 350° for 40-45 minutes. **Yield:** 8 servings.

SWEET POTATO SECRETS

SELECT sweet potatoes that are firm with no cracks or bruises. If stored in a cool, dark, well-ventilated place, they'll remain fresh for about 2 weeks. If the temperature is above 60°, they'll sprout sooner or become woody. Once cooked, sweet potatoes can be stored for up to 1 week in the refrigerator.

Frosty Cranberry Salad Cups

Instead of traditional cranberry sauce, consider these individual fruit salads.
They're a make-ahead treat terrific for potlucks.
—*Bernadine Bolte, St. Louis, Missouri*

1 can (16 ounces) jellied cranberry sauce
1 can (8 ounces) crushed pineapple, drained
1 cup (8 ounces) sour cream
1/4 cup confectioners' sugar
3/4 cup miniature marshmallows
Red food coloring, optional

In a bowl, combine all ingredients. Fill foil- or paper-lined muffin cups two-thirds full. Cover and freeze until firm, about 3 hours. **Yield:** 16 servings.

Dilly Bread Ring

(Pictured at right)

I made this bread when my boyfriend came to meet my family for the first time. It obviously made an impression on him, because we eventually got married! This batter bread requires no kneading, so even novice bakers will find it easy.

—Natercia Yailaian
Somerville, Massachusetts

2 packages (1/4 ounce *each*)
   active dry yeast
1/3 cup warm water
   (110° to 115°)
1/3 cup warm milk (110° to 115°)
6 tablespoons butter *or*
   margarine, softened
1/3 cup sugar
2 eggs
1 cup (8 ounces) sour cream
2 tablespoons minced fresh
   parsley
1 to 2 tablespoons dill weed
2 teaspoons salt
1-1/2 teaspoons minced chives
4-1/2 cups all-purpose flour

In a mixing bowl, dissolve yeast in warm water. Add milk, butter, sugar, eggs, sour cream, seasonings and 3 cups flour. Beat on low speed for 30 seconds. Beat on high for 3 minutes. Stir in remaining flour (batter will be sticky). Do not knead. Cover and let rise in a warm place until doubled, about 1 hour.

Stir dough down. Spoon into a greased 10-in. tube or fluted tube pan. Cover and let rise until nearly doubled, about 45 minutes. Bake at 375° for 30-35 minutes or until golden brown (cover loosely with foil if top browns too quickly). Cool for 10 minutes before removing from pan to a wire rack. **Yield:** 1 loaf.

After-Thanksgiving Turkey Soup

As much as my family loves Thanksgiving, they look forward to this cream soup using leftover turkey even more. It makes a big batch that we can enjoy for days.
—Valorie Walker, Bradley, South Carolina

1 leftover turkey carcass (from a 12- to 14-pound turkey)
3 medium onions, chopped
2 large carrots, diced
2 celery ribs, diced
1 cup butter *or* margarine
1 cup all-purpose flour
2 cups half-and-half cream
1 cup uncooked long grain rice
2 teaspoons salt
1 teaspoon chicken bouillon granules
3/4 teaspoon pepper

Place turkey carcass in a soup kettle or Dutch oven and cover with water. Bring to a boil. Reduce heat; cover and simmer for 1 hour. Remove carcass; cool. Set aside 3 qts. broth. Remove turkey from bones and cut into bite-size pieces; set aside.

In a soup kettle or Dutch oven, saute the onions, carrots and celery in butter until tender. Reduce heat; stir in flour until blended. Gradually add 1 qt. of reserved broth. Bring to a boil; cook and stir for 2 minutes or until thickened.

Add cream, rice, salt, bouillon, pepper, remaining broth and reserved turkey. Reduce heat; cover and simmer for 30-35 minutes or until rice is tender. **Yield:** 16 servings (about 4 quarts).

Winter Squash Souffle

My large family gets together quite often. To make it easy on the host, everyone brings a dish to pass, and we often swap recipes. I've shared this one many times.
—Colleen Birchill, Spokane, Washington

3 cups mashed cooked winter squash
1/4 cup shredded Swiss cheese
2 tablespoons butter *or* margarine, melted
2 tablespoons whipping cream
3/4 teaspoon salt
1/4 teaspoon pepper
1/4 teaspoon dried thyme
3 eggs, *separated*

In a large bowl, combine the squash, cheese, butter, cream, salt, pepper and thyme. Beat egg yolks; add to squash mixture. In a small mixing bowl, beat egg whites until stiff peaks form. Fold into squash mixture. Transfer to a greased 2-qt. baking dish.

Bake, uncovered, at 375° for 45-50 minutes or until a knife inserted near the center comes out clean. Serve immediately. **Yield:** 6-8 servings.

BAKING A WINTER SQUASH

TO BAKE winter squash for mashing, cut the squash in half; scoop out and discard seeds. Place cut side down in a greased baking dish. Bake, uncovered, at 350° for 45 to 60 minutes or until tender. Cool slightly. Scoop squash out of shell; mash. A 1-pound squash will yield about 2 cups mashed squash.

Almond-Cranberry Squash Bake

(Pictured at right)

When my husband and I visit family in North Dakota, I bring along the ingredients to make this casserole. It gets rave reviews every time I make it.
—*Ronica Skarphol Brownson*
Madison, Wisconsin

4 cups hot mashed butternut squash
4 tablespoons butter *or* margarine, softened, *divided*
1/2 teaspoon salt
1/2 teaspoon ground cinnamon
1/4 teaspoon ground allspice
1/4 teaspoon ground nutmeg
1 can (16 ounces) whole-berry cranberry sauce
1/2 cup sliced almonds
1/4 cup packed brown sugar

In a large bowl, combine the squash, 2 tablespoons butter, salt, cinnamon, allspice and nutmeg; mix well. Transfer to a greased 2-qt. baking dish. Stir cranberry sauce until softened; spoon over squash.

Combine almonds, brown sugar and remaining butter; mix well. Sprinkle over cranberry sauce. Bake, uncovered, at 350° for 50-60 minutes or until golden brown and bubbly. **Yield:** 8 servings.

Crunchy Apple Salad

This old-fashioned salad is part of my favorite meal that Mom used to make. Crunchy apples, celery and walnuts blend well with the creamy mayonnaise.
—*Julie Pearsall, Union Springs, New York*

4 large red apples, diced
1 cup chopped celery
1 cup raisins
1 cup chopped walnuts
1/2 cup mayonnaise

In a large bowl, combine the apples, celery, raisins and walnuts. Blend in mayonnaise. Cover and refrigerate until serving. **Yield:** 16 servings.

Giving Thanks

Sweets for Thanksgiving

EVEN after feasting on a succulent supper of turkey and all the trimmings, family and friends will have room for dessert when tempting treats—like Pumpkin Charlotte, Cranberry Raisin Pie and Refreshing Orange Ice (pictured at right)—crop up on your Thanksgiving table.

Each and every delicious cake, pie, cookie and dessert in this chapter is bursting with some of fall's most fabulous flavors, like pumpkin, cranberries, apples, nuts and more.

So these satisfying treats will not only enliven your holiday menus year after year, they'll also produce a bushel of warm compliments for the cook!

Cranberry Raisin Pie

(Pictured on page 142)

This pretty pie has a wonderful blend of tart and sweet flavors. I first sampled this dessert at a church dinner and finally tracked down the contributor for the recipe.
—*Betty White, Hutchinson, Kansas*

1-3/4 cups sugar
    3 tablespoons cornstarch
1-1/2 cups water
    2 cups cranberries
    1 cup raisins
    1 tablespoon lemon juice
Pastry for double-crust pie (9 inches)
    1 egg, beaten
Additional sugar

In a saucepan, combine sugar and cornstarch; gradually stir in water until smooth. Add cranberries and raisins; cook and stir over medium heat until mixture begins to boil. Cook and stir 12 minutes longer or until thickened and cranberries pop. Remove from the heat; stir in lemon juice. Cool slightly.

Line a 9-in. pie plate with bottom pastry; trim to 1 in. beyond edge of plate. Pour filling into crust. Roll out remaining pastry to fit top of pie. Cut vents using decorative cutters. Place top pastry over filling. Arrange pastry cutouts on top. Trim, seal and flute edges. Brush pastry with egg; sprinkle with sugar. Cover edges loosely with foil.

Bake at 400° for 20 minutes. Reduce heat to 350°. Remove foil; bake 15-20 minutes longer or until crust is golden brown and filling is bubbly. Cool on a wire rack. **Yield:** 6-8 servings.

Soft Gingersnaps

With molasses and spices, these cookies deliver the old-fashioned flavor everyone loves.
—*Shawn Barto, Clermont, Florida*

1-1/2 cups butter (no substitutes), softened
    2 cups sugar
    2 eggs
1/2 cup molasses
4-1/2 cups all-purpose flour
    3 teaspoons baking soda
    2 teaspoons ground cinnamon
    1 teaspoon ground ginger
    1 teaspoon ground cloves
1/2 teaspoon salt
1/2 teaspoon ground nutmeg
Additional sugar

In a mixing bowl, cream butter and sugar. Add eggs, one at a time, beating well after each addition. Beat in molasses. Combine the flour, baking soda, cinnamon, ginger, cloves, salt and nutmeg; gradually add to creamed mixture. Refrigerate for 1 hour or until dough is easy to handle.

Roll into 1-in. balls; roll in sugar. Place 2 in. apart on ungreased baking sheets. Bake at 350° for 8-12 minutes or until puffy and lightly browned. Cool for 1 minute before removing to wire racks. **Yield:** 11 dozen.

Pumpkin Charlotte

(Pictured at right and on page 143)

My mother-in-law gave me this recipe a while back and I just love it! I make it for my husband and his friends during hunting season and it's a big hit.
—Lorelle Edgcomb, Granville, Illinois

2 packages (3 ounces *each*)
  ladyfingers
2 packages (3 ounces *each*)
  cream cheese, softened
2 tablespoons sugar
2-1/4 cups whipping cream, *divided*
3 tablespoons confectioners'
  sugar, *divided*
1 cup cold milk
2 packages (3.4 ounces *each*)
  instant vanilla pudding mix
1/2 teaspoon ground cinnamon
1/4 teaspoon ground ginger
1/4 teaspoon pumpkin pie spice
1 can (15 ounces) solid-pack
  pumpkin
Additional ground cinnamon

Split ladyfingers; arrange on the bottom and upright around the sides of an ungreased 9-in. springform pan, trimming to fit if necessary. Set aside.

In a large mixing bowl, beat cream cheese and sugar until smooth. In a small mixing bowl, beat 1-3/4 cups whipping cream and 2 tablespoons confectioners' sugar until stiff peaks form. Set 1/2 cup aside. Fold remaining whipped cream into cream cheese mixture. Spread into prepared pan.

In a mixing bowl, combine the milk, pudding mixes and spices; beat on low speed for 1 minute. Add pumpkin; beat 1 minute longer. Fold in reserved whipped cream. Pour over cream cheese layer. Cover and refrigerate for 8 hours or overnight.

Just before serving, beat remaining cream and confectioners' sugar until stiff peaks form. Spoon over pumpkin layer. Sprinkle with cinnamon. Remove sides of pan. Refrigerate leftovers. **Yield:** 10-12 servings.

TIPS FOR WHIPPING CREAM

BEFORE whipping cream, refrigerate the bowl and beaters for about 30 minutes. Pour the cream into a deep, chilled bowl; whip on high (with sugar if instructed) until soft peaks form, if using as a garnish, or until stiff peaks form, if frosting a cake.

Refreshing Orange Ice

(Pictured on page 142)

This sherbet has been part of my family's Thanksgiving tradition for three generations.
We eat it along with the rest of the meal... the tangy, creamy flavor
complements the turkey and all the trimmings.
—*Carol Lydon, Philadelphia, Pennsylvania*

3 cups water, *divided*
1 cup sugar
1 can (12 ounces) frozen orange juice concentrate, thawed
2 tablespoons lemon juice
1/2 cup half-and-half cream

In a saucepan, bring 1 cup water and sugar to a boil, stirring frequently. Boil for 1 minute or until sugar is dissolved. Remove from the heat; stir in orange juice concentrate, lemon juice and remaining water. Transfer to a freezer-proof mixing bowl. Cover and freeze until firm.

Remove from the freezer. Beat until blended. Beat in cream. Cover and return to freezer. Remove from the freezer 20 minutes before serving. **Yield:** 10-12 servings.

Two-Tone Spice Cake

I'm known for bringing delectable desserts to church functions. The combination of spice cake
and sweet sour cream frosting is a pleasant surprise for people.
—*Peggy Leibitzke, San Diego, California*

10 tablespoons butter (no substitutes), softened
1 cup packed brown sugar
3 eggs
1-3/4 cups all-purpose flour
1-1/2 teaspoons baking powder
1-1/4 teaspoons ground cinnamon
1/2 teaspoon baking soda
1/2 teaspoon ground allspice
1/4 teaspoon salt
1/8 teaspoon ground nutmeg
3/4 cup sour cream
1/4 cup finely chopped nuts
SOUR CREAM FROSTING:
3/4 cup butter, softened
5 to 6 cups confectioners' sugar
1/3 cup sour cream
1-1/2 teaspoons vanilla extract

CHOCOLATE GLAZE:
4 squares (1 ounce *each*) semisweet *or* unsweetened chocolate
2 tablespoons butter

In a mixing bowl, cream butter and brown sugar. Add the eggs, one at a time, beating well after each addition. Combine the dry ingredients; add to the creamed mixture alternately with sour cream. Stir in nuts. Spread into two greased and floured 8-in. round baking pans.

Bake at 350° for 20-25 minutes or until a toothpick inserted near the center comes out clean. Cool for 10 minutes; remove from pans to wire racks to cool completely.

For frosting, in a mixing bowl, cream butter and confectioners' sugar. Beat in sour cream and vanilla. Spread between layers and over top and sides of cake.

In a microwave or heavy saucepan, melt chocolate and butter. Cool for 2 minutes; spread over top of cake, allowing some to drip down the sides. **Yield:** 12 servings.

Apple Walnut Pie

(Pictured at right)

My family is fond of any treat featuring apples, but this pie is the one they like best. Unlike some fruit pies, this crust doesn't become soggy, thanks to the addition of ground walnuts. Everyone agrees the flavor of nuts pairs well with apples in this fall favorite.
—*Evonne Wurmnest, Normal, Illinois*

3/4 cup ground walnuts
  2 tablespoons brown sugar
  2 tablespoons beaten egg
  1 tablespoon milk
  3 tablespoons butter *or* margarine, softened, *divided*
1/4 teaspoon vanilla extract
1-1/4 teaspoons lemon juice, *divided*
Pastry for double-crust pie (9 inches)
  5 cups sliced peeled tart apples (about 6 medium)
3/4 cup sugar
  2 tablespoons all-purpose flour
  1 teaspoon ground cinnamon
1/4 teaspoon ground nutmeg
1/4 teaspoon salt
Additional milk, optional

In a bowl, combine the walnuts, brown sugar, egg, milk, 1 tablespoon butter, vanilla and 1/4 teaspoon lemon juice. Line a 9-in. pie plate with bottom pastry; trim even with edge of plate. Spread nut mixture over crust.

In a large bowl, toss apples with remaining lemon juice. Combine the sugar, flour, cinnamon, nutmeg and salt; toss with apples. Spoon over the nut mixture; dot with remaining butter.

Roll out remaining pastry; make a lattice crust. Trim, seal and flute edges. Brush top with additional milk if desired. Bake at 375° for 50-60 minutes or until golden brown. Serve warm. **Yield:** 6-8 minutes.

FOIL COVER FOR PIE CRUST

IF THE EDGE of your pie crust is becoming too brown while baking, cover it with foil. It's easy to make a foil cover that can be washed and reused.

On a 12-inch disposable foil pizza pan, draw a 7-inch-diameter circle in the center. Cut out the circle and discard. Then simply center the foil over the pie to cover the crust.

Walnut-Crunch Pumpkin Pie

Friends and family look forward to this version of pumpkin pie all year.
A sweet crunchy topping goes so well with the nicely spiced filling.
—Edna Hoffman, Hebron, Indiana

2 eggs
1 can (15 ounces) solid-pack
  pumpkin
1 can (12 ounces) evaporated
  milk
3/4 cup packed brown sugar
2 teaspoons vanilla extract
1-1/2 teaspoons ground cinnamon
1/2 teaspoon salt
1/2 teaspoon ground ginger
1/2 teaspoon ground nutmeg
1 unbaked pastry shell (9 inches)
TOPPING:
1 cup chopped walnuts

3/4 cup packed brown sugar
1/4 cup butter *or* margarine, melted

In a mixing bowl, beat eggs. Add the pumpkin, milk, brown sugar, vanilla, cinnamon, salt, ginger and nutmeg; mix well. Pour into pastry shell.

Cover edges loosely with foil. Bake at 425° for 15 minutes. Reduce heat to 350°. Remove foil; bake 35-40 minutes longer or until set and a knife inserted near the center comes out clean. Cool on a wire rack for 2 hours.

Combine the topping ingredients; sprinkle over pie. Cover edges loosely with foil. Broil 3-4 in. from the heat for about 2 minutes or until golden brown. Remove foil. Store in the refrigerator. **Yield:** 6-8 servings.

Almond Tassies

A rich buttery crust holds a meringue filling flavored with almond paste. With their delicate,
dainty look, these cookies would be especially nice for a ladies' luncheon.
—Helen Verbeke, Clifton, New Jersey

2 cups butter (no substitutes),
  softened
1 cup sugar
2 egg yolks
3 cups all-purpose flour
1 teaspoon salt
FILLING:
1 can (8 ounces) almond paste
1 cup plus 1 tablespoon sugar,
  divided
2 egg yolks
1 teaspoon lemon juice
3 egg whites
1 teaspoon vanilla extract
1/2 cup finely chopped pecans

In a mixing bowl, cream the butter, sugar and egg yolks. Gradually add flour and salt. Divide dough into fourths; roll each portion into 12 small balls. Press each ball onto the bottom and up the sides of a greased miniature muffin cup; set aside.

For filling, combine almond paste, 1 cup sugar, egg yolks and lemon juice in a large mixing bowl. In a small mixing bowl, beat egg whites until soft peaks form; beat in vanilla and remaining sugar until stiff peaks form. Beat into the almond mixture.

Fill prepared cups three-fourths full. Sprinkle with pecans. Bake at 325° for 20-25 minutes or until lightly browned. Cool on wire racks for 10 minutes. Carefully remove tassies from pans. **Yield:** 4 dozen.

Pumpkin-Pecan Cake Roll

(Pictured at right)

I made this cake roll one Thanksgiving as a tasty change of pace from traditional pumpkin pie. The moist spice cake and creamy filling have made this dessert a family favorite for many functions.
—Iva Combs, Medford, Oregon

   3 **eggs**
   1 **cup sugar**
 3/4 **cup all-purpose flour**
 3/4 **cup cooked *or* canned pumpkin**
1-1/2 **teaspoons ground cinnamon**
   1 **teaspoon baking powder**
   1 **teaspoon ground ginger**
 1/2 **teaspoon salt**
 1/2 **teaspoon ground nutmeg**
   1 **teaspoon lemon juice**
   1 **cup finely chopped pecans**
Confectioners' sugar
FILLING:
   2 **packages (3 ounces *each*) cream cheese, softened**
 1/4 **cup butter *or* margarine, softened**
   1 **cup confectioners' sugar**
 1/2 **teaspoon vanilla extract**

Line a greased 15-in. x 10-in. x 1-in. baking pan with waxed paper and grease the paper; set aside. In a mixing bowl, beat eggs for 5 minutes. Add the sugar, flour, pumpkin, cinnamon, baking powder, ginger, salt and nutmeg; mix well. Add lemon juice. Spread batter evenly in prepared pan; sprinkle with pecans.

Bake at 375° for 15 minutes or until cake springs back when lightly touched. Cool for 5 minutes. Turn cake onto a kitchen towel dusted with confectioners' sugar. Gently peel off waxed paper. Roll up cake in towel, jelly-roll style, starting with a short side. Cool completely on a wire rack.

In a mixing bowl, combine the filling ingredients; beat until smooth. Unroll cake; spread filling over cake to within 1/2 in. of edges. Roll up again; place seam side down on a serving platter. Cover and refrigerate for at least 1 hour before serving. **Yield:** 12 servings.

Cranberry Chiffon Pie

After a hearty Thanksgiving meal where most of us eat too much, it's nice to offer this refreshing light dessert. The rosy color is a nice addition to the table.

—Iva Combs, Medford, Oregon

1 cup all-purpose flour
2 tablespoons sugar
1/2 cup cold butter *or* margarine
1/2 cup finely chopped walnuts
FILLING:
1 package (3 ounces) cranberry *or* strawberry gelatin
1/2 cup boiling water
1 cup whole-berry cranberry sauce
3/4 cup cranberry juice
1 tablespoon grated orange peel
1 cup whipping cream, whipped

In a bowl, combine the flour and sugar. Cut in butter until crumbly. Stir in walnuts. Press onto the bottom and up the sides of a greased 10-in. pie plate. Bake at 375° for 14-16 minutes or until set and edges are lightly browned. Cool on a wire rack.

For filling, in a bowl, dissolve gelatin in water. Stir in cranberry sauce, cranberry juice and orange peel. Cover and refrigerate until slightly thickened, about 1 hour. Fold in whipped cream. Pour into crust. Refrigerate for at least 3 hours. **Yield:** 6-8 servings.

Maple Raisin Oatmeal Cookies

(Pictured on opposite page)

My five children love maple and brown sugar oatmeal, so I decided to add those ingredients to my oatmeal cookies. The first time I made them, they vanished in just a few days!

—Karen Nienaber, Erskine, Minnesota

1 cup butter *or* margarine, softened
1 cup packed brown sugar
1/2 cup sugar
2 eggs
1 teaspoon maple flavoring
1-1/2 cups all-purpose flour
1 teaspoon baking soda
1 teaspoon ground cinnamon
1/2 teaspoon salt
3 cups quick-cooking oats
1 cup raisins

In a mixing bowl, cream the butter and sugars. Add eggs, one at a time, beating well after each addition. Beat in maple flavoring. Combine the flour, baking soda, cinnamon and salt; gradually add to the creamed mixture. Stir in oats and raisins. Drop by rounded teaspoonfuls 2 in. apart onto ungreased baking sheets. Bake at 350° for 10-12 minutes or until golden brown. Remove to wire racks to cool. **Yield:** 5-1/2 dozen.

Pumpkin Whoopie Pies

(Pictured at right)

My kids start begging me for these cake-like sandwich cookies as soon as autumn arrives. I haven't met a person yet who doesn't like these fun treats.
—Deb Stuber, Carlisle, Pennsylvania

1 cup shortening
2 cups packed brown sugar
2 eggs
1 teaspoon vanilla extract
3-1/2 cups all-purpose flour
1-1/2 teaspoons baking powder
1-1/2 teaspoons baking soda
1 teaspoon salt
1 teaspoon ground cinnamon
1 teaspoon ground ginger
1-1/2 cups cooked *or* canned
    pumpkin
FILLING:
1/4 cup all-purpose flour
Dash salt
3/4 cup milk
1 cup shortening
2 cups confectioners' sugar
2 teaspoons vanilla extract

In a mixing bowl, cream shortening and brown sugar. Add eggs, one at a time, beating well after each addition. Beat in vanilla. Combine the flour, baking powder, baking soda, salt, cinnamon and ginger; add to creamed mixture alternately with pumpkin.

Drop by rounded tablespoonfuls 2 in. apart onto greased baking sheets; flatten slightly with the back of a spoon. Bake at 400° for 10-11 minutes. Remove to wire racks to cool.

For filling, combine the flour and salt in a saucepan. Gradually whisk in milk until smooth; cook and stir over medium heat for 5-7 minutes or until thickened. Cover and refrigerate until completely cooled.

In a mixing bowl, cream shortening, confectioners' sugar and vanilla. Add chilled milk mixture; beat for 7 minutes or until fluffy. Spread on the bottom of half of the cookies; top with remaining cookies. Store in the refrigerator. **Yield:** about 2 dozen.

EASTER Gatherings

Whether you celebrate this holiday with a morning meal or a formal sit-down dinner, you'll discover a sunny selection of dishes in this chapter. Start your day with a bright-eyed brunch featuring such cheerful choices as egg casseroles, pancakes, French toast, waffles and salads. Or try a fellow cook's favorite Easter dinner menu that has an irresistible Italian twist.

Brunch Celebrates the Season

FLOWING dresses, pretty hats, fun-filled baskets, delicate daffodils...there's just something about Easter that signals the arrival of spring. Now is the time to put aside the heavy fare you served all winter and bring out a sunnier selection perfect for warmer weather.

To celebrate this season with family and friends, why not host a bright late-morning brunch featuring Swedish Pancakes, Fruit Salad with Poppy Seed Dressing and Crab-Spinach Egg Casserole?

In addition to these cheerful choices (shown at right), the following pages are blooming with a host of other innovative Easter brunch ideas...from egg dishes, salads and breads to pancakes, waffles, French toast and more.

RISE 'N' SHINE
SELECTION
(Clockwise from top right)

Crab-Spinach
Egg Casserole (p.158)

Swedish Pancakes (p.159)

Fruit Salad with
Poppy Seed Dressing (p.156)

Fruit Salad with Poppy Seed Dressing

(Pictured on opposite page and on page 154)

My family requests this yummy fruit salad every Easter.
The slightly sweet poppy seed dressing served on the side really makes it special.
—Joni Kingsley, Redlands, California

POPPY SEED DRESSING:
  1/3 cup red wine vinegar *or*
     cider vinegar
  3/4 cup sugar
    1 teaspoon ground mustard
  3/4 teaspoon salt
  3/4 cup vegetable oil
    1 tablespoon poppy seeds
SALAD:
    2 cups pineapple chunks
    2 cups green grapes
    2 medium firm bananas, sliced
    2 cups sliced fresh strawberries
Floral Ice Bowl (opposite page)
Lettuce *or* lemon leaves,* optional

In a blender or food processor, combine the vinegar, sugar, mustard and salt. While processing, gradually add oil in a steady stream. Stir in poppy seeds.

Just before serving, combine the fruits. Serve with poppy seed dressing in an ice bowl lined with lettuce or lemon leaves if desired. **Yield:** 10 servings.

*Editor's Note: If using lemon leaves, properly identify before picking and make sure the tree has not been treated with chemicals.

FAST FRUIT SALAD

TO SAVE TIME on the day of your brunch, you can prepare the dressing for Fruit Salad with Poppy Seed Dressing the night before and store it in a covered container at room temperature.

Also, cut up the pineapple and strawberries and measure the grapes; store in separate containers in the refrigerator. Just before guests arrive, slice the bananas and combine all the fruit.

Apricot Casserole

This sweet fruit dish is a terrific complement to salty ham on Easter morning.
Apricot is a tasty change from the more common pineapple.
—Janice Montiverdi, Sugar Land, Texas

    2 cans (15 ounces *each*) apricot
      halves
  1/2 cup plus 2 tablespoons butter
     or margarine, *divided*
    1 cup packed brown sugar
  1/4 cup all-purpose flour
1-1/3 cups crushed butter-flavored
     crackers (about 36 crackers)

Drain apricots, reserving 3/4 cup juice. Place apricots in a greased 11-in. x 7-in. x 2-in. baking dish. Melt 1/2 cup butter; add the brown sugar, flour and reserved juice. Pour over apricots.

Bake, uncovered, at 350° for 20 minutes. Melt remaining butter; toss with cracker crumbs. Sprinkle over top. Bake 15-20 minutes longer or until golden brown. **Yield:** 6-8 servings.

Floral Ice Bowl

(Pictured at right)

Bowl folks over at your Easter gathering with this frozen serving bowl from our Test Kitchen. It can be made days in advance and kept frozen until ready to use.

Assorted herbs and edible flowers such as mint, chamomile, pansies, nasturtiums, etc. *or* **colorful silk flowers and leaves**
1-quart and 2-1/2-quart freezer-proof glass bowls
Ice cubes
Freezer tape
Wooden skewer

If you are using herbs and edible flowers, wash blossoms and leaves and pat dry. If you are using silk flowers and leaves, wash them gently in warm sudsy water, rinse and let air-dry.

Fill the 2-1/2-qt. bowl half full with water. Arrange herbs and flowers or silk flowers and leaves to completely cover surface of the water. Place the 1-qt. bowl on top of flowers so there is about 1 in. of space between the bowls. Fill the 1-qt. bowl with ice cubes. Place freezer tape across both bowls to hold them in place.

Place the taped bowls in the freezer for 30 minutes or until ice crystals form on top of the water.

Using a wooden skewer, place additional herbs or leaves and flowers between the sides of the bowls. Return bowls to the freezer.

Checking periodically on the bowls, continue to add and reposition flow-ers as the water freezes. Freeze overnight.

Remove freezer tape and ice cubes. Fill the 1-qt. bowl with lukewarm water, then remove it. Dip the 2-1/2-qt. bowl in warm water and twist to loosen. Remove the ice bowl and return to the freezer until ready to use. **Yield:** 1 floral ice bowl (6 inches in diameter and 3 inches high).

MAKING A FLORAL ICE BOWL

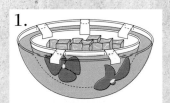

1. Place the 1-qt. bowl on top of the flowers in the 2-1/2-qt. bowl; fill the 1-qt. bowl with ice cubes. Place freezer tape across both bowls to hold them in place.

2. After freezing the bowls for about 30 minutes, place additional herbs or leaves and flowers between the sides of the bowls with a wooden skewer.

Crab-Spinach Egg Casserole

(Pictured on page 155)

*I've developed a strong interest in cooking over the years. As a matter of fact, I came up with
this casserole as a special breakfast for our daughter when she was home for a visit.*
—*Steve Heaton, Deltona, Florida*

8 eggs
2 cups half-and-half cream
2 cans (6 ounces *each*)
　crabmeat, drained
1 package (10 ounces) frozen
　chopped spinach, thawed and
　squeezed dry
1 cup dry bread crumbs
1 cup (4 ounces) shredded
　Swiss cheese
1/2 teaspoon salt
1/4 teaspoon pepper
1/4 teaspoon ground nutmeg
2 celery ribs, chopped

1/2 cup chopped onion
1/2 cup chopped sweet red pepper
3 medium fresh mushrooms, chopped
2 tablespoons butter *or* margarine

In a bowl, beat eggs and cream. Stir in the crab, spinach,
bread crumbs, cheese, salt, pepper and nutmeg; set aside. In
a skillet, saute the celery, onion, red pepper and mushrooms
in butter until tender. Add to the spinach mixture.

Transfer to a greased shallow 2-1/2-qt. baking dish. Bake,
uncovered, at 375° for 30-35 minutes or until golden brown
around the edges and center is set. Let stand for 10 minutes before serving. **Yield:** 12-16 servings.

Apple Pie Sandwiches

*I created this recipe one autumn when we had an abundant apple crop.
We enjoy these sandwiches for breakfast and dessert all year long.*
—*Gloria Jarrett, Loveland, Ohio*

2 cups diced peeled tart apples
1 cup water
1/2 cup plus 1 tablespoon sugar,
　divided
5 teaspoons cornstarch
1/2 teaspoon ground cinnamon
1/4 teaspoon ground nutmeg
2 teaspoons lemon juice
12 slices day-old bread
3 eggs
2/3 cup milk
2 teaspoons vanilla extract
Confectioners' sugar, optional

In a saucepan, cook apples and water over medium heat
for 10 minutes or until apples are tender. Combine 1/2 cup
sugar, cornstarch, cinnamon and nutmeg; stir into apple
mixture. Bring to a boil; cook and stir for 2 minutes or until thickened. Remove from the heat; stir in lemon juice.
Spread six slices of bread with 1/3 cup filling each; top
with remaining bread.

In a shallow bowl, beat the eggs, milk, vanilla and remaining sugar. Dip sandwiches in egg mixture. Cook on a
lightly greased hot griddle until golden brown on both sides.
Dust with confectioners' sugar if desired. **Yield:** 6 servings.

Swedish Pancakes

(Pictured at right and on page 155)

When we spend the night at my mother-in-law's house, our kids beg her to make these crepe-like pancakes for breakfast. They're a little lighter than traditional pancakes, so my family can eat a lot!
—Susan Johnson, Lyons, Kansas

  2 cups milk
  4 eggs
  1 tablespoon vegetable oil
1-1/2 cups all-purpose flour
  3 tablespoons sugar
  1/4 teaspoon salt
Lingonberries *or* **raspberries**
Seedless raspberry jam *or* **fruit spread, warmed**
Whipped topping

In a blender, combine the first six ingredients. Cover and process until blended. Heat a lightly greased 8-in. nonstick skillet; pour 1/4 cup batter in- to center of skillet. Lift and tilt pan to evenly coat bottom. Cook until top appears dry; turn and cook 15-20 seconds longer. Repeat with remaining batter, adding oil to skillet as needed. Stack pancakes with waxed paper or paper towels in between. Reheat in the microwave if desired.

Fold pancakes into quarters; serve with berries, raspberry jam and whipped topping. **Yield:** 20 pancakes.

EARLY EASTER EGGS

IN 3000 B.C., Persians began using colored eggs to herald the arrival of spring. Thirteenth-century Macedonians were the first Christians on record to use colored eggs in Easter celebrations.

Cinnamon Pecan Braids

Whenever there's a bake sale, I make these braids. They're so eye-catching that most of the loaves get snapped up by the people working the sale!
—Connie Dahmer, Marion, Illinois

1 package (1/4 ounce) active dry yeast
1 cup warm water (110° to 115°), *divided*
3 eggs, beaten
5 cups all-purpose flour
1/2 cup sugar
1/2 teaspoon salt
1 cup cold butter *or* margarine
FILLING:
1 cup butter *or* margarine, softened
1 cup packed brown sugar
1 cup chopped pecans
1 tablespoon ground cinnamon
GLAZE:
1-1/2 cups confectioners' sugar
1 tablespoon butter *or* margarine, melted
1/2 teaspoon vanilla extract
1 to 2 tablespoons milk

In a mixing bowl, dissolve yeast in 1/4 cup warm water. Add eggs and remaining water; mix well. In another bowl, combine the flour, sugar and salt. Cut in butter until crumbly. Beat into yeast mixture (do not knead). Cover and refrigerate overnight.

For filling, in a small mixing bowl, cream butter and brown sugar. Stir in pecans and cinnamon; set aside.

Turn dough onto a lightly floured surface; divide into four portions. Roll each into a 12-in. x 9-in. rectangle on a greased baking sheet. Spread filling lengthwise down center third of each rectangle.

On each long side, cut 3/4-in.-wide strips to the center to within 1/2 in. of the filling. Starting at one end, fold alternating strips at an angle across filling. Pinch ends to seal and tuck under. Cover and let rise in a warm place for 1 hour (dough will not double).

Bake at 350° for 18-20 minutes or until golden brown. Cool slightly before removing from pans to wire racks. Combine glaze ingredients; drizzle over cooled braids. **Yield:** 4 loaves.

Date Crumb Cake

This recipe makes a big pan perfect for holiday entertaining. Guests always comment on this cake's wonderful old-fashioned flavor.
—Shelly Korell, Bayard, Nebraska

2 cups all-purpose flour
1 cup sugar
3/4 cup shortening
2 eggs, lightly beaten
1 cup buttermilk
1 teaspoon baking powder
1 teaspoon baking soda
3/4 cup chopped dates
1/2 cup chopped walnuts

In a mixing bowl, combine flour and sugar. Cut in shortening until mixture resembles coarse crumbs; set aside 1 cup for topping. To the remaining crumb mixture, add eggs, buttermilk, baking powder and baking soda; beat until smooth. Fold in dates and walnuts.

Transfer to a greased 13-in. x 9-in. x 2-in. baking pan; sprinkle with reserved crumb mixture. Bake at 350° for 25-30 minutes or until a toothpick inserted near the center comes out clean. Cool on a wire rack. **Yield:** 12-15 servings.

Asparagus Hollandaise Puff

(Pictured at right)

This impressive puff earns many "oohs" and "aahs" from brunch guests. It's relatively easy to make, so I don't mind serving it often.
—Leslie Cunnian, Peterborough, Ontario

1 cup water
1/2 cup butter (no substitutes)
1/2 teaspoon salt
1/8 teaspoon white pepper
1 cup all-purpose flour
1 cup (4 ounces) shredded
   Swiss cheese
4 eggs
1 envelope hollandaise
   sauce mix
3/4 pound fresh asparagus
   (about 18 spears), trimmed
4 ounces thinly sliced ham,
   julienned

In a large saucepan, bring water, butter, salt and pepper to a boil. Add flour and cheese; stir until a smooth ball forms. Remove from the heat; let stand for 5 minutes. Add eggs, one at a time, beating well after each addition. Continue beating until mixture is smooth and shiny.

Spread dough over the bottom of a greased 10-in. quiche pan or pie plate, forming a shell by pushing dough from center toward the edges. Bake, uncovered, at 375° for 30 minutes or until puffed around the edges and golden brown.

Meanwhile, prepare hollandaise sauce according to package directions. Add 1/2 in. of water to a large skillet; add asparagus and bring to a boil. Reduce heat; cover and simmer until crisp-tender, about 4 minutes. Drain and keep warm.

Arrange ham and asparagus in center of puff. Drizzle with hollandaise sauce. Serve immediately. **Yield:** 8 servings.

Cheddar Pancakes

This is our favorite special-occasion breakfast. I usually
double the recipe and freeze leftovers for a quick midweek morning meal.
—Virginia Mae Folsom, Agincourt, Ontario

1 cup all-purpose flour
2 tablespoons sugar
2 teaspoons baking powder
1/2 teaspoon salt
1/4 teaspoon ground nutmeg
1 egg
1 cup milk
2 tablespoons vegetable oil
1 teaspoon vanilla extract
1 cup (4 ounces) shredded sharp
    cheddar cheese
Applesauce, warmed, optional

In a bowl, combine the flour, sugar, baking powder, salt and nutmeg. Combine the egg, milk, oil and vanilla; stir into dry ingredients just until moistened. Stir in cheese.

Pour batter by 1/4 cupfuls onto a lightly greased hot griddle; turn when bubbles form on top of pancakes. Cook until second side is golden brown. Serve with applesauce if desired. **Yield:** 8-10 pancakes.

French Toast Strata

I'm always on the lookout for different breakfast and brunch ideas. I like to serve
this easy make-ahead casserole when we have out-of-town guests.
—Jill Middleton, Baldwinsville, New York

1 loaf (1 pound) cinnamon
    bread, cubed
1 package (8 ounces) cream
    cheese, cubed
8 eggs
2-1/2 cups milk
6 tablespoons butter *or*
    margarine, melted
1/4 cup maple syrup
CIDER SYRUP:
1/2 cup sugar
4 teaspoons cornstarch
1/2 teaspoon ground cinnamon
1 cup apple cider
1 tablespoon lemon juice
2 tablespoons butter *or*
    margarine

Arrange half of the bread cubes in a greased 13-in. x 9-in. x 2-in. baking dish. Top with cream cheese and remaining bread. In a blender, combine eggs, milk, butter and maple syrup; cover and process until smooth. Pour over bread. Cover and refrigerate overnight.

Remove from the refrigerator 30 minutes before baking. Bake, uncovered, at 350° for 35-40 minutes or until a knife inserted near the center comes out clean and a thermometer reads at least 160°. Let stand for 10 minutes before serving.

For syrup, in a saucepan, combine sugar, cornstarch and cinnamon. Gradually whisk in cider and lemon juice. Bring to a boil; cook and stir for 2 minutes or until thickened. Stir in butter until melted. Serve warm with strata. **Yield:** 8 servings (1 cup syrup).

Holiday Ham

(Pictured at right)

When I was a young girl, ham made appearances at all of our holiday dinners. The old-fashioned flavor reminds folks of Grandma's kitchen.
—Betty Butler, Union Bridge, Maryland

  1 can (20 ounces) sliced
    pineapple
1/2 spiral-sliced fully cooked
    bone-in ham (8 to 10 pounds)
2/3 cup maraschino cherries
1-1/2 cups packed brown sugar
1/2 teaspoon seasoned salt

Drain pineapple, reserving juice. Place ham on a rack in a shallow roasting pan. Secure pineapple and cherries to ham with toothpicks. Combine brown sugar and seasoned salt; rub over ham. Gently pour pineapple juice over ham.

  Bake, uncovered, at 325° for 1-1/2 to 2 hours or until a meat thermometer reads 140° and ham is heated through. Baste frequently with brown sugar mixture. **Yield:** about 18-20 servings.

Strawberry Syrup

This recipe is a spin-off of my dad's homemade syrup. Our son requests it with fluffy pancakes whenever he and his family come to visit.
—Nancy Dunaway, Springfield, Illinois

  1 cup sugar
  1 cup water
1-1/2 cups mashed unsweetened
    strawberries

In a saucepan, bring sugar and water to a boil. Gradually add strawberries; return to a boil. Reduce heat; simmer, uncovered, for 10 minutes, stirring occasionally. Serve over pancakes, waffles or ice cream. **Yield:** about 2-1/2 cups.

Minty Pineapple Punch

(Pictured on opposite page)

People are surprised to learn that tea is an ingredient in this pleasant beverage.
It's a nice change from punch recipes that call for soda.
—Margaret McNeil, Memphis, Tennessee

3 medium lemons, halved
6 cups water
2 cups sugar
1-1/2 teaspoons vanilla extract
1-1/2 teaspoons almond extract
4 individual tea bags
4 cups boiling water
2 cans (46 ounces *each*)
 pineapple juice
Fresh mint, optional

Squeeze juice from lemons; set juice aside. Place lemon halves in a large saucepan; add water and sugar. Bring to a boil; boil for 5 minutes. Remove from the heat and discard lemons. Stir in extracts and reserved lemon juice.

Steep tea in boiling water for 5 minutes; discard tea bags. Stir tea and pineapple juice into lemon mixture. Chill. Serve over ice. Garnish with mint if desired. **Yield:** 5 quarts.

Sausage Mushroom Manicotti

If you're tired of pasta with tomato sauce, try this version instead.
A creamy sauce covering sausage-filled noodles makes it hard to resist.
—Kathy Taipale, Iron River, Wisconsin

1 pound bulk Italian sausage
1/2 cup thinly sliced green onions
1 garlic clove, minced
2 tablespoons butter *or*
 margarine
1 jar (4-1/2 ounces) sliced
 mushrooms, drained
1 can (10-3/4 ounces) condensed
 cream of mushroom soup,
 undiluted
1/2 cup sour cream
1/4 teaspoon pepper
1 package (8 ounces) manicotti
 shells, cooked and drained
SAUCE:
1 can (5 ounces) evaporated
 milk

1 jar (4-1/2 ounces) sliced mushrooms, drained
1 tablespoon minced fresh parsley
2 cups (8 ounces) shredded mozzarella cheese,
 divided

In a skillet, cook sausage over medium heat until no longer pink; drain and set aside. In the same skillet, saute onions and garlic in butter until tender. Add mushrooms; heat through. Transfer to a bowl; stir in the sausage, soup, sour cream and pepper. Stuff into manicotti shells. Place in a greased 13-in. x 9-in. x 2-in. baking dish.

In a saucepan, heat milk, mushrooms and parsley. Remove from the heat; stir in 1-1/2 cups cheese until melted. Pour over stuffed shells.

Cover and bake at 350° for 25 minutes. Uncover; sprinkle with remaining cheese. Bake 5-10 minutes longer or until cheese is melted. **Yield:** 7 servings.

Tangy Fruit Salsa with Cinnamon Chips

(Pictured at right)

Paired with sweet cinnamon chips, this fruit salsa is quickly gobbled up by friends and family. It makes a nice addition to a brunch buffet. Plus it's a great snack.
—Margaret McNeil
Memphis, Tennessee

1 tablespoon sugar
1/4 teaspoon ground cinnamon
4 flour tortillas (7 inches)

SALSA:
1 can (15 ounces) sliced peaches, drained and chopped
2 kiwifruit, peeled and chopped
1 cup sliced unsweetened strawberries
2 teaspoons lime juice
1 teaspoon sugar
1 teaspoon grated lime peel

Combine sugar and cinnamon. Spritz tortillas with nonstick cooking spray; sprinkle with cinnamon-sugar. Cut each tortilla into eight wedges; place in a single layer in an ungreased 15-in. x 10-in. x 1-in. baking pan. Bake at 400° for 8-10 minutes or until lightly browned. Remove to a wire rack to cool.

In a bowl, combine the salsa ingredients; mix gently. Serve with cinnamon chips. **Yield:** 2-1/4 cups salsa (32 chips).

Fluffy Bacon-Cheese Frittata

My four best friends and I frequently rely on this recipe. Alongside English muffins and fresh fruit, this frittata makes a hearty, wholesome breakfast.
—Sheryl Holsten, Alexandria, Minnesota

6 bacon strips, diced
1/3 cup chopped onion
5 eggs, *separated*
1-1/4 cups milk
3 tablespoons all-purpose flour
1/4 teaspoon paprika
1-1/2 cups (6 ounces) shredded
    Swiss cheese
1/4 to 1/2 teaspoon salt
1 cup (4 ounces) shredded sharp
    cheddar cheese
1 tablespoon minced fresh
    parsley

In a skillet, cook bacon over medium heat until crisp; remove to paper towels. Drain, reserving 1 tablespoon drippings. In the drippings, saute onion until tender. Remove from the heat; set aside.

In a large mixing bowl, beat egg yolks, milk, flour and paprika until smooth. Add Swiss cheese. In a small mixing bowl, beat egg whites and salt until stiff peaks form. Fold into cheese mixture.

Pour over onion in skillet; cover and cook on medium-low heat for 12-15 minutes or until almost set. Sprinkle with cheddar cheese and bacon. Cover and cook 5 minutes longer or until cheese is melted. Sprinkle with parsley. **Yield:** 6 servings.

Creamy Asparagus Soup

This is my version of a recipe I tasted while on vacation. When we got home, I tinkered around with ingredients until I came up with a winning combination.
—Lisa Hagdohl, Walbridge, Ohio

1 medium potato, peeled and
    diced
1 medium onion, chopped
5 green onions, chopped
1 medium carrot, chopped
1 celery rib, chopped
1/4 cup butter *or* margarine
1/4 cup all-purpose flour
1 teaspoon salt
1/4 teaspoon pepper
1 can (49-1/2 ounces) chicken
    broth
1 pound fresh asparagus,
    trimmed and cut into 2-inch
    pieces
1/2 cup half-and-half cream
1 cup (8 ounces) sour cream

2 bacon strips, cooked and crumbled
Additional sour cream
Asparagus tips, optional

In a Dutch oven or soup kettle, saute potato, onions, carrot and celery in butter until onions and celery are tender. Stir in flour, salt and pepper until blended. Gradually add broth. Bring to a boil; cook and stir for 2 minutes.

Add asparagus; reduce heat. Cover and simmer for 20-25 minutes or until vegetables are tender. Cool to lukewarm.

In a blender, puree vegetable mixture in small batches until smooth. Pour into a large bowl; stir in cream and sour cream until smooth.

Serve warm, or cover and refrigerate for at least 2 hours and serve chilled. Garnish with bacon, sour cream and asparagus tips if desired. **Yield:** 8-10 servings.

Peach Praline Muffins

(Pictured at right)

We eat a lot of muffins around our house. The kids love to nibble on them around the clock. This is a favorite.
— Paula Wiersma
Eastampton, New Jersey

1-2/3 cups all-purpose flour
   2 teaspoons baking powder
1/4 teaspoon salt
1/2 cup packed brown sugar
1/2 cup milk
1/3 cup vegetable oil
   1 egg
   1 teaspoon vanilla extract
   1 cup chopped fresh *or* frozen
    peaches, thawed and drained
1/2 cup chopped pecans
TOPPING:
1/4 cup packed brown sugar
1/4 cup chopped pecans
   1 tablespoon cold butter *or*
    margarine

In a large bowl, combine the flour, baking powder and salt. In another bowl, combine the brown sugar, milk, oil, egg and vanilla. Stir into dry ingredients just until moistened. Fold in peaches and pecans. Fill greased or paper-lined muffin cups two-thirds full.

   Combine topping ingredients until crumbly; sprinkle over batter. Bake at 400° for 15-18 minutes or until a toothpick comes out clean. Cool for 5 minutes before removing from pan to a wire rack. **Yield:** 1 dozen.

PEACH POINTERS

PURCHASE peaches that have an intense fragrance and that give slightly to palm pressure. Avoid those that are hard or have soft spots. A half pound will yield about 1 cup chopped peaches.

   Store ripe peaches in a plastic bag in the refrigerator for up to 5 days. To ripen peaches, place in a brown paper bag and store at room temperature for about 2 days.

   To easily remove the pit, cut the fruit from stem to stem all the way around, Twist the peach halves in opposite directions and lift out the pit.

Ham 'n' Swiss Strudel

*You just can't beat this strudel stuffed with ham, cheese and rice when you want
to serve a special breakfast or brunch. Fresh fruit rounds out the meal.*
—*Sally Coffey, Hilton, New York*

1-1/2 cups chicken broth
   3/4 cup uncooked long grain rice
      1 cup finely chopped onion
      1 tablespoon plus 1/2 cup butter
         or margarine, *divided*
     12 sheets phyllo dough
         (18 inches x 14 inches)
      4 ounces thinly sliced deli ham,
         julienned
      2 cups (8 ounces) shredded
         Swiss cheese
      1 teaspoon paprika

In a saucepan, bring broth to a boil; add rice. Reduce heat; cover and simmer for 15 minutes or until rice is tender and liquid is absorbed. In another saucepan, saute onion in 1 tablespoon butter until tender; add to rice.

Melt remaining butter. Place one sheet of phyllo dough on a work surface; brush with butter. Layer with remaining phyllo and butter (keep dough covered with waxed paper until ready to use). Spoon rice mixture over dough to within 1 in. of edges. Sprinkle with ham, cheese and paprika.

Fold short sides 1 in. over filling. Roll up jelly-roll style, starting with a long side. Brush with remaining butter. Place seam side down on a greased baking sheet. Bake at 375° for 25-30 minutes or until golden brown. Cool for 5 minutes before slicing. **Yield:** 10-12 servings.

AVOID A BRUNCH CRUNCH

YOU DON'T have to crack under the pressure of hosting an Easter breakfast or brunch. The key is selecting a good assortment of foods and getting a lot done the night before.

- When selecting recipes to serve, look for some make-ahead choices as well as some last-minute dishes. If children are part of the guest list, you may want to offer them the old standby of cereal and milk…they'll likely prefer it to some of your more "fancy" foods.
- The day before, iron tablecloths and napkins and set the table. Put out the serving dishes and utensils.
- Put condiments that are stored in the fridge (such as butter, jam, cream cheese, etc.) on the same shelf so you can quickly reach for them the next morning. Condiments stored at room temperature (like syrup and honey) can be poured into their serving pitchers and covered with plastic wrap.
- Get a head start on as many dishes as possible by chopping, slicing and dicing the night before.
- Measure the coffee the night before. Then make it in the morning and transfer it to a thermal carafe for serving. Make and refrigerate the juice. In the morning, transfer it to a pretty pitcher.
- Review your menu and make a list of what needs to be done in the morning before your guests arrive.

Scrambled Egg Brunch Bread

(Pictured at right)

This attractive bread is brimming with eggs, ham and cheese, making it a real meal in one. By using refrigerated crescent rolls, it's a snap to prepare.

—Julie Deal

China Grove, North Carolina

2 tubes (8 ounces *each*) refrigerated crescent rolls
4 ounces thinly sliced deli ham, julienned
4 ounces cream cheese, softened
1/2 cup milk
8 eggs
1/4 teaspoon salt
Dash pepper
1/4 cup chopped sweet red pepper
2 tablespoons chopped green onion
1 teaspoon butter *or* margarine
1/2 cup shredded cheddar cheese

Unroll each tube of crescent dough (do not separate rectangles). Place side by side on a greased baking sheet with long sides touching; seal seams and perforations. Arrange ham lengthwise down center third of rectangle.

In a mixing bowl, beat cream cheese and milk. Separate one egg; set egg white aside. Add the egg yolk, remaining eggs, salt and pepper to cream cheese mixture; mix well. Add red pepper and onion.

In a large skillet, melt butter; add egg mixture. Cook and stir over medium heat just until set. Remove from the heat. Spoon scrambled eggs over ham. Sprinkle with cheese.

On each long side of dough, cut 1-in.-wide strips to the center to within 1/2 in. of filling. Starting at one end, fold alternating strips at an angle across filling. Pinch ends to seal and tuck under. Beat reserved egg white; brush over dough. Bake at 375° for 25-28 minutes or until golden brown. **Yield:** 6 servings.

Italian-Style Easter Dinner

"MY HERITAGE flavors many of the foods I prepare," says Mary Ann Marino. "So it's no wonder my Easter meal has an undeniable Italian twist."

A traditional Easter entree for this West Pittsburgh, Pennsylvania cook, Italian Leg of Lamb marinates overnight and roasts the next day, making each savory slice tender and flavorful.

"For my oven-baked Parmesan Asparagus, a simple cheese topping pairs well with spring's finest vegetable," she states.

Instead of a whole ham, Mary Ann likes to prepare Glazed Ham Balls, which are delicious when served alongside Sweet Pineapple Casserole.

Concludes Mary Ann, "No Italian dinner is complete without dessert. Light and fluffy Cream Cheese Clouds are just dreamy after a big meal."

ELEGANT EASTER MEAL

(Clockwise from top left)

Italian Leg of Lamb (p. 172)

Sweet Pineapple Casserole (p. 174)

Parmesan Asparagus (p. 173)

Cream Cheese Clouds (p. 173)

Italian Leg of Lamb

(Pictured on page 170)

When this pleasantly seasoned roast appears on my Easter table, no one walks away hungry.
Garlic, lemon juice and seasonings make each bite of this succulent lamb irresistible.

1/2 to 2/3 cup lemon juice
1/2 cup olive *or* vegetable oil
2 tablespoons dried oregano
2 teaspoons ground mustard
1 teaspoon garlic powder
4 garlic cloves, minced
1 boneless leg of lamb
  (4 to 5 pounds)

In a bowl, combine the first six ingredients; mix well. Pour 1/2 cup into another bowl for basting; cover and refrigerate. Pour remaining marinade into a gallon-size resealable plastic bag; add lamb. Seal and turn to coat. Refrigerate for at least 2 hours or overnight.

Drain and discard marinade. Place lamb fat side up on a rack in a roasting pan. Bake, uncovered, at 325° for 3 to 3-1/2 hours or until meat reaches desired doneness (for rare, a meat thermometer should read 140°; medium, 160°; well-done, 170°). Baste occasionally with reserved marinade. **Yield:** 10-12 servings.

AN EASTER DINNER AGENDA

A Few Weeks Before:
- Order a 4- to 5-pound boneless leg of lamb from your butcher.
- Order tulips for the Tulip Centerpiece (see page 175).
- Prepare two grocery lists—one for non-perishable items to purchase now and one for perishable items to purchase a few days before Easter.

Two Days Before:
- Buy lamb and remaining grocery items.

The Day Before:
- Set the table.
- Buy the tulips, trim stems and place in cold water in a tall vase until you're ready to make the Tulip Centerpiece.
- Marinate the Italian Leg of Lamb in the refrigerator.
- Prepare and refrigerate the "clouds" for the Cream Cheese Clouds.
- Make the Glazed Ham Balls; chill.

Easter Day:
- Make the Tulip Centerpiece. (If the stems have started to curve, you may need to trim them before making the arrangement.)
- Bake the Italian Leg of Lamb.
- Reheat the Glazed Ham Balls, make Parmesan Asparagus and bake the Sweet Pineapple Casserole.
- Just before serving, top the Cream Cheese Clouds with strawberries and whipped topping.

Cream Cheese Clouds

(Pictured at right and on page 170)

This attractive dessert is like a meringue but without all of the fuss. The "clouds" are made the night before and quickly filled just before serving. In a pinch, I've used canned pie filling for the fresh strawberries.

  1 **package (8 ounces) cream cheese, softened**
3/4 **cup confectioners' sugar**
1/2 **teaspoon vanilla extract**
  1 **cup whipping cream**
  2 **quarts fresh strawberries, sliced**
  1 **carton (8 ounces) frozen whipped topping, thawed**

In a mixing bowl, beat the cream cheese, sugar and vanilla until fluffy. Gradually add cream, beating until thickened. Spoon mixture into 10 mounds on a waxed paper-lined baking sheet. Using the back of a spoon, shape into 3-in. cups. Freeze for 2 hours or overnight.

To serve, fill with strawberries and garnish with whipped topping. **Yield:** 10 servings.

Parmesan Asparagus

(Pictured on page 171)

Nothing could be more simple than this side dish. With just four ingredients, I assemble it in no time, then pop it in the oven for about 15 minutes. It turns out perfect every time.

  4 **pounds asparagus, trimmed**
1/4 **cup butter *or* margarine, melted**
  2 **cups shredded Parmesan cheese**
1/2 **teaspoon pepper**

Add 1/2 in. of water to a large skillet; add asparagus. Bring to a boil. Reduce heat; cover and simmer for 3-5 minutes or until crisp-tender. Drain.

Arrange asparagus in a greased 13-in. x 9-in. x 2-in. baking dish. Drizzle with butter; sprinkle with Parmesan cheese and pepper. Bake, uncovered, at 350° for 10-15 minutes or until cheese is melted. **Yield:** 10-12 servings.

Glazed Ham Balls

(Pictured at right)

My family prefers these to a traditional roasted ham. It seems they gobble them up as soon as I set them out. You can make them ahead and reheat the next day.

2 eggs
1-1/2 cups crushed saltines
  (about 45 crackers)
2 pounds ground fully
  cooked ham
1 pound ground pork
2 cups packed brown sugar
6 tablespoons cider vinegar
2 teaspoons ground mustard

In a bowl, combine the eggs and cracker crumbs. Crumble ham and pork over mixture and mix well. Shape into 1-1/2-in. balls. Place in two ungreased 15-in. x 10-in. x 1-in. baking pans. Bake, uncovered, at 350° for 40 minutes or until lightly browned.

Meanwhile, combine the brown sugar, vinegar and mustard in a saucepan. Bring to a boil; cook and stir for 2 minutes or until thickened. Drain ham balls; pour syrup over ham balls. Bake 10 minutes longer or until glazed. **Yield:** 4 dozen.

Sweet Pineapple Casserole

(Pictured above and on page 171)

This side dish has just the right amount of sweetness. So it's a great accompaniment to any meaty entree. Using canned pineapple makes it a snap to assemble.

2 eggs, beaten
2 cans (20 ounces *each*) crushed
  pineapple, undrained
1 cup sugar
1/4 cup cornstarch
1 teaspoon ground cinnamon
1 teaspoon butter *or* margarine

In a bowl, combine eggs and pineapple. In another bowl, combine sugar, cornstarch and cinnamon. Stir in pineapple mixture. Transfer to a greased 2-qt. baking dish. Dot with butter. Bake, uncovered, at 350° for 1-1/4 hours or until golden brown. **Yield:** 10-12 servings.

Tulip Centerpiece

(Pictured at right)

Fresh springtime flowers are an attractive addition to the Easter table. For a dramatic effect, make this surprisingly simple centerpiece calling for flowers and raffia. Guests will be impressed with your floral arrangement expertise!

**Large clear glass container and
  smaller container to fit inside**
Raffia in color of choice
**Tulips *or* other flowers in colors
  of choice**

Place a smaller container in the center of a larger clear glass container. Wrap colored raffia around the small container, filling the space between the two containers and completely hiding the inner vase.

Add some water to the small container only. Insert flowers, allowing stems to rest on the sides of the larger container. Place flowers in the center to complete the arrangement. (We used about 2-1/2 dozen flowers in our arrangement.) Carefully add more water to the small container.

MAKING A TULIP CENTERPIECE

1. Place small container in center of a large clear glass container and wrap colored raffia around to fill space between containers.

2. Add flowers to small container, allowing stems to rest on the sides of the larger container.

SPECIAL
Celebrations

Occasions throughout the year call for special
gatherings with family and friends. Bring the year to a
close with traditional fare for Hanukkah. Then host a
New Year's Eve buffet or quarterback a Super Bowl
pizza party. Having a bridal shower is a breeze with
our easy ideas, while a patriotic menu adds spark to
your Fourth of July festivities. For real kid appeal,
turn to a selection of sweet summer brownies
or spine-tingling Halloween treats.

Casual New Year's Eve Buffet

INSTEAD of heading out to an expensive New Year's Eve gala, welcome in the New Year at home with friends and family.

After breaking the bank on Christmas gifts, you can forgo fancy and prepare a down-home spread of flavorful, frugal fare.

Marinated Beef Sandwiches, Whole Wheat Dinner Rolls, Almond Good Luck Cake, Broccoli Salad Supreme and Almond Creme (shown at right) fill the bill for any budget.

Or turn the page for other appealing appetizers, main courses, side dishes and desserts.

Simple decorations like balloons, streamers, horns and party hats are inexpensive additions that make the evening fun and festive.

RING IN THE NEW YEAR
(Clockwise from top left)

Marinated Beef Sandwiches (p. 182)

Whole Wheat Dinner Rolls (p. 184)

Almond Good Luck Cake (p. 183)

Broccoli Salad Supreme (p. 180)

Almond Creme (p. 181)

Broccoli Salad Supreme

(Pictured on page 178)

People can't get enough of the sweet grapes and crunchy broccoli in this colorful salad. I appreciate its make-ahead convenience.
— *Terri Twyman, Bonanza, Oregon*

10 cups broccoli florets (about 3-1/2 pounds)
6 cups seedless red grapes (about 3 pounds)
1 cup sliced celery
6 green onions, sliced
2 cups mayonnaise
2/3 cup sugar
2 tablespoons cider vinegar
1 pound sliced bacon, cooked and crumbled
1-1/3 cups slivered almonds, toasted

In a large salad bowl, combine the broccoli, grapes, celery and onions. In a small bowl, combine the mayonnaise, sugar and vinegar. Pour over broccoli mixture and toss to coat. Cover and refrigerate for at least 4 hours or overnight. Just before serving, gently stir in bacon and almonds. **Yield:** about 20 servings.

Beef 'n' Bean Egg Rolls

Unlike traditional cabbage-filled egg rolls, this version uses Southwest-seasoned ground beef and beans. These are a regular part of our New Year's Eve "snack fest".
—*Laura Mahaffey, Annapolis, Maryland*

1/2 pound ground beef
1/4 cup chopped onion
2 tablespoons chopped green pepper
1 cup refried beans
1/4 cup shredded cheddar cheese
1 tablespoon ketchup
1-1/2 teaspoons chili powder
1/4 teaspoon ground cumin
32 wonton wrappers*
Oil for deep-fat frying
Salsa

In a large skillet, cook the beef, onion and green pepper over medium heat until meat is no longer pink; drain. Remove from the heat; stir in beans, cheese, ketchup, chili powder and cumin.

Position a wonton wrapper with one point toward you. Place 1 tablespoon meat mixture in the center. Fold bottom corner over filling; fold sides toward center over filling. Roll toward the remaining point. Moisten top corner with water; press to seal. Repeat with remaining wrappers and filling.

In an electric skillet or deep-fat fryer, heat oil to 375°. Fry egg rolls, a few at a time, for 2 minutes or until golden brown. Drain on paper towels. Serve with salsa. **Yield:** 32 egg rolls.

*Editor's Note: Fill wonton wrappers a few at a time, keeping others covered until ready to use.

Almond Creme

(Pictured at right and on page 178)

My mother often made this rich, velvety dessert for New Year's Eve. Now that I'm married, I plan to carry on the tradition.
—*Marcie McEachern, Dallas, Texas*

  2 **envelopes unflavored gelatin**
1/2 **cup water**
  3 **cups whipping cream**
  1 **cup sugar**
  4 **eggs, beaten**
  1 **teaspoon almond extract**
Fresh raspberries and chocolate curls, optional

In a saucepan, sprinkle gelatin over water. Let stand for 1 minute. Stir in cream and sugar. Cook and stir over medium-low heat for 5 minutes or until gelatin is dissolved.

Remove from the heat. Stir a small amount of hot mixture into eggs; return all to the pan, stirring constantly. Cook and stir over medium heat until a thermometer reads 160° (do not boil). Remove from the heat. Stir in almond extract.

Pour into dessert dishes. Refrigerate until set. Garnish with raspberries and chocolate curls if desired. **Yield:** 8 servings.

THE STRAIGHT STORY ON CHOCOLATE CURLS

FOR A SWEET TWIST, garnish your dessert with chocolate curls. There are two ways to make them.

- If you have a solid block of chocolate, warm it in the microwave for a few seconds. Then hold a vegetable peeler against a flat side of the block and carefully bring the blade toward you. Allow the curls to fall onto a plate or piece of waxed paper in a single layer.

- If you don't have a block of chocolate, melt chocolate chips, chocolate candy coating or chocolate bars. (The amount needed depends on the number of curls you want.)

Pour the chocolate onto the back of an inverted cookie sheet and spread to a smooth, thin layer. Let cool until firm and pliable, not brittle. With a cheese slicer, metal spatula or pancake turner and using even pressure, scrape a thin layer of chocolate. The chocolate will curl as you go. The slower you scrape, the wider your curls will be.

Slide a toothpick or wooden skewer through each curl to carefully lift it onto the dessert and arrange as desired.

Marinated Beef Sandwiches

(Pictured on page 178)

This recipe from my sister-in-law is especially good when entertaining for New Year's and football games. No one walks away hungry after eating one of these hearty sandwiches.
—Elizabeth Stoddart, West Lafayette, Indiana

1-1/2 cups water
3/4 cup packed dark brown sugar
3/4 cup soy sauce
2 tablespoons lemon juice
3 small onions, sliced
3 garlic cloves, minced
1-1/2 teaspoons ground ginger
1 boneless beef rump roast (about 4 pounds)
12 to 14 sandwich rolls, split

In a gallon-size resealable plastic bag, combine the first seven ingredients; add roast. Seal bag and turn to coat; refrigerate overnight, turning occasion-ally. Transfer roast and marinade to a Dutch oven. Cover and bake at 325° for 2-1/2 to 3 hours or until meat is tender. Thinly slice; serve beef and juice on rolls. **Yield:** 12-14 servings.

SERVING IN A SLOW COOKER

YOU CAN BAKE the beef for Marinated Beef Sandwiches the day before your party. Transfer the sliced beef and cooking juices to a slow cooker and refrigerate. The next day, reheat on low before your guests arrive. Serve on rolls.

Black-Eyed Pea Soup

Since we raise our own pigs, I like to use ground pork in this zesty soup. But I've used ground beef with equally good results. Green chilies give this dish some Southwestern flair.
—Mary Lou Chernik, Taos, New Mexico

1-1/2 pounds ground pork
1 large onion, chopped
2 garlic cloves, minced
3 cans (15-1/2 ounces *each*) black-eyed peas, rinsed and drained
2 cups water
1 can (14-1/2 ounces) stewed tomatoes
1 can (10 ounces) diced tomatoes and green chilies
1 can (4 ounces) chopped green chilies
1 tablespoon beef bouillon granules
1 tablespoon molasses
1 teaspoon Worcestershire sauce
1/2 teaspoon salt
1/4 teaspoon pepper
1/4 teaspoon ground cumin

In a large soup kettle or Dutch oven, cook the pork, onion and garlic over medium heat until meat is no longer pink; drain. Stir in the remaining ingredients; bring to a boil. Reduce heat; cover and simmer for 45 minutes. **Yield:** 12 servings (about 3 quarts).

Almond Good Luck Cake

(Pictured at right and on page 179)

I make this cake for every New Year's Eve dinner. It's said that the person who finds the one whole almond inside will have good luck during the upcoming year.
— *Vivian Nikanow, Chicago, Illinois*

<pre>
  1/2 cup chopped almonds
    1 tablespoon plus 2-1/3 cups
      all-purpose flour, divided
  1/3 cup butter (no substitutes),
      softened
  1/3 cup shortening
1-1/4 cups sugar, divided
    3 eggs, separated
    2 tablespoons lemon juice
    1 teaspoon grated lemon peel
    1 teaspoon vanilla extract
    1 teaspoon almond extract
    2 teaspoons baking powder
  1/2 teaspoon salt
  1/4 teaspoon baking soda
  3/4 cup milk
  1/2 teaspoon cream of tartar
    1 whole almond
APRICOT GLAZE:
  1/2 cup apricot preserves
    1 tablespoon orange juice
</pre>

Combine almonds and 1 tablespoon flour; sprinkle into a well-greased 10-in. fluted tube pan. Set aside. In a large mixing bowl, cream the butter, shortening and 1 cup sugar. Add egg yolks, one at a time, beating well after each addition. Stir in lemon juice, peel and extracts. Combine the baking powder, salt, baking soda and remaining flour; add to the creamed mixture alternately with milk.

In a small mixing bowl, beat egg whites and cream of tartar until soft peaks form. Beat in the remaining sugar, 1 tablespoon at a time, until stiff. Fold into batter. Pour into prepared pan. Insert whole almond into batter.

Bake at 350° for 40-45 minutes or until a toothpick inserted near the center comes out clean. Cool for 10 minutes before removing from pan to a wire rack.

For glaze, melt preserves in a microwave or saucepan; strain. Add orange juice; drizzle over warm cake. **Yield:** 12 servings.

Whole Wheat Dinner Rolls

(Pictured on page 179)

*Our family has come to expect my husband's grandma to make these rolls for every gathering.
With their simple down-home flavor, they're great for sandwiches or just topped with butter.*
—Kerry Luce, Woodstock, Vermont

3 to 4 cups all-purpose flour
3 cups whole wheat flour
1/2 cup sugar
2 packages (1/4 ounce *each*)
   active dry yeast
1 tablespoon salt
2 cups milk
1/2 cup vegetable oil
2 tablespoons molasses
2 eggs
GLAZE:
1 egg white
1 tablespoon water
Sesame *or* poppy seeds, optional

In a large mixing bowl, combine 1/2 cup all-purpose flour, whole wheat flour, sugar, yeast and salt. In a saucepan, heat milk, oil and molasses to 120°-130°. Add to dry ingredients. Add eggs; beat on low speed until moistened. Beat on medium for 3 minutes. Stir in enough remaining all-purpose flour to form a soft dough.

Turn onto a floured surface; knead until smooth and elastic, about 6-8 minutes. Place in a greased bowl, turning once to grease top. Cover and let rise in a warm place until doubled, about 1 hour.

Punch dough down. Divide in half; shape each portion into 12 balls. Place 1 in. apart in two greased 13-in. x 9-in. x 2-in. baking pans. Cover and let rise until doubled, about 45 minutes. Beat egg white and water until foamy; lightly brush over dough. Sprinkle with sesame or poppy seeds if desired. Bake at 350° for 20-25 minutes or until golden brown. **Yield:** 2 dozen.

Lacy Oat Sandwich Wafers

*These cookies appear on my table for various special occasions. I'm often asked for the recipe,
so I'm sure to have a few copies on hand.*
—Ruth Lee, Troy, Ontario

2/3 cup butter (no substitutes)
2 cups quick-cooking oats
1 cup sugar
2/3 cup all-purpose flour
1/4 cup milk
1/4 cup corn syrup
2 cups semisweet chocolate,
   milk chocolate, vanilla *or*
   white chips, melted

In a saucepan, melt butter over low heat. Remove from the heat. Stir in the oats, sugar, flour, milk and corn syrup; mix well. Drop by teaspoonfuls 2 in. apart onto foil-lined baking sheets. Bake at 375° for 8-10 minutes or until golden brown. Cool completely; peel cookies off foil.

Spread melted chocolate on the bottom of half of the cookies; top with remaining cookies. **Yield:** about 3-1/2 dozen.

Baked Deli Sandwich

(Pictured at right)

Frozen bread dough, easy assembly and quick baking time make this stuffed sandwich an appetizer I rely on often. This is one of my most-requested recipes. It's easy to double for a crowd or to experiment with different meats and cheeses.

—Sandra McKenzie
Braham, Minnesota

1 loaf (1 pound) frozen bread
   dough, thawed
2 tablespoons butter *or*
   margarine, melted
1/4 teaspoon garlic salt
1/4 teaspoon dried basil
1/4 teaspoon dried oregano
1/4 teaspoon pizza seasoning
1/4 pound sliced deli ham
6 thin slices mozzarella cheese
1/4 pound sliced deli smoked
   turkey breast
6 thin slices cheddar cheese
Pizza sauce, warmed, optional

On a baking sheet coated with non-stick cooking spray, roll dough into a small rectangle. Let rest for 5-10 minutes. In a small bowl, combine the butter and seasonings. Roll out dough into a 14-in. x 10-in. rectangle. Brush with half of the butter mixture.

Layer the ham, mozzarella cheese, turkey and cheddar cheese lengthwise over half of the dough to within 1/2 in. of edges. Fold dough over and pinch firmly to seal. Brush with remaining butter mixture.

Bake at 400° for 10-12 minutes or until golden brown. Cut into 1-in. slices. Serve immediately with pizza sauce if desired. **Yield:** 4-6 servings.

Family Traditions

WHEN my husband's Polish-Austrian parents immigrated to the United States, they brought along a wonderful New Year's Eve custom. Before the stroke of midnight, a coin is placed on every window ledge and above every doorway in the house. As the New Year enters the home through windows and doors, it carries along blessings of prosperity in the year to come. It's a fun tradition our two grown daughters now follow.

—Bonnie Ziolecki, Menomonee Falls, Wisconsin

Wild Rice Bread

Wild rice gives this tender bread a tasty nutty flavor. This recipe makes five loaves,
which are great for sharing. We enjoy slices warmed for dinner and toasted for breakfast.
—Susan Schock, Hibbing, Minnesota

2 packages (1/4 ounce *each*)
active dry yeast
4-1/2 cups warm water (110° to
115°), *divided*
8 tablespoons sugar, *divided*
1/2 cup molasses
1/2 cup vegetable oil
2 tablespoons salt
1-1/2 cups cooked wild rice
14 to 15 cups all-purpose flour

In a mixing bowl, dissolve yeast in 1 cup warm water. Add 1 tablespoon sugar; let stand for 5 minutes. Add the molasses, oil, salt and remaining water and sugar; mix well. Add wild rice. Stir in enough flour to form a soft dough. Turn onto a floured surface; knead until smooth and elastic, about 6-8 minutes. Place in a greased bowl, turning once to grease top. Cover and let rise in a warm place until doubled, about 1-1/2 hours.

Punch dough down. Cover and let rise until doubled, about 1 hour. Punch dough down. Turn onto a lightly floured surface; divide into five portions. Shape each into a loaf. Place in five greased 9-in. x 5-in. x 3-in. loaf pans. Cover and let rise until doubled, about 1 hour.

Bake at 375° for 25-35 minutes or golden brown. Remove from pans to wire racks to cool. **Yield:** 5 loaves.

Make-Ahead Coleslaw

A blend of vegetables adds pretty color and pleasant crunch to this coleslaw.
It's nice to rely on do-ahead dishes like this when feeding a crowd.
—Andrea Hutchison, Canton, Oklahoma

1 large head cabbage, shredded
(about 20 cups)
2 large onions, thinly sliced
2 celery ribs, thinly sliced
2 large carrots, shredded
1 large cucumber, thinly sliced
1 large green pepper, chopped
1 jar (4 ounces) diced
pimientos, drained
1-1/2 cups sugar
1-1/2 cups vinegar
1/2 cup vegetable oil
1 teaspoon salt

1 teaspoon celery seed
1 teaspoon ground mustard
1/2 teaspoon dried basil
1/2 teaspoon dried marjoram
1/4 teaspoon pepper

In a large salad bowl, combine the first seven ingredients; set aside. In a large saucepan, combine the remaining ingredients. Bring to a boil; boil for 1-2 minutes or until the sugar is dissolved. Pour over cabbage mixture and toss to coat. Cover and refrigerate overnight or up to 1 week. **Yield:** about 20 servings.

Black-Eyed Pea Salsa

(Pictured at right)

Colorful tomatoes, green pepper and red onion contrast nicely with black-eyed peas.
— *Lynn McAllister*
Mt. Ulla, North Carolina

2 cans (15-1/2 ounces *each*) black-eyed peas, rinsed and drained
2 medium tomatoes, chopped
1 cup chopped green pepper
1/2 cup chopped red onion
4 green onions, sliced
1 garlic clove, minced
1 cup Italian salad dressing
1/4 cup sour cream
1/4 cup minced fresh parsley
Tortilla chips

In a bowl, combine the first six ingredients. Combine the salad dressing, sour cream and parsley. Add to the pea mixture; toss to coat. Cover and refrigerate for at least 4 hours. Serve with tortilla chips. **Yield:** 5 cups.

Golden Shrimp Puffs

I first served these at a New Year's Eve get-together a few years ago. After receiving raves, they became part of my regular appetizer offerings throughout the year.
— *Patricia Slater, Baldwin, Ontario*

6 tablespoons butter (no substitutes)
3/4 cup water
1/4 teaspoon garlic salt
3/4 cup all-purpose flour
3 eggs
1 package (5 ounces) frozen cooked salad shrimp, thawed
1/4 cup chopped green onions
5 tablespoons grated Parmesan cheese, *divided*

In a saucepan, bring butter, water and garlic salt to a boil. Add flour all at once; stir until a smooth ball forms. Remove from the heat; let stand for 5 minutes. Add eggs, one at a time, beating well after each addition. Continue beating until mixture is smooth and shiny.

Stir in the shrimp, onions and 4 tablespoons Parmesan cheese. Drop by rounded teaspoonfuls 2 in. apart onto ungreased baking sheets. Sprinkle with remaining Parmesan cheese. Bake at 400° for 25-30 minutes or until golden brown. Serve warm. **Yield:** 4 dozen.

Cheddar Cheese Spread

A simple spread like this with some crackers is often all you need when entertaining. Letting the spread refrigerate overnight blends the flavors beautifully.
—Kathy Rairigh, Milford, Indiana

2 cartons (8 ounces *each*) sharp cheddar cheese spread
1 package (8 ounces) cream cheese, softened
1 teaspoon Worcestershire sauce
1/2 teaspoon garlic powder
1/2 teaspoon onion powder
1/8 teaspoon salt
1/8 teaspoon white pepper
Assorted crackers

In a mixing bowl, combine the first seven ingredients; beat until smooth. Cover and refrigerate overnight. Serve with crackers. **Yield:** 3 cups.

Crunchy Caramel Corn

Kids at our New Year's Eve parties gobble up this sweet and crunchy popcorn.
—Shelly Gromer, Long Beach, California

6 cups popped popcorn
3/4 cup salted peanuts
1/2 cup packed brown sugar
1/4 cup butter (no substitutes)
2 tablespoons light corn syrup
1/4 teaspoon salt
1/2 teaspoon vanilla extract
1/4 teaspoon baking soda

Place popcorn and peanuts in a large microwave-safe bowl; set aside. In another microwave-safe bowl, combine the brown sugar, butter, corn syrup and salt. Cover and microwave on high for 1 minute; stir. Microwave 2 minutes longer.

Stir in vanilla and baking soda. Pour over popcorn mixture. Microwave, uncovered, on high for 3 minutes, stirring several times. Spread on greased baking sheets to cool. Store in an airtight container. **Yield:** about 2 quarts.

Editor's Note: This recipe was tested in an 850-watt microwave.

POPCORN POINTERS

LEAN your ears this way for a few kernels of wisdom that will steer you toward perfect popcorn.

- 1 cup of unpopped kernels equals about 8 cups of popped popcorn.
- To pop popcorn on the stove, use a 3- or 4-quart pan with a loose-fitting lid to allow the steam to escape. Add 1/3 cup vegetable oil for every cup of kernels.
- Heat the oil to between 400° and 460° (if the oil smokes, it's too hot). Drop in one kernel, and when it pops, add the rest—just enough to cover the bottom of the pan with a single layer.
- Cover the pan and shake to spread the oil. When the popping begins to slow, remove the pan from the heat. The hot oil will continue to pop the remaining kernels.
- Don't pre-salt the kernels—this toughens the popcorn. If desired, salt the corn after it's popped.

Stuffed Shells Florentine

(Pictured at right)

For a little fancier New Year's gathering, I like to serve these pasta shells stuffed with cheese and spinach and topped with spaghetti sauce. Complete the meal with breadsticks and a tossed salad. Italian food is loved by all, and the aroma is warm and inviting.

— Trisha Kuster, Macomb, Illinois

1 package (12 ounces) jumbo pasta shells
1 egg, beaten
2 cartons (15 ounces *each*) ricotta cheese
1 package (10 ounces) frozen chopped spinach, thawed and squeezed dry
1/2 cup grated Parmesan cheese
1/2 teaspoon salt
1/2 teaspoon dried oregano
1/4 teaspoon pepper
1 jar (32 ounces) spaghetti sauce
Thin breadsticks, optional

Cook pasta shells according to package directions. Meanwhile, in a bowl, combine the egg, ricotta cheese, spinach, Parmesan cheese, salt, oregano and pepper; mix well. Drain shells; stuff with spinach mixture.

Place shells in a greased 13-in. x 9-in. x 2-in. baking dish. Pour spaghetti sauce over shells. Cover and bake at 350° for 30-40 minutes or until heated through. Serve with breadsticks if desired. **Yield:** 8-10 servings.

DRAINING JUMBO PASTA SHELLS

INSTEAD of draining jumbo pasta shells in a colander (which can cause them to tear), carefully remove them from the boiling water with a tongs. Pour out any water inside the shells and drain on lightly greased waxed paper until you're ready to stuff them.

Meatball Sub Sandwiches

Making these saucy meatballs in advance and reheating them saves me precious time when expecting company. These sandwiches are great casual fare for any get-together.
— *Deena Hubler, Jasper, Indiana*

2 eggs
1 cup dry bread crumbs
2 tablespoons finely chopped onion
2 tablespoons grated Parmesan cheese
1 teaspoon salt
1/2 teaspoon pepper
1/2 teaspoon garlic powder
1/4 teaspoon Italian seasoning
2 pounds ground beef
1 jar (28 ounces) spaghetti sauce
12 sandwich rolls, split

Additional Parmesan cheese, and sliced onion and green peppers, optional

In a large bowl, combine the first eight ingredients. Crumble beef over mixture and mix well. Shape into 1-in. balls. Place in a single layer in a 3-qt. microwave-safe dish.

Cover and microwave on high for 5 minutes. Turn meatballs; cook 5-6 minutes longer or until no longer pink. Drain. Add spaghetti sauce. Cover and microwave on high for 3-5 minutes or until heated through. Serve on rolls. Top with Parmesan cheese, onion and green peppers if desired. **Yield:** 12 servings.

Editor's Note: This recipe was tested in an 850-watt microwave.

Greek Chicken

This recipe earned me first place in a local cooking contest a few years ago. For special occasions, I add four to six sun-dried tomatoes (soaked and drained according to package directions) to the cheese mixture before blending.
— *Nina Ivanoff, Prince George, British Columbia*

4 boneless skinless chicken breast halves
2 packages (4 ounces *each*) feta *or* blue cheese
1 can (4-1/4 ounces) chopped ripe olives, drained
2 tablespoons olive *or* vegetable oil, *divided*
1/2 teaspoon dried oregano
2 tablespoons dry white wine *or* chicken broth
1 teaspoon sugar
1 teaspoon balsamic vinegar
1 garlic clove, minced

1/4 teaspoon dried thyme
1 medium onion, sliced

Flatten chicken breasts to 1/8-in. thickness; set aside. In a food processor or blender, combine the cheese, olives, 1 tablespoon oil and oregano; cover and process until mixture reaches a thick chunky paste consistency. Spread over chicken breasts; roll up and tuck in ends. Secure with a wooden toothpick.

In a bowl, combine wine or broth, sugar, vinegar, garlic, thyme and remaining oil. Pour into an ungreased 2-qt. baking dish. Top with onion. Place chicken over onion. Cover and bake at 350° for 30 minutes. Uncover and baste with pan juices. Bake 15-20 minutes longer or until chicken juices run clear. **Yield:** 4 servings.

Hazelnut Mocha Torte

(Pictured at right)

This dessert is reminiscent of fine European cakes. I recently made it for my mother, who is German, and it brought back many fond memories for her.
—Elizabeth Blondefield
San Jose, California

6 egg whites
1/4 teaspoon cream of tartar
1 cup sugar
2 cups ground hazelnuts
1/4 cup all-purpose flour
MOCHA GANACHE:
8 squares (1 ounce *each*) semisweet chocolate
1 cup whipping cream
3 tablespoons butter (no substitutes)
2 teaspoons instant coffee granules
BUTTERCREAM:
2/3 cup sugar
1/4 cup water
4 egg yolks, lightly beaten
1 teaspoon vanilla extract
1 cup butter
1/4 cup confectioners' sugar
Additional ground hazelnuts
Whole hazelnuts and chocolate leaves

CHOCOLATE LEAVES

WASH mint, lemon or rose leaves; set aside to dry. Melt 1 cup semisweet chocolate chips and 1 tablespoon shortening. Brush evenly on underside of leaves. Chill until set, about 10 minutes. Apply a second layer; chill until set. Gently peel leaf away from chocolate. Cover and refrigerate until ready to use.

In a mixing bowl, beat egg whites until foamy. Add cream of tartar; beat until soft peaks form. Gradually add sugar, beating until sugar is dissolved and stiff peaks form. Combine hazelnuts and flour; fold into batter, 1/4 cup at a time. Spoon into two greased 9-in. round baking pans lined with waxed paper. Bake at 300° for 25-30 minutes or until cake springs back when lightly touched. Cool for 10 minutes before removing from pans to wire racks.

In a heavy saucepan, combine the ganache ingredients; cook and stir over low heat until chocolate and butter are melted. Remove from the heat. Set saucepan in ice; stir for 3-4 minutes or until thickened. Remove from ice and set aside.

For buttercream, combine sugar and water in a heavy saucepan. Bring to a boil; cook over medium-high heat until sugar is dissolved. Remove from the heat. Add a small amount of hot mixture to egg yolks; return all to pan. Cook and stir 2 minutes longer. Remove from the heat; stir in vanilla. Cool to room temperature. In a mixing bowl, cream butter until fluffy. Gradually beat in cooked sugar mixture. Beat in confectioners' sugar. If necessary, refrigerate until buttercream reaches spreading consistency.

Place one cake layer on a serving plate. Spread with half of ganache to within 1/4 in. of edges. Top with second cake layer and remaining ganache. Freeze for 5 minutes. Spread buttercream over top and sides of cake. Gently press ground hazelnuts into sides of cake. Garnish with whole hazelnuts and chocolate leaves. Refrigerate. **Yield:** 12-16 servings.

Super Bowl Pizza Party

IF YOU want to a score a touchdown with the Super Bowl fans in your family, just quarterback a pizza party!

To defeat hunger in a hurry, turn to this guaranteed-to-please game plan: Start with a winning combination of appetizing "pies"...then toss in a bowl brimming with salad greens or fresh fruit, generous slices of buttery garlic bread or some potato chips and, for dessert, homemade or store-bought cookies or brownies.

With tender crusts and a variety of toppings, Four-Cheese Pizza, Pepper Sausage Pizza and Deluxe Turkey Club Pizza (pictured at right) will score points with football followers of every age.

FOOTBALL FAN FAVORITES
(Clockwise from top right)

Four-Cheese Pizza (p. 196)

Pepper Sausage Pizza (p. 195)

Deluxe Turkey Club Pizza (p. 194)

Deluxe Turkey Club Pizza

(Pictured on page 192)

This unique recipe has become my family's favorite. In winter, we often stay home on Saturday nights to rent movies and indulge in generous slices of this pizza.
—*Philis Bukovcik, Lansing, Michigan*

1 tube (10 ounces) refrigerated pizza crust
1 tablespoon sesame seeds
1/4 cup mayonnaise*
1 teaspoon grated lemon peel
1 medium tomato, thinly sliced
1/2 cup cubed cooked turkey
4 bacon strips, cooked and crumbled
2 medium fresh mushrooms, thinly sliced
1/4 cup chopped onion
1-1/2 cups (6 ounces) shredded Colby/Monterey Jack cheese

Unroll pizza dough and press onto a greased 12-in. pizza pan; build up edges slightly. Sprinkle with sesame seeds. Bake at 425° for 12-14 minutes or until edges are lightly browned.

Combine mayonnaise and lemon peel; spread over crust. Top with tomato, turkey, bacon, mushrooms, onion and cheese. Bake for 6-8 minutes or until cheese is melted. Cut into slices. **Yield:** 8 slices.

*Editor's Note: Reduced-fat or fat-free mayonnaise may not be substituted for regular mayonnaise.

GAME PLAN FOR YOUR PARTY

YOU WON'T be defeated by last-minute details at your pizza party if you follow these timely tips.

- If you plan on baking more than one pizza at a time, look for recipes with the same baking temperature.
- Instead of serving only hot pizzas, offer a cold variety (like Pesto Pizza Squares on page 196 or Taco Pan Pizza on page 199) that can be made ahead.
- For each pizza, chop and measure as many ingredients as you can the night before and refrigerate in small resealable plastic bags. Write the name of each pizza on a large resealable plastic bag and fill with the appropriate smaller bags. This not only saves you time, but also makes it easier for guests to jump in and help assemble pizzas on party day.
- If a recipe instructs you to prebake the crust, do so the morning of the party. Store the cooled crust loosely covered at room temperature.

Pepper Sausage Pizza

(Pictured at right and on page 193)

Fresh spinach gives this recipe from our Test Kitchen a tasty twist. That leafy green plus yellow peppers, snow-white mushrooms and tomato sauce make this a colorful addition to your pizza buffet table.

3 to 4 cups all-purpose flour, *divided*
1 package (1/4 ounce) quick-rise yeast
1 teaspoon sugar
1 cup warm water (120° to 130°)
1/4 cup olive *or* vegetable oil
2 teaspoons salt
1 teaspoon dried basil
1/2 teaspoon pepper
1/2 cup shredded Parmesan cheese, *divided*
3 cups torn fresh spinach
1 can (15 ounces) pizza sauce
4 cups (16 ounces) shredded mozzarella cheese, *divided*
1/2 pound bulk pork sausage, cooked and drained
1 medium onion, chopped
1/2 pound fresh mushrooms, sliced
1/2 medium sweet yellow pepper, chopped
1-1/2 teaspoons pizza seasoning
3 tablespoons minced fresh basil, optional

In a mixing bowl, combine 1 cup flour, yeast and sugar. Add water; beat until smooth. Add the oil, salt, dried basil, pepper, 1/4 cup Parmesan cheese and 2 cups flour; beat until blended. Stir in enough remaining flour to form a soft dough. Turn onto a floured surface; knead until smooth and elastic, about 6-8 minutes. Cover and let rest for 5 minutes.

Meanwhile, place spinach in a microwave-safe bowl; cover and microwave on high for 30 seconds or just until wilted. Uncover and set aside.

Press dough into a greased 15-in. x 10-in. x 1-in. baking pan. Spread with pizza sauce; sprinkle with 2-1/2 cups mozzarella cheese, sausage, onion, spinach, mushrooms and yellow pepper. Top with remaining Parmesan and mozzarella. Sprinkle with pizza seasoning. Bake at 450° for 20 minutes or until crust is golden brown. Sprinkle with fresh basil if desired. Cut into squares. **Yield:** 12-15 slices.

Four-Cheese Pizza

(Pictured on page 193)

Although this pizza doesn't have sauce, it gets unforgettable flavor from a blend of cheeses,
vegetables and garlic. Using frozen bread dough appeals to folks who don't care to bake.
— Doris Johns, Hurst, Texas

1 loaf (16 ounces) frozen bread
    dough, thawed
1 large sweet red pepper,
    chopped
1 large green pepper, chopped
1 cup (4 ounces) shredded
    mozzarella cheese
3/4 cup shredded Swiss cheese
1/2 cup grated Parmesan cheese
1/2 cup crumbled feta cheese
2 tablespoons minced fresh
    parsley
1 tablespoon minced fresh basil
    or 1 teaspoon dried basil

3 plum tomatoes, thinly sliced
1 tablespoon olive *or* vegetable oil
2 garlic cloves, minced

On a lightly floured surface, roll dough into a 15-in. circle. Transfer to a greased 14-in. pizza pan; build up edges slightly. Prick dough several times with a fork. Bake at 400° for 8-10 minutes or until lightly browned. Remove from the oven.

Reduce heat to 375°. Sprinkle chopped peppers, cheeses, parsley and basil over crust. Arrange tomato slices over top. In a small bowl, combine oil and garlic; brush over tomatoes. Bake for 15-20 minutes or until cheese is melted. Let stand for 5 minutes before cutting. **Yield:** 8 slices.

Pesto Pizza Squares

Our Test Kitchen offers this alternative to traditional baked pizzas. With pesto sauce, tomatoes,
olives and fresh mushrooms, it's a flavorful variation of the more common vegetable pizza.

2 tubes (8 ounces *each*)
    refrigerated crescent rolls
1 cup tightly packed fresh basil
1/4 cup tightly packed fresh
    parsley
1/4 cup tightly packed fresh
    cilantro
2 garlic cloves
1/3 cup olive *or* vegetable oil
1/4 cup grated Parmesan cheese
1/4 cup sour cream
1/4 cup whipped cream cheese
3 plum tomatoes
3/4 cup chopped fresh mushrooms
1/3 cup sliced ripe olives

Unroll crescent dough into a greased 15-in. x 10-in. x 1-in. baking pan; press seams together and build up edges. Prick dough with a fork. Bake at 375° for 11-13 minutes or until golden brown; cool completely on a wire rack.

In a food processor, combine the basil, parsley, cilantro, garlic, oil and Parmesan cheese; cover and puree until smooth. Transfer to a bowl; add sour cream and cream cheese. Spread over crust.

Halve tomatoes lengthwise and thinly slice widthwise; arrange over basil mixture. Top with mushrooms and olives. Refrigerate until serving. Cut into bite-size squares. **Yield:** 3 dozen.

Baked Potato Pizza

(Pictured at right)

I make this creative pizza for Super Bowl parties. The sour cream, bacon, onions and cheese make every bite taste just like a loaded baked potato.
—Gina Pierson, Centralia, Missouri

1 package (6 ounces) pizza crust mix
3 medium unpeeled potatoes, baked and cooled
1 tablespoon butter *or* margarine, melted
1/4 teaspoon garlic powder
1/4 teaspoon Italian seasoning *or* dried oregano
1 cup (8 ounces) sour cream
6 bacon strips, cooked and crumbled
3 to 5 green onions, chopped
1-1/2 cups (6 ounces) shredded mozzarella cheese
1/2 cup shredded cheddar cheese

Prepare crust according to package directions. Press dough into a lightly greased 14-in. pizza pan; build up edges slightly. Bake at 400° for 5-6 minutes or until crust is firm and begins to brown.

Cut potatoes into 1/2-in. cubes. In a bowl, combine butter, garlic powder and Italian seasoning. Add potatoes and toss. Spread sour cream over crust; top with potato mixture, bacon, onions and cheeses. Bake at 400° for 15-20 minutes or until cheese is lightly browned. Let stand for 5 minutes before cutting. **Yield:** 8 slices.

SUGGESTIONS FOR SERVING PIZZAS

YOU WON'T FUMBLE getting food on the table with these guidelines.

- Put two pizzas with the same baking temperature into the oven. (If possible, have two different varieties for folks to sample.) Each pizza should be on its own shelf. Halfway through the baking time, rotate the pizzas, moving the pizza on the higher rack to the lower rack and vice versa. You may need to add 5 to 10 minutes to the baking time.
- Bake other pizzas as soon as the first two come out of the oven. This gives people a chance to finish their first plate of food and allows you to add hot fresh food to the table.
- While pizzas are baking, set out the cold pizzas and other food.

Buffalo Chicken Calzones

I'm always looking for creative ways to jazz up pizza. I came up with this
"pizza turnover" to incorporate my love of buffalo chicken wings.
—Ruth Ann Riendeau, Twin Mountain, New Hampshire

  1 can (8 ounces) pizza sauce
  2 teaspoons plus 1/2 cup hot
    pepper sauce, *divided*
1-1/4 pounds boneless skinless
    chicken breasts, cubed
  3 celery ribs, chopped
  3 tablespoons butter *or*
    margarine
Dash Cajun seasoning
  2 tubes (10 ounces *each*)
    refrigerated pizza crust dough
1-1/2 cups (6 ounces) shredded
    Monterey Jack cheese
  4 ounces crumbled blue cheese
Cornmeal

In a bowl, combine pizza sauce and 2 teaspoons hot pepper sauce; set aside. In a skillet, saute chicken and celery in butter for 3-5 minutes or until chicken is no longer pink. Stir in Cajun seasoning and remaining hot pepper sauce; cover and simmer for 10-15 minutes or until heated through.

Unroll pizza dough; divide each portion in half. On a floured surface, roll each into an 8-in. circle. Spread pizza sauce mixture over half of each circle to within 1 in. of edges. Top with chicken mixture and cheeses. Fold dough over filling; pinch edges to seal.

Sprinkle greased baking sheets with cornmeal. Place calzones over cornmeal. Bake at 400° for 10-12 minutes or until golden brown. **Yield:** 4 calzones.

Breakfast Pizza

When my boys were in high school, they often tired of traditional breakfast foods.
To keep them interested, I would make this pizza. It's also a great appetizer.
—Judy Skinner, Fort Collins, Colorado

  1 tube (8 ounces) refrigerated
    crescent rolls
  1 pound bulk pork sausage
  1 cup frozen shredded hash
    brown potatoes, thawed
  1 jar (4-1/2 ounces) sliced
    mushrooms, drained
  6 bacon strips, cooked and
    crumbled
1/2 cup sliced ripe olives
  1 cup (4 ounces) shredded
    cheddar cheese
  1 cup (4 ounces) shredded
    mozzarella cheese
  5 eggs
1/4 cup milk
1/2 teaspoon salt
  2 tablespoons grated Parmesan cheese

Unroll crescent dough and separate into triangles; place on a greased 12-in. pizza pan. Press seams together and build up edges; set aside.

In a skillet, cook sausage over medium heat until no longer pink; drain and cool slightly. Sprinkle sausage, hash browns, mushrooms, bacon and olives over dough. Top with cheddar and mozzarella cheeses.

In a bowl, beat eggs, milk and salt; pour over pizza. Sprinkle with Parmesan cheese. Bake at 375° for 25-30 minutes or until golden brown. Let stand for 10 minutes before cutting. **Yield:** 6-8 slices.

Taco Pan Pizza

(Pictured at right)

Our Test Kitchen knows that pizza and tacos are favorite foods in lots of families. So they came up with this recipe that cleverly combines the two. A variety of toppings can be used to suit your tastes.

1 tube (10 ounces) refrigerated pizza crust
1/2 cup sour cream
1/3 cup mayonnaise
2 tablespoons minced fresh cilantro *or* parsley
1 jalapeno pepper, seeded and chopped*
1 teaspoon sugar
1/2 teaspoon chili powder
1/4 teaspoon salt
1/4 teaspoon ground cumin
1 medium ripe avocado, peeled and cubed
2 teaspoons lime juice
2 medium tomatoes, chopped
1/4 cup chopped green onions
1/3 cup sliced ripe olives
1 cup (4 ounces) shredded Mexican cheese blend *or* cheddar cheese

Unroll pizza dough and place in a greased 15-in. x 10-in. x 1-in. baking pan; flatten dough and build up edges slightly. Prick dough several times with a fork. Bake at 425° for 10-11 minutes or until lightly browned. Cool on a wire rack.

Meanwhile, in a bowl, combine the sour cream, mayonnaise, cilantro, jalapeno, sugar, chili powder, salt and cumin. Spread over cooled crust. Toss avocado with lime juice; arrange over sour cream mixture. Sprinkle with tomatoes, onions, olives and cheese. Refrigerate until serving. Cut into squares. **Yield:** 16-20 slices.

***Editor's Note:** When cutting or seeding hot peppers, use rubber or plastic gloves to protect your hands. Avoid touching your face.

PERSONAL "PIES" FOR KIDS

CONSIDER having some small Italian bread shells and assorted toppings for the kids. They can have fun making pizzas to suit their tastes, and you don't have to worry about them not liking the pizzas you've prepared.

Bridal Shower Reigns Supreme

EVERYTHING will be coming up roses for the bride-to-be when you shower her with a party and presents!

Hosting this get-together is a breeze when you rely on the appetizers, entrees, side dishes and desserts featured on the following pages.

As guests arrive, offer dainty cups of refreshing Cranberry Raspberry Punch, then call the ladies to the linen-topped table showcasing Orange-Avocado Chicken Salad, Creamy Crab Salad and Parmesan Cheese Straws (shown at right). This menu is especially easy because much of the preparation can be done ahead of time.

While the guest of honor opens pretty packages, present some delectable desserts and freshly brewed coffee or tea.

HERE COMES THE BRIDE
(Clockwise from top right)

Cranberry Raspberry Punch (p. 204)

Creamy Crab Salad (p. 204)

Parmesan Cheese Straws (p. 202)

Orange-Avocado
Chicken Salad (p. 203)

Parmesan Cheese Straws

(Pictured on page 200)

*These rich and buttery breadsticks are a fun change from regular dinner rolls
and are fairly easy to make. They're great alongside salads and soups.*
—*Mitzi Sentiff, Greenville, North Carolina*

1/2 cup butter (no substitutes),
    softened
2/3 cup grated Parmesan cheese
  1 cup all-purpose flour
1/4 teaspoon salt
1/8 teaspoon cayenne pepper
1/4 cup milk

In a small mixing bowl, beat butter and Parmesan cheese until well blended. Add the flour, salt and cayenne; mix well. Divide dough in half. On a lightly floured surface, roll each portion into an 18-in. x 3-in. rectangle. Cut into 3-in. x 1/2-in. strips.

Place 1 in. apart on lightly greased baking sheets; brush with milk. Bake at 350° for 8-10 minutes or until lightly browned. Remove to wire racks to cool. Store in an airtight container. **Yield:** 6 dozen.

Creamy Coconut Chocolate Pie

*I've used this recipe many times through the years for showers and luncheons.
The women I've served it to like the fluffy chocolate filling.*
—*Joan Sturrus, Grand Rapids, Michigan*

  3 cups finely crushed cream-
    filled sandwich cookies (about
    30 cookies)
1/2 cup butter *or* margarine,
    melted
FILLING:
  5 cups miniature marshmallows
  1 cup milk
Pinch salt
  1 teaspoon vanilla extract
1/2 cup chopped pecans
  1 square (1 ounce) unsweetened
    chocolate, grated
  1 cup whipping cream, whipped

TOPPING:
1/2 cup flaked coconut, toasted
1/3 cup confectioners' sugar
  1 cup whipping cream, whipped
Chocolate curls *or* grated chocolate

For crust, combine crushed cookies and butter; press onto the bottom and up the sides of a 9-in. pie plate. Chill until firm. For filling, combine marshmallows, milk and salt in a heavy saucepan. Cook and stir over low heat until marshmallows are melted. Refrigerate until cool, about 1-1/2 hours.

In a bowl, gently fold vanilla, pecans and grated chocolate into whipped cream. Fold into chilled marshmallow mixture. Pour into crust. Sprinkle with coconut. Fold confectioners' sugar into whipped cream; spread over coconut. Garnish with chocolate curls or grated chocolate. Refrigerate for at least 2 hours before serving. **Yield:** 8 servings.

Orange-Avocado Chicken Salad

(Pictured at right and on page 200)

Orange sections and avocado slices surround this hearty salad, making for a pretty presentation. It's a refreshing summer main dish for both lunch and dinner.
—Shelia Garcia, Mantachie, Mississippi

1/4 cup lime juice
   2 teaspoons salt, *divided*
   4 cups cubed cooked chicken
   2 cups frozen peas, thawed
   1 cup coarsely chopped carrots
1/2 cup thinly sliced celery
1/3 cup minced fresh parsley
   1 cup mayonnaise *or* salad
      dressing
   3 tablespoons orange juice
1/4 teaspoon pepper
Torn salad greens
   6 medium navel oranges, peeled
      and sectioned
   4 medium ripe avocados, peeled
      and sliced
1/4 cup thinly sliced green onions

In a small bowl, combine lime juice and 3/4 teaspoon salt; cover and refrigerate. In a large bowl, combine the chicken, peas, carrots, celery and parsley. Combine the mayonnaise, orange juice, pepper and remaining salt; pour over chicken mixture and toss to coat.

Cover and refrigerate for at least 1 hour.

Place greens on a serving platter or individual plates. Top with chicken salad; arrange orange sections and avocado slices around salad. Sprinkle with green onions. Drizzle with lime juice mixture. **Yield:** 12 servings.

SEEDING AND PEELING AVOCADOS

THE EASIEST avocados to peel and slice are those that are ripe yet firm. (Very ripe, soft avocados are best used for mashing.)

Cut the avocado in half lengthwise. Twist the halves in opposite directions to separate. Carefully tap the seed with the blade of a sharp knife. Rotate the knife to loosen the seed and lift it out.

To remove the peel, scoop out the flesh from each half with a large metal spoon, staying close to the peel. Slice; dip slices in lemon juice to prevent them from turning brown.

Creamy Crab Salad

(Pictured on page 201)

This easy-on-the-pocket salad beautifully dresses up economical imitation crab.
My husband's grandmother gladly shared the recipe.
—Barb Stanton, Winona, Minnesota

1 package (16 ounces) medium
   shell pasta
1 package (16 ounces) imitation
   crabmeat, flaked
3 green onions, thinly sliced
1/2 cup chopped carrot
1/2 cup chopped cucumber
1/2 cup chopped green pepper
1 cup (8 ounces) sour cream
1 cup mayonnaise
1/3 cup sugar
1 tablespoon seasoned salt
2 teaspoons cider vinegar
1-1/2 to 2 teaspoons pepper
Leaf lettuce, optional

Cook pasta according to package directions; drain and rinse in cold water. Place in a large bowl; add crab, onions, carrot, cucumber and green pepper. Combine the sour cream, mayonnaise, sugar, seasoned salt, vinegar and pepper; pour over salad and toss to coat. Cover and chill for at least 2 hours. Serve in a lettuce-lined bowl if desired. **Yield:** 10-12 servings.

Cranberry Raspberry Punch

(Pictured on page 201)

The blushing bride-to-be and her guests will ask for refills of this pretty pink punch.
It's not too sweet, so my family never tires of it at events throughout the year.
—Susan Rogers, Wilmington, Massachusetts

1 package (16 ounces) frozen
   sweetened sliced strawberries,
   thawed
1 can (12 ounces) frozen
   lemonade concentrate, thawed
1 can (11-1/2 ounces) frozen
   cranberry raspberry juice
   concentrate, thawed
2 liters ginger ale, chilled

2 liters club soda, chilled
1 quart raspberry *or* orange sherbet

Place the strawberries, lemonade concentrate and cranberry raspberry concentrate in a blender; cover and process until smooth. Transfer to a punch bowl. Gently stir in ginger ale and club soda. Top with scoops of sherbet. Serve immediately. **Yield:** about 5 quarts.

Pretty Petit Fours

(Pictured at right)

Add a delicate touch to your dessert table with these bite-size cakes from our Test Kitchen. We decorated the tops with roses to follow our floral theme, but feel free to try your hand at other designs.

1/4 cup butter *or* margarine, melted
1/4 cup shortening
1 cup sugar
1 teaspoon vanilla extract
1-1/3 cups all-purpose flour
2 teaspoons baking powder
1/2 teaspoon salt
2/3 cup milk
3 egg whites

GLAZE:
2 pounds confectioners' sugar
2/3 cup plus 2 tablespoons water
2 teaspoons orange extract

FROSTING:
6 tablespoons butter *or* margarine, softened
2 tablespoons shortening
1/2 teaspoon vanilla extract
3 cups confectioners' sugar
3 to 4 tablespoons milk
Gel, liquid *or* paste food coloring

In a large mixing bowl, cream the butter, shortening and sugar. Beat in vanilla. Combine the flour, baking powder and salt; add to creamed mixture alternately with milk. In a small mixing bowl, beat egg whites until soft peaks form; gently fold into batter.

Pour into a greased 9-in. square baking pan. Bake at 350° for 20-25 minutes or until a toothpick inserted near the center comes out clean. Cool for 10 minutes before removing from pan to a wire rack to cool completely.

Cut a thin slice off each side of cake. Cut cake into 1-1/4-in. squares. Place 1/2 in. apart on a rack in a 15-in. x 10-in. x 1-in. pan.

In a mixing bowl, combine glaze ingredients. Beat on low speed just until blended; beat on high until smooth. Apply glaze evenly over tops and sides of cake squares, allowing excess to drip off. Let dry. Repeat if necessary to thoroughly coat squares. Let dry completely.

For frosting, in a mixing bowl, cream butter, shortening and vanilla. Beat in confectioners' sugar and enough milk to achieve desired consistency. Place 1/2 cup each in two bowls; tint one pink and one green.

Cut a small hole in the corner of a pastry or plastic bag; insert #104 tip. Fill with pink frosting; pipe a rosebud on each petit four. Insert #3 round tip into another pastry or plastic bag; fill with green frosting. Pipe a leaf under each rose. **Yield:** 2-1/2 dozen (3 cups frosting).

Puff Pillow Buns

I entered this recipe at the 1971 Iowa State Fair and won first place. You can conveniently make the dough the night before, then shape and bake the buns the next morning.
—Shirley Marti, Lansing, Iowa

1 package (1/4 ounce) active dry yeast
1/4 cup warm water (110° to 115°)
1/2 cup warm milk (110° to 115°)
1/3 cup butter *or* margarine, melted
1/4 cup sugar
1 teaspoon salt
1/2 teaspoon lemon extract
2 eggs
3 to 3-1/2 cups all-purpose flour

FILLING:
1 package (8 ounces) cream cheese, softened
1/4 cup milk
1 teaspoon vanilla extract
2 tablespoons butter *or* margarine, melted

ICING:
1 cup confectioners' sugar
2 tablespoons butter *or* margarine, softened

1/2 teaspoon vanilla extract
1 to 2 tablespoons milk

In a mixing bowl, dissolve yeast in warm water. Add the milk, butter, sugar, salt, lemon extract, eggs and 1 cup flour. Beat until smooth. Stir in enough remaining flour to form a soft dough. Turn onto a floured surface; gently knead for 2-3 minutes. Place in a greased bowl, turning once to grease top. Cover and refrigerate for 2 hours or overnight.

Punch dough down. Turn onto a floured surface; divide into four portions. Roll one portion into a 9-in. x 6-in. rectangle (refrigerate remaining portions until ready to roll out). Cut into 3-in. squares.

In a mixing bowl, beat cream cheese, milk and vanilla until smooth. Place about 2 teaspoons filling in the center of each square. Moisten corners with water; bring over center of filling and pinch corners tightly in center. Repeat with remaining dough and filling. Place seam side up 2 in. apart on greased baking sheets; brush with melted butter. Cover and let rise in a warm place until doubled, about 45 minutes.

Bake at 400° for 10-12 minutes or until lightly browned. Remove from pans to wire racks. Combine icing ingredients; spread over warm buns. **Yield:** 2 dozen.

Mexican Wedding Cakes

As part of a Mexican tradition, I tucked these tender cookies into small gift boxes for the guests at my sister's wedding a few years ago. Most folks gobbled them up before they ever got home!
—Sarita Johnston, San Antonio, Texas

2 cups butter (no substitutes), softened
1 cup confectioners' sugar
4 cups all-purpose flour
1 teaspoon vanilla extract
1 cup finely chopped pecans
Additional confectioners' sugar

In a mixing bowl, cream butter and sugar. Gradually add flour; mix well. Beat in vanilla. Stir in pecans. Shape tablespoonfuls into 2-in. crescents. Place 2 in. apart on ungreased baking sheets. Bake at 350° for 12-15 minutes or until lightly browned. Roll warm cookies in confectioners' sugar; cool on wire racks. **Yield:** about 6 dozen.

Strawberry Wedding Bell Cookies

(Pictured at right)

To ring in a joyous occasion like a bridal shower or wedding, I'm often asked to make these festive cookies. You can use different flavors of jam to suit your tastes.
—Laurie Messer, Bonifay, Florida

1 cup butter (no substitutes), softened
1 package (3 ounces) cream cheese, softened
1/4 cup sugar
1 teaspoon vanilla extract
2 cups all-purpose flour
1/4 teaspoon salt
1/2 cup strawberry jam
Confectioners' sugar

In a mixing bowl, cream butter, cream cheese and sugar. Beat in vanilla. Combine flour and salt; gradually add to the creamed mixture. Divide dough into fourths. Cover and refrigerate for 2 hours or until easy to handle.

On a lightly floured surface, roll out each portion of dough to 1/8-in. thickness. Cut with floured 2-in. round cookie cutters. Place 1 in. apart on ungreased baking sheets. Spoon 1/4 teaspoon jam in the center and spread to within 1/4 in. of edge.

Shape into a bell by folding edges of dough to meet over filling. Bake at 375° for 8-10 minutes or until lightly browned. Remove to wire racks to cool. Dust with confectioners' sugar. **Yield:** about 5 dozen.

Family Traditions

INSTEAD of making a "bouquet" from ribbons and bows at the bridal shower, our family gives the guest of honor a nosegay of silk flowers with silver dollars (minted in the year of the wedding) tied on with colorful ribbon. The bride-to-be then uses this memento at the wedding rehearsal and saves it as a keepsake for years.
—Betty McLean, Fort Myers, Florida

Shrimp Pasta Salad

A Thousand Island-type dressing adds some zip to this pasta and shrimp salad.
My family prefers it to oil-based salad dressings.
—Mrs. Herbert Waalkens, Albert Lea, Minnesota

1 package (16 ounces) small
   shell pasta
1 package (10 ounces) frozen
   cooked salad shrimp, thawed
1/2 cup chopped celery
1/2 cup chopped onion, *divided*
2 hard-cooked eggs, chopped,
   divided
1/4 cup minced fresh parsley
1 cup mayonnaise
1/4 cup chili sauce

1 tablespoon chopped dill pickle *or* dill pickle relish
1/2 teaspoon Worcestershire sauce
1/2 teaspoon seasoned salt

Cook pasta according to package directions; drain and rinse in cold water. Place in a bowl; add the shrimp, celery, 1/4 cup onion, half of the chopped eggs and parsley.

In a small bowl, combine the mayonnaise, chili sauce, pickle, Worcestershire sauce, seasoned salt, and remaining onion and eggs. Stir into pasta mixture. Cover and refrigerate until serving. **Yield:** 10 servings.

Marinated Mozzarella Cubes

(Pictured on opposite page)

Being from America's Dairyland, I'm always on the lookout for new ways to serve cheese.
I received this delicious recipe from a friend a few years ago and am happy to share it with others.
—Arline Roggenbuck, Shawano, Wisconsin

1 pound mozzarella cheese, cut
   into 1-inch cubes
1 jar (7 ounces) roasted red
   peppers, drained and cut into
   bite-size pieces
6 fresh thyme sprigs
2 garlic cloves, minced
1-1/4 cups olive *or* vegetable oil
2 tablespoons minced fresh
   rosemary
2 teaspoons Italian seasoning
1/4 teaspoon crushed red pepper
   flakes
Bread *or* **crackers**

In a quart jar with a tight-fitting lid, layer a third of the cheese, peppers, thyme and garlic. Repeat layers twice. In a small bowl, combine the oil, rosemary, Italian seasoning and pepper flakes; mix well. Pour into jar; seal and turn upside down. Refrigerate overnight, turning several times. Serve with bread or crackers. **Yield:** 12-16 servings.

Mmmmarinated Mozzarella!

MAKE a few extra batches of Marinated Mozzarella Cubes; divide among quart or pint jars. Tuck each jar into a pretty basket along with bread or crackers and give away the baskets as party favors.

After eating the cheese and peppers from the jar, use the olive oil for cooking or as a dip for fresh bread.

Spinach-Cheese Mushroom Caps

(Pictured at right)

Dainty finger foods like these mushrooms are a nice way to welcome guests into your home. A hearty spinach filling will tide folks over until the meal is served.
—*Sandy Herman, Marietta, Georgia*

24 large fresh mushrooms
1/4 cup chopped onion
2 garlic cloves, minced
1 tablespoon olive *or* vegetable oil
1 package (8 ounces) cream cheese, softened
1 package (10 ounces) frozen chopped spinach, thawed and well drained
1/2 cup plus 2 tablespoons shredded Parmesan cheese, *divided*
1/2 cup crumbled feta cheese
1 bacon strip, cooked and crumbled
1/2 teaspoon salt

Remove stems from mushrooms; set caps aside. Finely chop the stems. In a skillet, saute the chopped mushrooms, onion and garlic in oil until tender.

In a mixing bowl, beat cream cheese until smooth. Add the spinach, 1/2 cup Parmesan cheese, feta cheese, bacon, salt and mushroom mixture. Spoon into mushroom caps. Sprinkle with the remaining Parmesan cheese. Place on a baking sheet. Bake at 400° for 15 minutes or until golden brown. **Yield:** 2 dozen.

MAKE THE MUSHROOMS AHEAD

INSTEAD of assembling Spinach-Cheese Mushroom Caps as guests arrive, stuff them in the morning and place on a baking sheet. Cover with a damp paper towel; refrigerate until baking time.

Artichoke Chicken Lasagna

*Chicken, artichokes and a cream sauce make this lasagna more special
than the usual tomato and beef variety. Everyone will love it!*
— Donna Boellner, Annapolis, Maryland

2/3 cup butter *or* margarine,
   divided
1/3 cup all-purpose flour
1 teaspoon salt, *divided*
1/4 teaspoon ground nutmeg
1/8 teaspoon pepper
3 cups milk
1-3/4 pounds boneless skinless
   chicken breasts, cut into thin
   strips and halved
2 cans (14 ounces *each*)
   water-packed artichoke
   hearts, drained and
   quartered
1 teaspoon dried thyme
9 lasagna noodles, cooked and
   drained
1 cup grated Parmesan cheese

In a saucepan, melt 1/3 cup butter. Stir in flour, 1/2 teaspoon salt, nutmeg and pepper until smooth. Gradually stir in milk. Bring to a boil; cook and stir for 2 minutes or until thickened. In a skillet, cook chicken in remaining butter until juices run clear. Stir in artichokes, thyme and remaining salt; heat through.

In a greased 13-in. x 9-in. x 2-in. baking dish, layer about 1/3 cup white sauce, three noodles, 1/2 cup sauce, 1/3 cup Parmesan cheese and about 3 cups chicken mixture. Repeat layers. Top with remaining noodles, sauce and Parmesan cheese. Bake, uncovered, at 350° for 35-40 minutes or until bubbly and golden brown. Let stand for 10 minutes before cutting. **Yield:** 12 servings.

Frozen Fruit Slush

*A fresh fruit salad can take some time to prepare and needs last-minute assembly.
That's why I often rely on this make-ahead frozen fruit dish when entertaining a crowd.*
—Judy McHone, Springfield, Illinois

2-1/2 cups water
1 cup sugar
1 can (6 ounces) frozen orange
   juice concentrate, thawed
3/4 cup lemonade concentrate
4 large firm bananas, sliced
1 can (29 ounces) sliced
   peaches, undrained and
   chopped

1 can (20 ounces) pineapple chunks, undrained
1 can (15 ounces) mandarin oranges, drained
1 package (10 ounces) frozen sweetened sliced
   strawberries, thawed
1 jar (6 ounces) maraschino cherries, undrained

In a large bowl, combine all ingredients. Cover and freeze for at least 8 hours or until firm. Remove from the freezer 45 minutes before serving. **Yield:** 18 servings (3/4 cup each).

Lovely Table For the Ladies

(Pictured above)

WHEN hosting a party just for women, add a little more feminine flair. For starters, place white or ivory linen cloths on your table, then drape tulle netting over the top. Place Napkin Roses (instructions at right) on each plate.

You can further enhance the floral effect by setting out a spray of fresh flowers. Or beside each place setting, put the blossom of a fresh-cut flower in a small, shallow clear bowl filled with water. (To prop up the flower, we first filled the bowl with clear marbles.)

CREATING NAPKIN ROSES

GUESTS will shower you with compliments when they see this fresh idea for Napkin Roses. To start, lay a square napkin flat with the right side down.

1. Fold napkin in half diagonally. Fold right corner three-quarters of the way up, aligning open edges.

2. Hold newly folded edge a few inches from the bottom; alternately finger-pleat and roll napkin to opposite corner, following bottom edge. Secure rose with ribbon and tie in a bow.

Festive Fare For July Fourth

IF YOU are in charge of the Fourth of July festivities this year, why not try a revolutionary idea and forgo ordinary hamburgers and hot dogs?

Instead, add some sizzle to your menu with on-the-grill goodies such as Sesame Chicken Kabobs and Sweet 'n' Spicy Grilled Pork Chops. Then pay tribute to the finest summer produce with Picnic Potato Salad and Melon with Minted Lime Dip. For the finale, Lemon Nut Star Cookies will trigger many "oohs" and "aahs" from your flag-waving family. (All recipes are shown at right.)

So when planning a patriotic picnic, spark your creativity by turning to the true-blue favorites in this chapter.

BACKYARD BARBECUE
(Clockwise from top right)

Picnic Potato Salad (p. 220)

Sesame Chicken Kabobs (p. 216)

Lemon Nut Star Cookies (p. 215)

Sweet 'n' Spicy
Grilled Pork Chops (p. 214)

Melon with Minted Lime Dip (p. 218)

Sweet 'n' Spicy Grilled Pork Chops

(Pictured on page 212)

This started out as a mild sauce that I decided to "spice up". You'll find it's easy to adjust the seasonings to suit your family's taste. I also like to use the sauce on boneless skinless chicken breasts.
—*Gladys Peterson, Beaumont, Texas*

1 can (14-1/2 ounces) diced tomatoes, drained
1 can (10 ounces) diced tomatoes with chilies, undrained
1/2 cup raisins
1/4 cup currant jelly
4-1/2 teaspoons cider vinegar
1/4 teaspoon *each* garlic powder, salt and crushed red pepper flakes
12 boneless pork chops (3/4 inch thick)

In a blender, combine the tomatoes, raisins, jelly, vinegar and seasonings; cover and process until smooth. Pour into a 1-qt. saucepan; bring to a boil. Reduce heat; simmer, uncovered, for 20 minutes or until thickened. Set aside 3/4 cup for serving.

Coat grill rack with nonstick cooking spray before starting grill. Grill pork chops, uncovered, over medium heat, for 4 minutes. Turn; brush with sauce. Grill 4-6 minutes longer or until meat juices run clear. Serve with reserved sauce. **Yield:** 12 servings.

FOOD SAFETY TIPS FOR SUMMER

SUMMER is prime time for memorable picnics and cookouts with friends and family. But the last thing you want to bring home from these fun-filled outings is food poisoning, so follow these precautions. (Also see Properly Packing a Cooler on page 220.)

- When packing the cooler or picnic basket, wrap raw meat, poultry and fish separately from cooked foods in airtight plastic containers or resealable plastic bags.
- It's a good idea to have two sets of cutting boards, grilling utensils and platters—one for uncooked foods and one for cooked items.
- Pack a meat thermometer to ensure you're grilling meat and poultry to the proper temperature.
- Prevent the spread of bacteria by washing fruits and vegetables before putting in the basket or cooler.
- Pack clean foil, plastic wrap and resealable plastic bags to store leftovers.
- If you won't have access to soap and water at the picnic, bring along moist towelettes, antibacterial soap that doesn't require water or a spray bottle with soapy water.
- Hot foods should be eaten within 2 hours of being made.
- Remove foods from the cooler just before cooking or serving.
- Food should not stand out longer than 2 hours. (On days above 85°, 1 hour is the maximum.) Promptly store hot and cold leftovers in an ice-filled cooler. If no ice remains in the cooler when you get home, play it safe and discard the food.

Lemon Nut Star Cookies

(Pictured at right and on page 212)

Family and friends will say "Hooray!" when they see these star-spangled cookies from our Test Kitchen. Make these treats throughout the year by using different cookie cutters and food coloring.

1 cup butter (no substitutes), softened
2 cups confectioners' sugar
2 eggs
2 tablespoons lemon juice
4 teaspoons half-and-half cream
2 teaspoons grated lemon peel
3-1/4 cups all-purpose flour
1/2 cup ground almonds
1/2 teaspoon baking soda
1/8 teaspoon salt
GLAZE:
2 cups confectioners' sugar
1/4 cup light corn syrup
2 tablespoons lemon juice
Red and blue food coloring

In a mixing bowl, cream butter and confectioners' sugar. Add eggs, one at a time, beating well after each addition. Beat in the lemon juice, cream and lemon peel. Combine the flour, almonds, baking soda and salt; gradually add to creamed mixture. Cover and refrigerate for 2 hours or until easy to handle.

On a lightly floured surface, roll out dough to 1/8-in. thickness. Cut with a floured star-shaped cookie cutter. Place 1 in. apart on ungreased baking sheets. Bake at 350° for 8-10 minutes or until lightly browned. Remove to wire racks to cool.

For glaze, combine confectioners' sugar, corn syrup and lemon juice until smooth. Divide into three bowls. Tint one portion red and one portion blue; leave the third portion plain. Spread over cookies; let stand overnight for glaze to harden. **Yield:** about 5-1/2 dozen.

Sesame Chicken Kabobs

(Pictured on page 213)

This colorful dish is a favorite of mine for entertaining. I marinate the chicken and cut up the peppers the night before. Then the next day, I just assemble the kabobs and grill.
—Cindy Novak, Antioch, California

1/3 cup sherry *or* chicken broth
1/3 cup soy sauce
2 green onions, chopped
3 tablespoons apricot preserves
1 tablespoon vegetable oil
2 garlic cloves, minced
1/2 teaspoon ground ginger *or* 2 teaspoons minced fresh gingerroot
1/2 teaspoon hot pepper sauce
3 teaspoons sesame seeds, toasted, *divided*
1-1/2 pounds boneless skinless chicken breasts, cut into 1-inch cubes
1 medium sweet red pepper, cut into 1-inch pieces
1 medium sweet yellow pepper, cut into 1-inch pieces

In a bowl, combine the sherry or broth, soy sauce, onions, preserves, oil, garlic, ginger, hot pepper sauce and 1-1/2 teaspoons sesame seeds. Pour 1/3 cup into another bowl for basting; cover and refrigerate. Pour remaining marinade into a large resealable plastic bag; add chicken. Seal bag and turn to coat; refrigerate for 2-3 hours or overnight, turning occasionally.

Drain and discard marinade. On metal or soaked wooden skewers, alternately thread chicken and peppers. Grill, uncovered, over medium heat for 6 minutes, turning once. Baste with reserved marinade. Grill 5-10 minutes longer or until meat juices run clear, turning and basting frequently. Sprinkle with remaining sesame seeds. **Yield:** 6 servings.

Zucchini Salad

My husband and I have a big garden and grow a variety of vegetables, including lots of zucchini. That abundant summer produce stars in this simple salad.
—Shirley Smith, Wichita, Kansas

4 medium zucchini, sliced (about 5 cups)
1 can (14 ounces) water-packed artichoke hearts, drained and chopped
2 jars (4-1/2 ounces *each*) sliced mushrooms, drained
1 can (2-1/4 ounces) sliced ripe olives
1 can (8 ounces) sliced water chestnuts, drained
1 envelope ranch salad dressing mix
1 cup Italian salad dressing
Leaf lettuce, optional

In a bowl, combine the zucchini, artichokes, mushrooms, olives and water chestnuts. Combine the ranch dressing mix and Italian dressing; pour over vegetables and toss to coat. Cover and refrigerate for several hours or overnight. Drain; serve in a lettuce-lined bowl if desired. **Yield:** 8 servings.

Caesar Chicken Potato Salad

(Pictured at right)

Here in Texas, we seem to have summer year-round. So quick-to-fix dishes like this that get you in and out of the kitchen are popular.
—Sarita Johnston, San Antonio, Texas

    4 cups quartered small white *or*
      red potatoes
  3/4 pound boneless skinless
      chicken breasts, cubed
    1 tablespoon vegetable oil
    1 package (10 ounces) mixed
      salad greens
    1 small red onion, sliced and
      separated into rings
  3/4 cup Caesar salad dressing
  1/3 cup croutons
    2 tablespoons shredded
      Parmesan cheese

Place potatoes in a large saucepan and cover with water. Cover and bring to a boil over medium-high heat; cook for 15-20 minutes or until tender. Meanwhile, in a skillet, saute chicken in oil for 5-10 minutes or until juices run clear. Drain potatoes; add to chicken.

Place greens and onion in a serving bowl. Top with chicken mixture. Drizzle with dressing; sprinkle with croutons and Parmesan cheese. Serve immediately. **Yield:** 4 servings.

Family Traditions

JULY FOURTH was truly kids' day in the little Arkansas town where I reared my children. We bought small flags and yards of crepe-paper streamers to decorate wagons, tricycles, bicycles—anything with wheels. All the local kids would then participate in the town parade, each hoping to win the grand prize.
—*Mary Lewis*
Memphis, Tennessee

Melon with Minted Lime Dip

(Pictured on page 212)

For a refreshing summer side dish for any meal, our Test Kitchen
recommends these marinated melon balls with a cool, creamy dip.
You can also serve this fruity treat as a light dessert.

1/4 **cup sugar**
1/4 **cup water**
6 **tablespoons lime juice**
2 **tablespoons minced fresh**
 mint
2 **teaspoons grated lime peel**
1-1/2 **teaspoons ground ginger** *or* **2**
 tablespoons grated fresh
 gingerroot
8 **cups melon balls** *or* **cubes**
MINTED LIME DIP:
1 **cup (8 ounces) sour cream**
2 **tablespoons sugar**
1 **tablespoon lime juice**
2 **teaspoons grated lime peel**

In a bowl, combine the sugar, water, lime juice, mint, lime peel and ginger. Add melon balls. Cover and refrigerate for 1-6 hours. Thread melon onto wooden skewers or toothpicks. In a bowl, combine dip ingredients. Serve with melon. **Yield:** 8 cups fruit (1 cup dip).

CHILLING DIP AT PICNICS

WHEN serving dip on a hot day, it's important to keep it cool. If you don't have a ceramic dip set (shown on page 212 with the Minted Lime Dip), use what you have on hand.

Fill a large glass or plastic serving bowl with ice cubes, crushed ice or ice packs. Fill a smaller bowl with dip and set on top of the ice. Replace the ice as it melts.

If you're taking the dip to an outing, put the dip in a small bowl (plastic is best for traveling because it won't break), cover with plastic wrap and put in a cooler. Assemble the ice-filled serving bowl when you get to the picnic.

Patriotic Fruit Pizza

(Pictured at right)

When strawberry season arrives, folks who know me anticipate this flavorful fruity dessert. It's very pretty and always gets lots of compliments wherever I take it.
—Amy Murdoch
Union Grove, Wisconsin

1-1/2 cups all-purpose flour
1/4 cup confectioners' sugar
1 cup cold butter (no substitutes)
1 package (4-3/4 ounces) strawberry Danish dessert*

FILLING:
1 package (8 ounces) cream cheese, softened
1 cup sugar
1/4 teaspoon vanilla extract
3 cups sliced fresh strawberries
1 cup fresh blueberries

In a bowl, combine the flour and confectioners' sugar. Cut in butter until mixture begins to hold together. Press into a 12-in. tart or pizza pan; build up edges slightly. Bake at 350° for 10 minutes or until golden brown. Cool for 15 minutes. Cook Danish dessert according to package directions for pie glaze; cool to room temperature.

In a mixing bowl, beat cream cheese, sugar and vanilla. Spread over crust. Arrange strawberries in an 8- to 10-in. circle in center of pizza. Sprinkle blueberries around strawberries. Pour half of the Danish dessert over strawberries (save remaining glaze for another use). Refrigerate until serving. Cut into wedges. **Yield:** 8-10 servings.

*Editor's Note: Look for strawberry Danish dessert in the gelatin aisle of your grocery store.

Strawberry Sherbet

When our boys were young and always hungry, we'd head to our strawberry patch and gather fruit for this sherbet. This treat was a must for company.
—Ruth Guse, Stillwater, Minnesota

4 quarts fresh strawberries, sliced
4 cups sugar
2-2/3 cups milk
2/3 cup orange juice
1/8 teaspoon ground cinnamon, optional

In a large bowl, combine strawberries and sugar; let stand for 1-1/2 to 2 hours or until very juicy. Process in small batches in a blender until pureed. Strain seeds; pour strawberry juice into a bowl. Stir in milk, orange juice and cinnamon if desired.

Freeze in batches in an ice cream freezer according to manufacturer's directions. Refrigerate remaining mixture until it can be frozen. **Yield:** about 4 quarts.

Picnic Potato Salad

(Pictured on page 213)

What would a picnic be without potato salad? In this recipe, mint adds a tasty twist on the traditional. Because it contains oil instead of mayonnaise, it travels well to picnics.
—Sheri Neiswanger, Ravenna, Ohio

10 medium red potatoes, cubed
2/3 cup vegetable oil
2 tablespoons cider vinegar
4 teaspoons honey
1 teaspoon dried basil
1 teaspoon ground mustard
1/2 teaspoon salt
1/2 teaspoon dried thyme
1/4 teaspoon dried marjoram

1/4 teaspoon dried mint
Dash cayenne pepper

Place potatoes in a large saucepan and cover with water. Cover and bring to a boil over medium-high heat; cook for 15-20 minutes or until tender. Drain and place in a large bowl. Combine the remaining ingredients; pour over potatoes and toss to coat. Cool to room temperature. Cover and refrigerate until serving. **Yield:** 12 servings.

PROPERLY PACKING A COOLER

COOLERS serve as portable refrigerators when going on picnics. These tips will help your coolers—and the items inside—stay well-chilled for the duration of your outing.

- Cold foods (especially those containing mayonnaise) and beverages should be thoroughly chilled before being put in insulated coolers.
- Beverage coolers tend to be opened frequently during a picnic. So use one cooler for beverages and one for cold food.
- Transport hot food in a separate insulated cooler. Wrap the hot items in newspapers or dish towels, then pack the dishes tightly in a cooler lined with dish towels.
- Prechill coolers by placing a few ice cubes inside and closing the lid about an hour before filling.
- Right before you leave for the picnic, pack the cooler in the opposite order of how you'll be using the items. That means the foods you need first should be on top, so they're easily accessible.
- Put blocks of ice or ice packs on the bottom of the cooler. Layer with food or beverages, then top with ice cubes or crushed ice.
- A full cooler will stay colder longer than a partially filled one, so pick the right size cooler. If your food or beverages don't fill the cooler, add more ice.
- Don't put coolers in a hot trunk, especially if traveling quite a distance. Put them in the backseat of your air-conditioned car. Surround with blankets, sleeping bags and clothes to insulate even more.
- While at the picnic, keep coolers in the shade, cover with blankets and keep the lids closed as much as you can.
- If possible, replenish the ice as it melts. If you don't have access to more ice, don't drain the cold water from the cooler…it keeps things cold almost as well as ice.

Red, White And Blue Chili

(Pictured at right)

Instead of the usual picnic fare, I surprised family and guests with this mild-flavored dish one Independence Day. They were delighted with the blue tortilla chips and colorful chili.
—Dotty Parker, Christmas Valley, Oregon

  1 medium green pepper, diced
1/4 cup diced onion
  2 garlic cloves, minced
  1 tablespoon vegetable oil
  2 cans (14-1/2 ounces *each*)
     Mexican diced tomatoes,
     undrained
  2 cans (14-1/2 ounces *each*)
     chicken broth
  2 cups shredded cooked chicken
  2 cans (15-1/2 ounces *each*)
     great northern beans, rinsed
     and drained
  1 can (16 ounces) kidney beans,
     rinsed and drained
  1 envelope chili seasoning
  1 tablespoon brown sugar
  1 teaspoon salt
1/4 teaspoon pepper
Blue tortilla chips

In a Dutch oven or soup kettle, saute the green pepper, onion and garlic in oil until tender. Stir in the tomatoes, broth, chicken, beans, chili seasoning, brown sugar, salt and pepper. Bring to a boil. Reduce heat; cover and simmer for 45 minutes. Serve with tortilla chips. **Yield:** 8 servings (about 2 quarts).

Summertime Salsa

My friends and I make batches of this salsa every year. We tuck a few jars away
so we can enjoy the flavor of summer when the weather turns cooler.
—Pat Shearer, Coutts, Alberta

10 cups chopped seeded peeled tomatoes (about 6 pounds)
5 cups chopped onions
3-1/2 cups chopped green peppers (about 1-1/2 pounds)
1-1/2 cups chopped sweet red peppers (about 3/4 pound)
1-1/4 cups white vinegar
6 jalapeno peppers, seeded and finely chopped*
3 garlic cloves, minced
3 teaspoons salt
1-1/2 teaspoons crushed red pepper flakes
1/2 teaspoon sugar
1/2 teaspoon mustard seed
1/2 teaspoon chili powder
1/4 teaspoon pepper

Combine all ingredients in a large kettle; bring to a boil. Reduce heat; simmer, uncovered, for 1-3/4 hours or until mixture reaches desired thickness. Pour hot mixture into hot jars, leaving 1/4-in. headspace. Adjust caps. Process in a boiling-water bath for 15 minutes. **Yield:** about 6 pints.

*Editor's Note: When cutting or seeding hot peppers, use rubber or plastic gloves to protect your hands. Avoid touching your face.

Honey-Ginger Barbecued Ribs

Grilling season just wouldn't be the same without these tender, finger-licking-good ribs.
My family loves how ginger enhances the slightly sweet marinade.
—Linda Tuchband, Overland Park, Kansas

4 to 5 pounds pork spareribs
2 cups chicken broth
1 cup soy sauce
3/4 cup ketchup
1/2 cup pineapple juice
1/2 cup honey
1 garlic clove, minced
1/2 teaspoon pepper
1/4 teaspoon ground ginger *or* 1 teaspoon minced fresh gingerroot
GLAZE:
2/3 cup honey
2 tablespoons soy sauce
1/4 teaspoon ground ginger *or* 1 teaspoon minced fresh gingerroot

Place ribs on a rack in a shallow baking pan; cover with foil. Bake at 325° for 1-1/2 hours; cool. In a bowl, combine the broth, soy sauce, ketchup, pineapple juice, honey, garlic, pepper and ginger. Place ribs in a gallon-size resealable plastic bag; add marinade. Seal bag; refrigerate overnight, turning occasionally.

Drain and discard marinade. In a small bowl, combine glaze ingredients; set aside. Grill ribs, uncovered, over medium heat for 20-25 minutes or until heated through, brushing with glaze during the last 10 minutes. **Yield:** 4-6 servings.

Fourth of July Ice Cream Cake

(Pictured at right)

This eye-catching dessert is actually easy to prepare and keeps well in the freezer for days. It's nice to be able to serve cake and ice cream in one slice.
—Anne Scholovich
Waukesha, Wisconsin

1 prepared angel food cake
  (10 inches)
2 quarts strawberry ice cream,
  softened
1 quart vanilla ice cream,
  softened
2-1/2 cups whipping cream
2 tablespoons confectioners'
  sugar
Decorative mini paper flags,
  optional

Cut cake horizontally into four equal layers. Place bottom layer on a serving plate; spread with half of the strawberry ice cream. Immediately place in freezer. Spread second cake layer with vanilla ice cream; place over strawberry layer in freezer. Spread third cake layer with remaining strawberry ice cream; place over vanilla layer in freezer. Top with remaining cake layer.

In a mixing bowl, beat cream until soft peaks form. Add sugar; beat until stiff peaks form. Frost top and sides of cake. Freeze until serving. Decorate with mini flags if desired. **Yield:** 12-14 servings.

Sweet Summer Brownies

WHEN the kids settle down after a day of fun in the sun, re-energize them with a sweet selection of brownies.

Chewy, gooey, sometimes nutty and always good, scrumptious squares are prepared in one pan and usually bake in a flash. So they're great when you want to offer a sweet summer treat but don't want to spend hours in a hot kitchen making cookies.

You'll find this classic dessert in a flavorful assortment of variations, such as Ice Cream Brownie Mountain, Cinnamon Brownies and Brownie Pizza (at right).

So set out a plate piled high with irresistible brownies—don't forget the cold milk!—and watch them disappear.

Cinnamon Brownies

(Pictured on page 224)

No frosting is needed on top of these chewy, fudge-like brownies.
This nice, basic bar has a burst of cinnamon in every bite.
—Christopher Wolf, Belvidere, Illinois

1-2/3 cups sugar
  3/4 cup butter *or* margarine,
      melted
    2 tablespoons strong brewed
      coffee
    2 eggs
    2 teaspoons vanilla extract
1-1/3 cups all-purpose flour
  3/4 cup baking cocoa
    1 tablespoon ground cinnamon
  1/2 teaspoon baking powder
  1/4 teaspoon salt

    1 cup chopped walnuts
Confectioners' sugar

In a mixing bowl, beat the sugar, butter and coffee. Add eggs and vanilla. Combine the flour, cocoa, cinnamon, baking powder and salt; gradually add to the sugar mixture and mix well. Stir in walnuts.

    Spread into a greased 13-in. x 9-in. x 2-in. baking pan. Bake at 350° for 18-22 minutes or until a toothpick inserted near the center comes out clean (do not overbake). Cool on a wire rack. Dust with confectioners' sugar. **Yield:** 2 dozen.

Almond Macaroon Brownies

Even when we were in the middle of remodeling our old farmhouse, I made time to bake at least
three times a week. This is a little fancier brownie that's great for guests.
—Jayme Goffin, Crown Point, Indiana

    6 squares (1 ounce *each*)
      semisweet chocolate
  1/2 cup butter (no substitutes)
  2/3 cup sugar
    2 eggs
    1 teaspoon vanilla extract
    1 cup all-purpose flour
  1/3 cup chopped almonds
TOPPING:
    1 package (3 ounces) cream
      cheese, softened
  1/3 cup sugar
    1 egg
    1 tablespoon all-purpose flour
    1 cup flaked coconut

  1/3 cup chopped almonds
  16 whole almonds
    1 square (1 ounce) semisweet chocolate, melted

In a microwave-safe bowl, heat chocolate and butter until melted; stir until smooth. Whisk in sugar, eggs and vanilla until smooth. Add flour and chopped almonds; mix well. Spread into a greased 8-in. square baking pan.

    In a mixing bowl, combine cream cheese, sugar, egg and flour; beat until smooth. Stir in coconut and chopped almonds. Spread over brownie layer. Evenly place whole almonds over topping. Bake at 350° for 35-40 minutes until a toothpick inserted near the center comes out with moist crumbs (do not overbake). Cool on a wire rack. Drizzle with melted chocolate. **Yield:** 16 brownies.

Ice Cream Brownie Mountain

(Pictured at right and on page 225)

If you like ice cream cake as my family does, you'll love this easy-to-make version. It's a fun, festive dessert for birthdays and other occasions, especially in summer.
— *Mirien Church, Aurora, Colorado*

> 4 eggs
> 2 cups sugar
> 1/2 cup vegetable oil
> 1-1/2 cups all-purpose flour
> 2/3 cup baking cocoa
> 1 teaspoon baking powder
> 1/2 teaspoon salt
> 1/2 cup chopped peanuts
> 1 quart vanilla ice cream, softened
> 1 carton (8 ounces) frozen whipped topping, thawed
> 2 tablespoons chocolate syrup
> Colored nonpareils and chopped peanuts, optional

In a mixing bowl, beat the eggs, sugar and oil. Combine flour, cocoa, baking powder and salt; gradually add to sugar mixture and mix well. Stir in peanuts. Spread into a greased 13-in. x 9-in. x 2-in. baking pan. Bake at 350° for 25-28 minutes or until a toothpick inserted near the center comes out with moist crumbs (do not overbake). Cool on a wire rack.

Line a 2-1/2-qt. bowl with a double layer of plastic wrap. Break brownies into pieces about 2 in. square; set aside a third of the pieces. Line the bottom and sides of prepared bowl with remaining brownie pieces, pressing firmly to completely cover to within 1 in. of rim. Fill brownie-lined bowl with ice cream, pressing down firmly. Top with reserved brownie pieces, covering ice cream completely. Cover and freeze overnight.

To serve, uncover and invert onto a serving plate. Let stand for 10 minutes before removing bowl and plastic wrap. Spread whipped topping over top and sides of dessert; drizzle with chocolate syrup. Garnish with nonpareils and peanuts if desired. Cut into wedges with a sharp knife. **Yield:** 10-12 servings.

Frosted Brownies

You can't go wrong with this traditional treat. These fudgy frosted squares travel well to potlucks and picnics and are sure to be one of the first desserts to disappear.
—Pat Yaeger, Naples, Florida

   4 squares (1 ounce *each*)
     unsweetened chocolate
   1 cup vegetable oil
   2 cups sugar
   4 eggs
   1 teaspoon vanilla extract
   1 cup all-purpose flour
1/4 teaspoon salt
   1 cup chopped walnuts
FROSTING:
   2 tablespoons butter (no
     substitutes)
   2 squares (1 ounce *each*)
     unsweetened chocolate
2-1/2 cups confectioners' sugar
1/4 cup milk
   1 teaspoon vanilla extract

In a large microwave-safe bowl, heat chocolate until melted; cool for 10 minutes. Add oil and sugar; mix well. Stir in eggs and vanilla. Add flour and salt; mix well. Stir in the nuts. Pour into a greased 13-in. x 9-in. x 2-in. baking pan. Bake at 350° for 25-30 minutes or until a toothpick inserted near the center comes out with moist crumbs (do not overbake). Cool on a wire rack.

   For frosting, melt butter and chocolate; stir until smooth. Cool to room temperature. In a mixing bowl, combine the chocolate mixture, sugar, milk and vanilla until smooth. Frost brownies. **Yield:** 2-1/2 dozen.

FAST FROSTING

AFTER removing a pan of brownies from the oven, sprinkle with chocolate chips. Let stand until the chocolate melts. Spread with a rubber spatula.

Caramel Macadamia Nut Brownies

One bite and you'll agree this is the most delectable brownie you'll ever sink your teeth into. Eat it with a fork to enjoy every last morsel of chocolate, caramel and nuts.
—Jamie Bursell, Juneau, Alaska

   1 teaspoon plus 3/4 cup butter
     (no substitutes), *divided*
   3 squares (1 ounce *each*)
     unsweetened chocolate
   3 eggs
1-1/2 cups packed brown sugar
   2 teaspoons vanilla extract
3/4 cup all-purpose flour
1/4 teaspoon baking soda

CARAMEL LAYER:
3/4 cup sugar
   3 tablespoons water
1/4 cup whipping cream
   2 tablespoons butter (no substitutes)
TOPPING:
1-1/2 cups semisweet chocolate chips
   1 cup milk chocolate chips
   1 jar (3-1/2 ounces) macadamia nuts, coarsely
     chopped

Line a 9-in. square baking pan with foil; grease the foil with 1 teaspoon butter and set aside. In a microwave-safe bowl, heat chocolate and remaining butter until melted; cool for 10 minutes. In a mixing bowl, beat eggs and brown sugar; stir in chocolate mixture and vanilla. Combine flour and baking soda; add to chocolate mixture.

Pour into prepared pan. Bake at 325° for 40 minutes or until a toothpick inserted near the center comes out with moist crumbs (do not overbake). Cool on a wire rack.

In a heavy saucepan, combine sugar and water. Cook and stir over medium heat for 4-5 minutes or until sugar is dissolved. Cook over medium-high heat without stirring until syrup is golden, about 5 minutes; remove from the heat.

In a small saucepan, heat cream over low heat until small bubbles form around edge of pan. Gradually stir cream into syrup (mixture will boil up). Cook and stir over low heat until blended. Stir in butter until melted. Remove from the heat; cool slightly.

Pour over brownies to within 1/4 in. of edges. Sprinkle with chips and nuts. Bake at 325° for 5 minutes (do not let chips melt completely). Cool completely on a wire rack. Refrigerate for 4 hours. Lift out of the pan; remove foil. Cut into bars. **Yield:** 20 brownies.

Brownie Pizza

(Pictured at right and on page 224)

Kids of all ages will find this a delightfully different way to serve brownies. Use whatever toppings you like to suit your family's tastes.
—Loretta Wohlenhaus
Cumberland, Iowa

3/4 cup butter *or* margarine,
    softened
  1 cup sugar
  1 egg
  1 teaspoon vanilla extract
1-1/2 cups all-purpose flour
  1/4 cup baking cocoa
  1/2 teaspoon baking powder
  1/4 teaspoon salt
  3/4 cup milk chocolate M&M's,
    divided
  1/2 cup chopped walnuts, *divided*
  1/4 cup miniature marshmallows
  1/4 cup flaked coconut

In a mixing bowl, cream butter and sugar. Beat in egg and vanilla. Combine the flour, cocoa, baking powder and salt; gradually add to creamed mixture and mix well. Stir in 1/2 cup M&M's and 1/4 cup walnuts.

Spread onto a greased 14-in. pizza pan to within 1/2 in. of edges. Sprinkle with remaining M&M's and walnuts. Top with marshmallows and coconut. Bake at 350° for 15-20 minutes or until a toothpick inserted near the center comes out clean. Cool on a wire rack. Cut into wedges. **Yield:** 10-12 servings.

Butterscotch Pecan Brownies

Starting with my mother's basic brownie, I made up this version as I went along.
It tastes just like candy, so you'll want to cut it into small squares.
— Donna Hampton, Warr Acres, Oklahoma

2 squares (1 ounce *each*)
  unsweetened chocolate
1/3 cup shortening
2 eggs
1 cup sugar
3/4 cup all-purpose flour
1/2 teaspoon baking powder
1/2 teaspoon salt
1/2 cup chopped pecans
FILLING:
1/4 cup butter *or* margarine
1/2 cup sugar
1/4 cup evaporated milk
3/4 cup marshmallow creme
1/2 teaspoon vanilla extract
1/4 cup chopped pecans
CARAMEL LAYER:
24 caramels
1/4 cup whipping cream
TOPPING:
1 cup semisweet chocolate chips
1/4 cup butterscotch chips
1/4 cup chopped pecans

In a microwave-safe bowl, melt chocolate and shortening; stir until smooth. Cool slightly. In a mixing bowl, beat eggs and sugar; stir in chocolate mixture. Combine flour, baking powder and salt; gradually stir into chocolate mixture. Stir in pecans. Spread into a greased 13-in. x 9-in. x 2-in. baking pan. Bake at 350° for 18-20 minutes or until a toothpick inserted near the center comes out clean. Cool on a wire rack.

For filling, melt butter in a heavy saucepan over medium heat. Add sugar and milk; bring to a gentle boil. Reduce heat to medium-low; boil and stir for 5 minutes. Remove from the heat; stir in marshmallow creme and vanilla. Add pecans. Spread over top of brownies. Refrigerate until set.

Combine the caramels and cream in a saucepan. Cook and stir over low heat until melted and smooth; cook and stir 4 minutes longer. Spread over filling. Refrigerate until set.

Melt the chocolate and butterscotch chips; stir until smooth. Stir in pecans; spread over caramel layer. Refrigerate for at least 4 hours or overnight. Remove from the refrigerator 20 minutes before cutting. Cut into 1-in. squares. **Yield:** about 8 dozen.

FOILED AGAIN!

TO EASILY cut brownies, line the baking pan with foil, leaving 3 inches hanging over each end. Grease the foil if the recipe instructs. After the baked brownies have cooled, use the foil to lift them out. Cut into bars and discard the foil. This not only makes it easier to cut the bars but saves cleanup time and prevents your pans from getting scratched.

Decadent Brownie Pie

(Pictured at right)

I guarantee this will be the richest,
fudge-like brownie you've ever tasted.
Slices can be dressed up or down
with an assortment of toppings.
—Stephanie Vozzo, Belvidere, New Jersey

2/3 cup butter *or* margarine,
    softened
1-1/4 cups sugar
1/2 cup light corn syrup
2 eggs
1-1/4 cups all-purpose flour
1/2 cup baking cocoa
1/2 teaspoon salt
3 tablespoons milk
2 cups chopped walnuts
GANACHE:
1 cup whipping cream
8 squares (1 ounce *each*)
    semisweet chocolate,
    chopped
Optional toppings—mint Andes
    candies, raspberries and fresh
    mint, caramel ice cream topping
    and whipped cream

In a mixing bowl, cream butter and sugar. Add corn syrup; mix well. Add eggs, one at a time, beating well after each addition. Combine the flour, cocoa and salt; add to creamed mixture alternately with milk. Fold in walnuts. Spread into a greased 10-in. springform pan. Bake at 325° for 55-60 minutes or until a toothpick inserted 1 in. from side of pan comes out clean. Cool on a wire rack.

For ganache, in a saucepan, bring cream to a boil. Remove from the heat; stir in chocolate until melted. Cool completely.

Remove sides of springform pan. Place a wire rack over waxed paper; set brownie on rack. Pour ganache over the brownie; spread over top and let drip down sides. Let stand until set. Cut into wedges; garnish with desired toppings. Store in the refrigerator. **Yield:** 10-12 servings.

Halloween "Spooktacular"

AS THE clock ticks closer to the witching hour of Halloween, don't be haunted by the headaches of hosting a frighteningly fun party for the youngsters in your family.

Entertaining can be eerily easy! The trick lies in offering an awesome assortment of kid-approved snacks and beverages.

Little ghosts and goblins will have a smashing good time at your Halloween bash when they spy a spooky spread of Orange Witches' Brew Punch, Bewitching Ice Cream Cones, Marshmallow Ghosts, Frightening Fingers and Black Cat Cookies (pictured at right).

All of the ghoulish goodies on the following pages will get you and your guests into the spirit of this magical holiday!

Marshmallow Ghosts

(Pictured on page 232)

Kids of all ages can help prepare these easy-to-make treats. With just three ingredients that I often keep on hand, they can be put together at a moment's notice.
—Nancy Foust, Stoneboro, Pennsylvania

12 ounces white candy coating
1-1/2 cups miniature marshmallows
Chocolate decorating gel *or*
  assorted candies

In a microwave, melt candy coating; stir until smooth. Cool slightly. Stir in marshmallows until coated. Drop by heaping tablespoonfuls onto waxed paper; smooth and flatten into ghost shapes. Decorate with gel or candies for eyes. Cool completely. Store in an airtight container. **Yield:** about 15 servings.

Frightening Fingers

(Pictured on opposite page and page 232)

These cookies have become somewhat famous at the school our children attend. One year, I made more than 150 of these "fingers" for their classroom Halloween parties.
—Natalie Hyde, Cambridge, Ontario

1 cup butter (no substitutes),
  softened
1 cup confectioners' sugar
1 egg
1 teaspoon vanilla extract
1 teaspoon almond extract
2-3/4 cups all-purpose flour
1 teaspoon baking powder

1 teaspoon salt
Red decorating gel
1/2 cup sliced almonds

In a mixing bowl, cream butter and sugar. Beat in the egg and extracts. Combine the flour, baking powder and salt; gradually add to the creamed mixture. Divide dough into fourths. Cover and refrigerate for 30 minutes or until easy to handle.

  Working with one piece of dough at a time, roll into 1-in. balls. Shape balls into 3-in. x 1/2-in. fingers. Using the flat tip of a table knife, make an indentation on one end of each for fingernail. With a knife, make three slashes in the middle of each finger for knuckle.

  Place 2 in. apart on lightly greased baking sheets. Bake at 325° for 20-25 minutes or until lightly browned. Cool for 3 minutes. Squeeze a small amount of red gel on nail bed; press a sliced almond over gel for nail, allowing gel to ooze around nail. Remove to wire racks to cool. **Yield:** about 5 dozen cookies.

Bewitching Ice Cream Cones

(Pictured at right and on page 233)

Both young and old members of my family request these frozen treats every Halloween. It's been a fun tradition around here for many years.
— Edie DeSpain, Logan, Utah

8 chocolate sugar ice cream cones
1 tube chocolate decorating gel
8 thin round chocolate wafers (2-1/4-inch diameter)
1 quart pistachio, mint *or* ice cream of your choice
Black shoestring licorice
16 semisweet chocolate chips
8 candy corn candies
Red decorating gel

Coat edge of ice cream cones with decorating gel; press chocolate wafer against gel to make brim of hat. Set aside.

Drop eight scoops of ice cream onto a waxed paper-lined baking sheet. Cut licorice into strips for hair; press into ice cream. Add chocolate chips for eyes and candy corn for noses. Pipe red gel for mouths.

Flatten scoops slightly to hold hats in place; position hats over heads. Freeze for at least 2 hours or until hats are set. Wrap each in plastic wrap after solidly frozen. **Yield:** 8 servings.

DEVILISH DECORATIONS

A SLEW of simple spooky decorations can set a spirited mood at your Halloween party. In addition to pumpkins and balloons, try these tricks.

- With a black marker, draw ghostly eyes and mouths on old white sheets. Drape over the bristle ends of brooms and prop up against walls.
- Cut out shapes of bats from black construction paper and suspend them from the ceiling with black thread and tape.
- For an eerie glow, replace some of your regular lightbulbs with green or orange bulbs, which can be found at hardware and party supply stores.
- Greet guests with spooky sounds from a purchased cassette or compact disc.
- Pick up a bag of spider webbing from a party supply store. Place in corners throughout the house and attach black plastic spiders. Also scatter spiders on tables, mantels and counters.

Candy Corn Clay Pot

(Pictured on opposite page)

Instead of omitting a centerpiece for a children's Halloween party, create one that will give the youngsters "paws". Just paint a clean clay pot, then fill it with candy corn and Black Cat Cookies. The kids can dip into this clever container for snacks. Or keep the display intact and use it as a door prize.

Ruler and pencil
New 6-inch clay pot
Two wide flat rubber bands
Sponge brush
Acrylic craft paints—white, yellow and orange
Craft knife
Candy corn
Black Cat Cookies (recipe on opposite page)

Use ruler and pencil to measure and lightly mark a line around clay pot 2 inches from the top rim of the pot and 1-1/2 inches from the bottom of the pot. Center a rubber band over each marked line.

With sponge brush and white paint, basecoat bottom and top sections of clay pot, taking care not to allow paint to puddle along edges of rubber bands. Also basecoat inside of rim. Let dry. Add an additional coat of white paint to bottom section only. Let dry. Paint outside top section and inside of rim yellow. Let dry.

When paint is thoroughly dry, use craft knife to score paint along painted edges of the rubber bands to break any paint seal that might have formed.

Position edge of bottom rubber band along the white painted edge and top rubber band along the yellow painted edge for painting guides. Paint center section orange. Let dry. Carefully remove rubber bands as before. Line the pot with plastic wrap; fill with candy corn and cookies.

MAKING A CANDY CORN CLAY POT

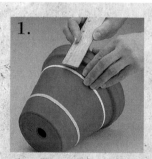  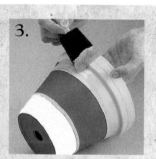 

1. With a ruler and pencil, mark a line 2 inches from top rim and 1-1/2 inches from bottom of pot. Center rubber bands over each line.

2. Basecoat bottom and top sections and inside of rim with white paint. Let dry. Add a second coat of white paint to the bottom section. Let dry.

3. Paint the outside top section and inside rim yellow. Let dry.

4. Reposition rubber bands. Paint the center section orange. Let dry. Carefully remove rubber bands. Line the pot with plastic wrap before filling.

Black Cat Cookies

(Pictured at right and on page 232)

Our children look forward to helping me bake these cute cat cookies each year. They've become experts at making the faces with candy corn and red-hots.
—Kathy Stock, Levasy, Missouri

1 cup butter (no substitutes), softened
2 cups sugar
2 eggs
3 teaspoons vanilla extract
3 cups all-purpose flour
1 cup baking cocoa
1/2 teaspoon baking powder
1/2 teaspoon baking soda
1/2 teaspoon salt
24 wooden craft *or* Popsicle sticks
48 candy corn candies
24 red-hot candies

In a mixing bowl, cream butter and sugar. Beat in eggs and vanilla. Combine the flour, cocoa, baking powder, baking soda and salt; gradually add to the creamed mixture. Roll dough into 1-1/2-in. balls. Place 3 in. apart on lightly greased baking sheets.

Insert a wooden stick into each cookie. Flatten with a glass dipped in sugar. Pinch top of cookie to form ears. For whiskers, press a fork twice into each cookie. Bake at 350° for 10-12 minutes or until cookies are set. Remove from the oven; immediately press on candy corn for eyes and red-hots for noses. Remove to wire racks to cool. **Yield:** 2 dozen.

Orange Witches' Brew Punch

(Pictured on page 233)

This slushy punch requires no ice ring to keep it cold. It's not too sweet, so it appeals to everyone. Use this refreshing beverage for any celebration.
—Susan Johnson, Lyons, Kansas

1 package (6 ounces) orange gelatin
1/2 to 1 cup sugar
2 cups boiling water
1 can (46 ounces) apricot nectar
1 can (46 ounces) pineapple juice
3/4 cup lemon juice
4 liters ginger ale, chilled

In a large bowl, dissolve gelatin and sugar in water. Stir in the apricot nectar, pineapple juice and lemon juice.

Freeze in two 2-qt. freezer containers. Remove from the freezer 2-3 hours before serving. Place contents of one container in a punch bowl; mash with potato masher. Stir in ginger ale just before serving. Repeat. **Yield:** about 8 quarts.

Three-in-One Popcorn Crunch

Folks with a sweet tooth will dig into these bite-size snacks. Candy corn is a colorful addition, so this mouth-watering mix is suitable for any autumn event.
—Carma Blosser, Livermore, Colorado

4 quarts popped popcorn
2 cups dry roasted peanuts
1-1/3 cups sugar
1-1/3 cups packed brown sugar
1 cup dark corn syrup
1/2 cup water
1/2 cup butter (no substitutes)
1/2 teaspoon salt
1-1/2 cups candy corn

Place popcorn and peanuts in large buttered heatproof containers or bowls; set aside. In a large heavy saucepan, combine the sugars, corn syrup, water, butter and salt. Cook over medium heat until a candy thermometer reads 285° (soft-crack stage), stirring occasionally.

Pour over popcorn mixture; stir gently to coat. Stir in candy corn. Drop into bite-size pieces onto waxed paper. Cool completely. Store in an airtight container. **Yield:** 6 quarts.

Editor's Note: We recommend that you test your candy thermometer before each use by bringing water to a boil; the thermometer should read 212°. Adjust your recipe temperature up or down based on your test.

Witch Hat Treats

(Pictured at right)

Here's a clever twist on ordinary marshmallow cereal treats. They add to the festive feeling around Halloween.
—*Nancy Foust, Stoneboro, Pennsylvania*

   3 tablespoons butter *or* margarine
   1 package (10 ounces) large marshmallows
 1/2 cup peanut butter
   6 cups crisp rice cereal
1-1/2 cups milk chocolate chips
   1 teaspoon shortening
Orange frosting
Chocolate jimmies
Black rope licorice

In a large microwave-safe bowl, melt butter on high for about 45 seconds. Add marshmallows; stir to coat. Microwave on high for 45 seconds; stir. Microwave 45 seconds longer or until smooth. Stir in peanut butter. Immediately add cereal; stir gently until coated. Press into a greased 13-in. x 9-in. x 2-in. pan.

In a small microwave-safe bowl, heat chocolate chips and shortening on 70% power for 1 minute. Heat in 10- to 20-second intervals until melted; stir until smooth. Spread over cereal mixture. Cool completely.

Cut into 2-1/2-in. x 2-in. triangles with a thin base on bottom of triangle for hat brim. Decorate with frosting, jimmies for the buckle and licorice for the brim. **Yield:** 2 dozen.

Editor's Note: This recipe was tested in an 850-watt microwave.

CREEPY CAULDRON

TO CREATE the spooky scene shown at right and on page 232, purchase dry ice from your local grocery store's seafood department or ice supplier. Using tongs or thick gloves, place the dry ice in a watertight container; cover with water. Warm water will create more smoke, but it will disappear quickly. Cooler water will produce less dense smoke, but it will last longer. If the amount of smoke decreases during your party, add more dry ice and water.

Editor's Note: Do not handle dry ice with your bare hands. Use tongs or thick gloves. Keep dry ice out of the reach of children.

Festival of Lights Feast

HANUKKAH ("Festival of Lights") is an 8-day celebration commemorating the victory of the Jews over the Syrians and the rededication of the temple in Jerusalem.

To celebrate this holiday in November or December, our Test Kitchen created a memorable menu featuring traditional foods such as Savory Beef Brisket, Festive Tossed Salad, Latkes (crispy potato pancakes), Challah (braided bread) and Glazed Lebkuchen (honey spice bars).

Tables are typically decorated with the colors of blue, silver and gold, menorahs (candelabra with nine candles, used in Jewish worship) and dreidels (four-sided toy tops marked with Hebrew letters that children play with during Hanukkah).

HIGHLIGHTS OF
HANUKKAH
(Clockwise from top right)

Glazed Lebkuchen (p. 244)

Challah (p. 245)

Latkes (p. 243)

Savory Beef Brisket (p. 242)

Festive Tossed Salad (p. 244)

Savory Beef Brisket

(Pictured on page 240)

Caramelized onions give beef and carrots great flavor.
You'll be surprised to see just how easy it is to prepare this fork-tender brisket.

1 fresh beef brisket* (5 to 6 pounds)
2 teaspoons all-purpose flour
1/4 to 1/2 teaspoon coarsely ground pepper
1/4 cup vegetable oil
8 small onions, sliced and separated into rings
2 tablespoons tomato paste
1-1/2 teaspoons coarse salt
2 garlic cloves, quartered
2 pounds carrots, cut into 1-inch pieces

Lightly dust brisket with flour; sprinkle with pepper. In a Dutch oven, brown brisket in oil on both sides over medium-high heat. Remove and keep warm. In the drippings, saute onions until golden brown, about 15 minutes. Return meat to pan. Combine tomato paste, salt and garlic; spoon over meat.

Cover and bake at 375° for 1-1/2 hours. Slice meat across the grain; return to pan, overlapping slices. Add carrots. Cover and bake 1-1/4 to 1-3/4 hours longer or until meat is tender. **Yield:** 12-15 servings.

***Editor's Note:** This is a fresh beef brisket, not corned beef.

TIMETABLE FOR HANUKKAH DINNER

A Few Weeks Before:
- Order a 5- to 6-pound fresh beef brisket from your butcher.
- Prepare two grocery lists—one for nonperishable items that can be purchased now and one for perishable items that need to be purchased a few days before your Hanukkah meal.

The Day Before:
- Buy remaining grocery items, including the beef brisket.
- Set the table.
- For the Festive Tossed Salad, make the dressing; cover and refrigerate. Cut up all the salad ingredients; place in separate airtight containers or resealable plastic bags and refrigerate.
- Bake the Challah and Glazed Lebkuchen; cover and store at room temperature.

The Day of Hanukkah Dinner:
- In the morning, peel the potatoes for the Latkes. Place in a bowl; cover with cold water and refrigerate until ready to grate.
- Make the Savory Beef Brisket and Latkes.
- Remove the salad dressing from the refrigerator. Just before serving, assemble the Festive Tossed Salad; shake the dressing and pour over the salad.
- Set out the Challah.
- Serve the Glazed Lebkuchen for dessert.

Latkes

(Pictured at right and on page 241)

These thin onion and potato pancakes make a tasty accompaniment to any meal. The key to their crispness is draining all the liquid from the grated potatoes and onion before frying.

> 2 pounds russet potatoes, peeled
> 1 medium onion
> 1/2 cup chopped green onions
> 1 egg, lightly beaten
> 1 teaspoon salt
> 1/4 teaspoon pepper
> Oil for deep-fat frying
> Applesauce

Coarsely grate potatoes and onion; drain any liquid. Place in a bowl; add green onions, egg, salt and pepper. In an electric skillet, heat 1/8 in. of oil to 375°. Drop batter by heaping tablespoonfuls into hot oil. Flatten to form patties. Fry until golden brown; turn and cook the other side. Drain on paper towels. Serve with applesauce. **Yield:** 2 dozen.

DEEP-FAT FRYING FACTS

YOU'LL soon be frying foods like a pro with these timely pointers.

- If you don't have a deep-fat fryer or electric fry pan with a thermostat, you can use a kettle or Dutch oven together with a thermometer so you can accurately regulate the temperature of the oil.
- Always follow the oil temperature recommended in recipes. If the oil is too hot, the foods will brown too fast and not be done in the center. If the oil is below the recommended temperature, the foods will absorb oil and taste greasy.
- To avoid splattering, carefully place foods into the hot oil and never add any liquids to hot oil.
- Don't overload your fryer. You'll have better results if you fry in small batches.
- To keep fried foods warm until the entire recipe is cooked, drain fried foods on paper towel, then place on an ovenproof platter. Cover loosely with foil and place in a 200° oven.

Festive Tossed Salad

(Pictured on page 240)

The light homemade dressing wonderfully coats a colorful combination of salad greens, vegetables, pickles and olives. This salad has something for everyone.

8 cups torn salad greens
1 medium tomato, cut into wedges
1 cup cubed peeled cucumber
1 medium sweet red pepper, julienned
1 celery rib, sliced
1/4 cup chopped green onions
4 sweet pickles, chopped
1 tablespoon chopped ripe olives

DRESSING:
1/4 cup olive *or* vegetable oil
2 tablespoons lemon juice
1 teaspoon salt
1 teaspoon sugar
1/4 teaspoon ground mustard
1/8 teaspoon garlic powder

In a large salad bowl, combine the first eight ingredients. In a jar with a tight-fitting lid, combine the dressing ingredients; shake well. Pour over salad; gently toss to coat. Serve immediately. **Yield:** 12 servings.

Glazed Lebkuchen

(Pictured on page 241)

Honey and spices give great flavor to these cake-like bars topped with a thin sugar glaze. They're especially popular around the holidays.

3/4 cup honey
1/2 cup sugar
1/4 cup packed brown sugar
2 eggs
2-1/2 cups all-purpose flour
1-1/4 teaspoons ground cinnamon
1 teaspoon baking soda
1/4 teaspoon ground cloves
1/8 teaspoon ground allspice
3/4 cup chopped slivered almonds
1/2 cup finely chopped citron
1/2 cup finely chopped candied lemon peel
FROSTING:
1 cup confectioners' sugar
3 tablespoons hot milk *or* water

1/4 teaspoon vanilla extract
Candied cherries and additional citron

In a saucepan, bring honey to a boil. Remove from the heat; cool to room temperature. In a mixing bowl, combine honey and sugars; mix well. Add eggs, one at a time, beating well after each addition. Combine the flour, cinnamon, baking soda, cloves and allspice; gradually add to honey mixture. Stir in nuts, citron and lemon peel (mixture will be thick).

Press into a greased 15-in. x 10-in. x 1-in. baking pan. Bake at 350° for 20-28 minutes or until top springs back when lightly touched. Meanwhile, combine the confectioners' sugar, milk and vanilla; mix well. Spread over bars while warm. Immediately cut into bars. Decorate with cherries and citron. Cool in pan on a wire rack. **Yield:** about 2 dozen.

Challah

(Pictured at right and on page 241)

*Eggs lend to the richness of this
traditional braided bread.
The attractive golden color and delicious
flavor make it hard to resist.
For instructions on braiding bread,*
turn to page 51.

2 packages (1/4 ounce *each*)
   active dry yeast
1 cup warm water (110° to
   115°)
1/2 cup vegetable oil
1/3 cup sugar
1 tablespoon salt
5 eggs
6 to 6-1/2 cups all-purpose flour
1 teaspoon cold water
1 tablespoon sesame *or* poppy
   seeds, optional

In a mixing bowl, dissolve yeast in
warm water. Add the oil, sugar, salt, 4
eggs and 4 cups of flour. Beat until
smooth. Stir in enough remaining flour
to form a firm dough. Turn onto a
floured surface; knead until smooth
and elastic, about 6-8 minutes. Place in
a greased bowl, turning once to grease
top. Cover and let rise in a warm place
until doubled, about 1 hour.

Punch dough down. Turn onto a
lightly floured surface; divide in half. Divide each portion
into thirds. Shape each piece into a 15-in. rope. Place three
ropes on a greased baking sheet and braid; pinch ends to seal
and tuck under. Repeat with remaining dough. Cover and
let rise until doubled, about 1 hour.

Beat cold water and remaining egg; brush over braids.
Sprinkle with sesame or poppy seeds if desired. Bake at 350°
for 30-35 minutes or until golden brown. Remove to wire
racks to cool. **Yield:** 2 loaves.

REFERENCE INDEX

Use this index as a guide to the many helpful hints, decorating ideas and step-by-step instructions throughout the book.

GENERAL RECIPE INDEX

This handy index lists every recipe by food category, major ingredient and/or cooking method.

Alphabetical Index

Refer to this index for a complete alphabetical listing of all the recipes in this book.

Here's *Your* Chance To Be Published!

Send us your special-occasion recipes and you could have them featured in a future edition of this classic cookbook.

YEAR AFTER YEAR, the recipe for success at every holiday party or special-occasion celebration is an attractive assortment of flavorful food.

So we're always on the lookout for mouth-watering appetizers, entrees, side dishes, breads, desserts and more...all geared toward the special gatherings you attend or host throughout the year.

Here's how you can enter your family-favorite holiday fare for possible publication in a future *Holiday & Celebrations Cookbook*:

Print or type each recipe on one sheet of 8-1/2" x 11" paper. Please include your name, address and daytime phone number on each page. Be specific with directions, measurements and the sizes of cans, packages and pans.

Please include a few words about yourself, when you serve your dish, reactions it's received from family and friends and the origin of the recipe.

Send to "Celebrations Cookbook", 5925 Country Lane, Greendale WI 53129 or E-mail to *recipes@reimanpub.com*. Write "Celebrations Cookbook" on the subject line of all E-mail entries and *include your full name, postal address and phone number on each entry.*

Contributors whose recipes are printed will receive a complimentary copy of this hardcover book...so the more recipes you send, the better your chances of "being published"!